Pirandello & Film

NINA
DAVINCI NICHOLS

·

JANA
O'KEEFE BAZZONI

·

PREFACE BY
MAURICE CHARNEY

·

University of Nebraska Press

Lincoln & London

1995

The
Scenario for a silent
film based on *Six Charac-*
ters © 1993 by Nina deVinci Nichols

© 1995 by the University of Nebraska Press
All rights reserved. Manufactured in the United States
of America. The paper in this book meets the minimum re-
quirements of American National Standard for Information Sciences – Permanence of Paper for Printed
Library Materials, ANSI z39.48-1984

Library of Congress Catalog-
ing in Publication
Data
Nichols, Nina daVinci, 1935–
Pirandello and film / Nina daVinci Nichols,
Jana O'Keefe Bazzoni; preface by Maurice Charney.
p. cm. Includes bibliographical references and index.
ISBN 0-8032-3336-1 (cl: alkaline paper) 1. Pirandello, Luigi,
1867–1936—Film and video adaptations. 2. Pirandello,
Luigi, 1867–1936—Motion picture plays.
I. Bazzoni, Jana O'Keefe, 1941– .
II. Title. PQ4835.I7Z7175
1995 852'.912—dc20
94-32071
CIP

Contents

Contents

Illustrations

Preface

Pirandello's long essay on humor and the comic, *L'umorismo* (*On Humor*) (1908), is a key statement of his ideas.[1] The essay was written not long after Freud's "The Joke and Its Relation to the Unconscious" (1905) and Henri Bergson's treatise, *"Laughter,"* an essay on the meaning of the comic (1900). Pirandello does not specifically mention either of these studies but uses some of the same sources, especially Theodor Lipps on the aesthetics and philosophy of comedy.[2] In terms of intellectual history, it is interesting that humor and comedy should have been such important topics at the beginning of the twentieth century. Following on major investigations into psychology during the last quarter of the nineteenth century, philosophers were increasingly fascinated by the irrational. Freud, Bergson, and Pirandello all turned to the irrational in their concern with the hidden springs of comedy, its latent energies, and its close connections with everything bitter, forbidden, and tragic.

Pirandello's essay uses concepts that are familiar in psychoanalysis, chiefly that humor emerges from *il sentimento del contrario*, the "feeling of the opposite." This is consistent with his emphasis on the farcical quality of tragedy, on the absurdity of ordinary events, and on the gravity, formality, and melodramatic character of the ridiculous happenings of daily life – all very Sicilian in its mixture of exaggerated passion, personal honor, and an overblown sense of self-importance.[3] The magnetic attraction of opposites and the deep pull of paradoxes in human experience have psychoanalytic roots. As we know, for instance, Pirandello was preoccupied with madness, as if he believed that to be a poet or a true humorist one had to surrender oneself to a force one hardly understood. To his mind, the poet and the humorist are people possessed, so that their imaginative creations spring from a source other than the ordinary self. Thus, the characters of his famous play, *Sei personaggi in cerca d'autore* (*Six Characters in Search of an Author*, hereafter *Six Characters*), exist autonomously outside the consciousness of their author, who is capable not only of creating them but of destroying them as well. We can see, moreover, in his filmscripts for *Six Characters* that Pirandello was particularly fascinated by schizoid states; indeed, he seemed unable to avoid playing with disturbing autobiographical themes. His own mad wife, for example, reappears as a character in his works so vividly that the distinction between the actual life of the artist and his life as a creative spirit is thoroughly blurred.

Il sentimento del contrario, at the heart of Pirandello's conception of humor, is therefore more a general term for the workings of the imagination than a specific synonym for comedy. Pirandello's idea has close affinities with Poe's "imp of the perverse" in the sense that it is profoundly antirational. Everything is based on contraries and paradoxes because one side of an equation stimulates the existence of its opposite. Imagination unearths a chaos of polarities that war against one another but that also complement one another. These fundamental contradictions derive

> from the discord which feeling and meditation discover whether between real life and the human ideal or between human aspirations and human frailty and miseries, and whose main effect is a certain perplexity between weeping and laughing; the skepticism which gives color to all humorous observations and descriptions; and, finally, the minutely and even cunningly analytical process of that skepticism. (*On Humor*, 109)

The analytical process of skepticism could be illustrated by artistic composition, which proceeds practically and rationally to lay out its contradictions.

Pirandello defines the comic even more broadly in psychological terms, positing a temperament like his own, effortlessly producing black comedy, tragic buffoonery, and the grotesque as a natural result of perception. The following passage expresses this idea of split consciousness more metaphorically:

> The condition of a man who is constantly somewhat off key, who is like a violin and a double bass at the same time; of a man in which a thought cannot originate without the opposite or contrary thought originating at the same time, and who finds that for each reason he has to say *yes*, there arises one or more that compels him to say *no* and keep him suspended in perplexity for the rest of his life; of a man who cannot give into a feeling without suddenly perceiving something inside him which mocks, disturbs, disconcerts and taunts him – is a condition which, in its very abnormality, can only be bitterly comic. (*On Humor*, 124)

This passage is close to the Freudian association between the comic and the repressed, "which mocks, disturbs, disconcerts and taunts" a person. The "bitterly comic" tries to deal with anxiety by controlling and mastering it through laughter. Pirandello defines comedy as "a diabolical imp that takes apart the mechanism of each image . . . [I]t [Comedy] releases the mainspring, and the whole mechanism squeaks convulsively" (125). Defining the comic as a squeaking mechanism allies it with the Bergsonian sense that comedy arises when something mechanical is affixed onto the living. Leone Gala, in *Il qiuoco delle parti* (*The Rules of the Game*), for instance, advises his rival to read Bergson in order to understand the power of intuition as the core of human nature. He leaves implicit that all other impulses make life mechanical, and hence comic.

As an essay on the imagination, *L'umorismo* lays out Pirandello's assumptions about creativity. He was a natural, fecund writer who seemed to work extremely quickly, as if he were merely cataloging the items of his possession – his "demons," as it were. Writing seemed to be a therapeutic process by which he dealt with his inspiration, or madness, or the madness that surrounded him. It was a form of exorcism. In Pirandello's astute Preface to *Six Characters*, written for the play's revised version in 1925, he gives his characters an obsessive, intensely passionate, and "real" quality that is most unsettling to us dramatically.[4] The characters come on-stage and tell their story – or at least significant pieces of it – with a nightmarish urgency. They say they need an author to give them life, but they already seem to be bursting with abundant, melodramatic life.

The Preface also toys with other paradoxes relating to characters. Pirandello says that "the play was really conceived in one of those spontaneous illuminations of the fantasy when all the elements of the mind answer to each other's call and work in divine accord" (Preface, 368). This is a romantic and inspirational view of artistic creation in which the conscious, constructive role of the author is minimized.[5] Pirandello continues to insist that the play is not written out in a final, immutable form but is in flux, in process:

> The stage – a stage which accepts the fantastic reality of the six characters – is no fixed, immutable datum. Nothing in this play exists as given and preconceived. Everything is in the making, is in motion, is a sudden experiment: even the place in which this unformed life, reaching after its own form, changes and changes again contrives to shift position organically. (Preface, 373)

In this remarkable statement Pirandello seems coyly to forswear authorship altogether. He is obviously thinking of the characters as a *commedia dell'arte* troupe improvising the play from fixed character assumptions and traditional *lazzi,* or stage business. The characters are on their own and do not really need an author; all they need is a stage on which to present their predetermined scenarios.

The Preface returns to ideas first presented in *L'umorismo:* everything is multifaced and multifaceted, and comedy and tragedy are hopelessly intermingled. One implies the other and cannot exist without the other as in some endless system of oppositions. Thus *Six Characters* winds up as a farrago, an olio of disparate ingredients:

> a mixture of tragic and comic, fantastic and realistic, in a humorous situation that was quite new and infinitely complex, a drama which is conveyed by means of the characters, who carry it within them and suffer it, a drama, breathing, speaking, self-propelled, which seeks at all costs to find the means of its own presentation; and the comedy of the vain attempt at an improvised realization of the drama on stage. (Preface, 366)

The play is a true grotesque, then, because as it proceeds, the level of misunderstanding only increases. No recognition or fulfillment comes at the end – only absurdity, a feeling of great tenderness and sadness, and a melodramatic sort of clownishness.

* * *

Pirandello and Film emphasizes Pirandello's close connection with cinema from the turn of the century. This may surprise some students of Pirandello, since his involvement with film has been seriously underplayed. Gaspare Giudice's popular biography, for example, devotes only five pages to Pirandello and cinema, and these are added to its last chapter. Of first importance to the film aspect of his career is his 1915 novel, *Si gira! (Shoot!),* which reflects his extensive personal experience with cinema and his theories about film and modernity. We know, for example, that Pirandello began visiting studios in 1904 during the very earliest years of film production – the Italian film industry flourished until just after the First World War. Pirandello not only wrote many informal scripts for these companies but also sold script ideas. Several Italian writers had a close relation to film studios, although most films were short and undeveloped. They were certainly not at all literary. In assessing Pirandello's involvement with the medium, we should bear in mind that Pirandello had a lifelong connection with film in a practical way. Unlike his literary writings, much of his early contribution to cinema, like films themselves, has disappeared.

Si gira! also is notable in its suggestion of complex theories anticipating the views of French, Russian, but especially German intellectuals of the 1920s. That the novel is ambivalent about the artistic possibilities of early cinema should not surprise us since Pirandello was ambivalent about any art that circumvented subjectivity. Serafino Gubbio, the novel's cameraman, is an early version of a film director overwhelmingly aware of his mechanical function as a recorder of what the camera sees. The novel's conflict between photographic realism and the passions generated by film production is irreconcilable, however, and the studio becomes the setting for tragedy. The unreality of script and camerawork is set against the unstable reality of actors, culminating in the deadly reality of the tiger in the "Lady and the Tiger" story being filmed. Melodrama of the most histrionic sort is casually mixed with emotional posturing to create a "humoristic" sense in which the real and the unreal are confounded. The strangely modern absurdity one feels in *Si gira!* makes it a disturbingly original novel and the first to be firmly anchored in the nascent film industry.

Many of the aesthetic assumptions of *Si gira!* anticipate those of *Six Characters*, whose first performance in Rome on May 10, 1921, caused a riot. Audiences were not prepared for a modernist play with a fragmentary, discontinuous plot suggesting incest between a father and his stepdaughter. Instead of a coherent story to fall back on, the play supplied hints and possibilities of a lurid nature. At the same time, it seemingly was about nothing more narratively exigent than the nature of dramatic creation. The Author disclaimed any responsibility for his characters, and the theatrical Director perversely refused to understand what the six characters were telling him. In a play inherently deprived of any possibility of a satisfactory ending, the six characters may go on searching for a sympathetic and adequate author ad infinitum.

At least forty-nine attempts (and probably more that were not recorded) to film the great play failed. The play lends itself extremely well to film, perhaps better than any other work of Pirandello apart from *Il fu Mattia Pascal* (*The Late Mattia Pascal*), which Marcel L'Herbier made into an excellent art film in 1925. Pirandello's own filmscript, however, differs strikingly from the play and should be understood as a wholly separate work. As the second part of this book indicates, Pirandello wrote several versions for the film project of which the fullest and best is the *Film-Novelle*. Consisting of 119 takes, that version represents much more than a sketch of a possible shooting script. It clearly has a strong affinity to German Expressionist films of the time in its use of chiaroscuro, phantasmagorical images, urban street scenes, illusory transformations of character, and its sense of decadence in scenes set in a high fashion establishment and brothel. Despite its suggestive sexual scenes, however, the script is highly moralistic.

Pirandello develops his own role as Author, ending the film with a grand production of *Six Characters* complete with Audience. He uses the *mise-en-abyme* idea of a play-within-a-film skillfully to develop ironies between the anguish of the Author as a person and the unctuous self-satisfaction of the Author as a public figure. In the last take (119) "the Author appears in front of the curtain and takes a calm, dignified bow while the audience applauds wildly." Yet he is haunted by the fact that he personally has caused the death of some of his characters and saddled them all with abundant quantities of grief. His profound despair about his ambiguous artistic role is the real upshot and final revenge of *il sentimento del contrario*. Another kind of troubling psychological angst that appears in the filmscript is only hinted at in the play. Among the last takes, for example, the Daughter, dressed as a courtesan in a splendid evening gown, is watching Pirandello's play on-stage. The Daughter's escort is an elderly gentleman just seen at the fashion establishment: "Suddenly, her eyes fill with horror and she stares at him as if seeing a ghost. His face has metamorphosed into that of the Mother's first husband. . . . The Daughter leaps from her seat with a shrill cry" (115).

Pirandello and Film traces Pirandello's continuing interest in cinema as an expression of multiple and shifting realities. In some prescient senses, illuminated by the book, his humoristic ideas are better suited to film than to fiction and drama, especially his ideas about a black comedy of irresolution and discontinuity, and of a flight from comfortable closure that is typically postmodern. While this book is scholarly and historical, it also holds forth the promise that some farsighted creative person will take up the challenge of Pirandello's filmscript for *Six Characters in Search of an Author* and develop it in the context of late twentieth-century assumptions. It is a tantalizing possibility.

A word about the making of *Pirandello and Film*. In writing the book, Nina daVinci Nichols calls upon her experience as critic and editor of many scholarly works on drama, from Shakespearean to nineteenth- and twentieth-century plays. Jana O'Keefe Bazzoni brings to the book her expertise in twentieth-century Italian theater from F. T. Marinetti to Dario Fo. Her scholarly writings on Pirandello reflect her interest in translation, dramatic theory, and theatrical staging. Passages from languages other than English have been newly translated by the authors unless otherwise noted. Titles remain in the original language so as to avoid confusing the reader with variant translations and a work's variant forms, from fiction to drama and film. The exception to this rule is *Six Characters in Search of an Author,* so much a part of the English language and so central to this book.

Maurice Charney

NOTES

1. I refer to the translation by Antonio Illiano and Daniel P. Testa.

2. Theodor Lipps's *Komik und Humor* (1898) is cited several times in Pirandello's essay. *Note: L'umorismo* is essentially a scholarly work drawing on major theoreticians of the period. Pirandello already had written two important essays related to the subject matter of "L'umorismo," so the material was much on his mind. Olga Ragusa believes the essay was put together hastily from a course Pirandello held at the Istituto Superiore de Magistero in Rome (see *Luigi Pirandello,* 30).

3. See Charney, "How Pirandellian Is Shakespeare?" in *Hamlet's Fictions,* New York: Routledge, 1988, 26–34, revised from "Shakespearean and Pirandellian: *Hamlet* and *Six Characters in Search of an Author,*" *Modern Drama* 24 (1981): 323–29.

4. Although this is referred to as a Preface by convention, Pirandello himself entitled his comments "Come e perché ho scritto *Sei personaggi in cerca d'autore.*"

5. *Note: L'umorismo* also refers to the German romantic writer Ludwig Tieck for comparative definitions and meanings of humor. Throughout the essay, Pirandello's view of the creative process echoes ideas about a work's organic unity similar to those of Schlegel and perhaps Coleridge to a lesser extent.

Acknowledgments

Our thanks go to many people who supported the project. To Benito Ortolani, who most generously made the correspondence between Pirandello and Marta Abba available to us in manuscript form. To Robert Lantz, for sharing his boyhood recollections of his father, Adolf, and of Pirandello, and for lending us a rare copy of the German filmscript in his private collection. To Michael Kowal, Mark Bledstein, Paul Bernard Newman, Frank Sypher, and Hannah Charney for consulting on translations. To Leo Charney for his appendix situating Pirandello in the philosophy of film during the 1920s and 1930s. To the many librarians at special collections who assisted in the research, especially those at Museo Biblioteca dell'Attore, Genoa; Centro sperimentale di cinematografia, Cineteca nazionale, Rome; The New York Public Library for the Performing Arts; Reinhardt Archives, SUNY Binghamton; and Special Collections, Spencer Library, The University of Kansas.

Our deepest gratitude to Eric Bentley and Mario Fratti, who encouraged us to undertake the book.

Research for *Pirandello and Film* was funded in part by the National Endowment for the Humanities, the Research Foundation of the City University of New York, Baruch College, and Rutgers University.

Chronologies

« 1 »

The first chronology consists of film works initiated or completed during Pirandello's lifetime. Several options and proposals have been included to suggest the range of activity on Pirandello's properties in various periods, many with reference to *Six Characters in Search of an Author*. Dating of projects is approximate since not all negotiations were recorded and since many negotiations overlapped and continued for years. The inclusion of significant events in Pirandello's life and work serve as landmarks to his film career. Titles appearing in italics or within quotation marks signify published works.

1867 Born in Girgenti, Sicily, on June 28

1894 Marries Antonietta Portulano

    Publishes first collection of short stories

1904–14 Visits the studios of Film d'Arte Italiana, Rome, witnessing film production; begins gathering material for his novel on filmmaking, *Si gira!* (*Shoot!*)

    Offers film subjects to Nino Martoglio at Cines Film Company, later Cinecittà

    Iue eroi (original scenario; The two heroes), given to Nino Martoglio at Morgana and later produced (?) by Cines

    Visits Cines studios throughout this period

1915 *Si gira!* (*Shoot!*) is published serially in *Nuova antologia* (June–August)

    L'altro figlio (story; "The Other Son"). Carmine Gallone proposes and obtains approval for a film scenario

1916 *Si gira!* is published as a single volume under the new title *Quaderni di Serafino Gubbio, Operatore* (*The Notebooks of Serafino Gubbio, Cameraman*)

    Tespi Film founded with Mario Corsi and Arnaldo Frateili as artistic directors, Pirandello as literary consultant

1917   *Cosí è (se vi pare)* (*Right You Are [If You Think So]*), his first full-length, nondialect play, is performed

Negotiations begin on the sale of "Il viaggio" (story; "Adriana Takes a Trip")

Papà mio, mi piaccion tutti! (story; Father dear, they all like me!); Pirandello contributes scenes and episodes directed by Giuseppe Forti

1918   *Il lume dell'altra casa* (story; The light across the way), written and directed by Ugo Gracci, produced by Silentium Film. The first of eight silent films based on Pirandello's works

1919   *Lo scaldino* (story; The footwarmer), directed by Augusto Genina; produced by Itala Film (Turin) and Tespi Film (Rome); released in 1921 as *Senza amore* (Loveless loves)

Il crollo (The collapse), based on the play *Lumie di Sicilia* (*Sicilian Limes*); directed by Mario Gargiulo; produced by Flegrea

Collaborates anonymously on *Pantera di neve* (Snow panther) with Arnaldo Frateili for Tespi Film

1920   *Ma non è una cosa seria*, based on the play *But It's Not Serious*, directed by Augusto Camerini; screenplay by Arnaldo Frateili; and on the stories "La Signora Speranza" and "Non è una cosa seria" ("It's Nothing Serious"); produced by Nova Film of Rome

1921   *Sei personaggi in cerca d'autore* (*Six Characters in Search of an Author*). First performance in Rome

Il viaggio ("Adriana Takes a Trip"), directed by Gennaro Righelli; written by Righelli in collaboration with Adriano Piacitelli; starring Maria Jacobini; produced by Feat (Rome)

La rosa (story; "The Rose," 1914), directed by Arnaldo Frateili, screenplay by Frateili with Stefano Pirandello; produced by Tespi Film

1924   Teatro degli undici o dodici (Theater of the eleven or twelve) is founded with state support; later renamed Teatro d'Arte di Roma

1925   *Feu Mathias Pascal* (*Il fu Mattia Pascal*), directed by Marcel L'Herbier

Publishes a Preface to *Sei personaggi* (*Six Characters*), together with a revised version of the play

Republishes *Si gira!* (*Shoot!*), returning to this version of the title

1926   *Enrico IV* (play; *Henry IV*) is produced and directed by Amleto Palermi from a script by Adolf Lantz, called *Die flucht in die nacht* (Flight at night). The film is shot in Germany and in Italy and stars Conrad Veidt

Austrian release is entitled *Die lebende Maske* (The living mask); French release is entitled *Le Fou* (The madman)

Writes the *Prologo* (*Prologue*) to a screen adaptation of *Six Characters in Search of an Author*

Proposals to film *Six Characters* from: Geschaftsstelle Verband Deutscher Filmautoren-Berlin (Pirandello asks for 100,000 lire and that Marta Abba play the Stepdaughter); Hans Feist; and Amleto Palermi, who offers $5000

Sells option for *La nuova colonia* (play; *The New Colony*, 1928), based on the 1911 novel *Suo marito* (Her husband); details missing

1928   Takes up residence in Berlin

Proposals to film *Six Characters:* Ferreira and Albert Megale request a 2½-month option; Fellner & Somlo GmbH of Berlin offer a contract with Friedrich Murnau as director; a proposal from UFA-ENAC by Tomaso Bisi, the Italian production company formed by Mussolini with UFA; a proposal from Terrafilm-SASP (Stefano Pittaluga Co.)

1928–29   Writes the German *Film-Novelle* for a silent film based on *Six Characters* in collaboration with Adolf Lantz

1928–36   Collaborates with his son Stefano Landi on eight possible scenarios or subjects drawing on the story "Ignare"; titles respond to requests from different producers. Amor sacro (Sacred love), Vergine madre (Virgin Mother), Fiamme all'occidente (Flames in the west), Mai figlio nacque in vano (No child is born in vain), Fuga in Egitto (Flight into Egypt), L'oscuro richiamo (The dark call), La via del perdono (The way of forgiveness), Il figlio dell'uomo cattivo (The evil man's son)

1929   Visits London to see *The Jazz Singer* as guest of Paramount

Essay, "Se il film parlante abolirà il teatro?" ("Will Talkies Abolish the Theater?") appears in *Corriere della Sera*, June 16

Adapts *L'abito nuovo* (story; The new suit), to star Emil Janning, for director Joe May. No production records

Proposals to film *Six Characters* from: Fritz Wreede; Otto Kahn of Paramount; Philips (? British International Pictures); ENAC (to be produced by the new Cinecitta)

Writes *Vergine madre* (Virgin Mother) for Anna May Wong, to be directed by Richard Eichberg for British International Pictures

Negotiates with Eichberg for two films, one for Anna May Wong and another unspecified. Contract and production details incomplete

Terra-film makes an offer for "Nel segno" (Bull's eye) (1913)

Rights sold to Stefano Pittaluga of Cines for the stories "In silenzio" ("In Silence"), "Lontano" (Faraway), and "Donna Mimma" ("The Diploma—A Sketch")

1930   The Pirandello/Lantz *Film-Novelle* based on *Six Characters* is published in German together with the play's 1925 Preface ("Come e perché ho scritto i *Sei personaggi* . . .")

La canzone dell'amore (Song of love) based on "In silenzio" (story; "In Silence"), directed by Gennaro Righelli for Cines; the first Italian sound film to be distributed

La dernière berceuse (The last lullaby), French version of *La canzone dell'amore*; *Liebeslied* (Love song), dubbed German version of *La canzone dell'amore*

Nascere (screenplay; Birth) written by Francesco DiCocco, based on "Donna Mimma" (story; "The Diploma—A Sketch"); never produced

Metro-Goldwyn-Mayer (MGM) offers a three-month residency in Hollywood (renewable) to negotiate sound film subjects, to be contracted separately. (LP asks $15,000 per three months plus minimum of one subject option paid in first three months, another paid option in second period)

Signs a publicized option contract with Jesse Lasky of Paramount (for $1½ million) for *Six Characters* plus four other pictures, possibly including "Il capretto nero" (story; "The Little Black Kid"); option never acted upon

Several subjects proposed for the United Artists European network by Hugo von Hofmannsthal's son, agent covering Berlin, Paris, London, Rome, and Madrid

Paramount acquires the rights to "Il lume dell'altra casa" (story; The light across the way)

?Writes Aspetta e vedrai (screen subject; Wait and see); no production records

Il piacere dell'onestà (play; *The Pleasure of Honesty*), is optioned by Amleto Palermi for Tonfilm italiana

1931   Negotiates with Berta Cutti of Universal for *Come prima, meglio di prima* (As before, better than before) for $12,500

MGM negotiates for the *Film-Novelle* of *Six Characters*; they consider offering $80,000 if Pirandello acts the Author's role

1932   *As You Desire Me* (play; *Come tu mi vuoi*), starring Greta Garbo, Erich von Stroheim, and Melvin Douglas, directed by George Fitzmaurice for MGM

Lends his name to the film subject *Giuoca, Pietro!* (Play, Peter!), written principally by his son Stefano Landi

Proposals to film *Six Characters* from: Fines, a French company; Irving Thalberg of MGM; and Carl Laemmle of Universal

Signs with Cines for four subjects including *L'esclusa* (novel; The outcast), one per year

1933   *Giuoca, Pietro!* (*Play, Peter!*) is made into a documentary by Walter Ruttmann under the title *Acciaio* (Steel)

Renegotiates with Irving Thalberg of MGM regarding *Six Characters*

Offers the German *Film-Novelle* to Carl Laemmle of Universal Pictures with the provision that he adapt it for a sound film

American rights for a "talkie" of *La nuova colonia* (play; *The New Colony*) sold to Lee Shubert

Rights to the film *Come prima, meglio di prima* (As before, better than before) in American and Italian versions sold to Universal Pictures

1934   Wins the Nobel Prize for Literature

Proposals regarding *Six Characters* from: an unspecified American company; from Pinker and Davis; and from the financing company for Cinematographique d'Paris

Receives offers for film subjects from five studios through British agent, Curtis-Brown Ltd.

Alexander Korda requests a subject for his London Film Year

Enrico IV (play; *Henry IV*), second version, directed by Giorgio Pàstina

Writes an adaptation of *Trovarsi* (play; *To Find Oneself*), retitled "The Two Seas" for Greta Garbo at MGM

1935   Receives five requests for film rights to *Il piacere dell'onestà* (play; *The Pleasure of Honesty*): from Paramount, for Edward G. Robinson; MGM, for Ruben Mamoulian; David O. Selznick; Ernst Lubitsch; and Hans Bartsch Plays, agent

Remake of the film *Ma non è una cosa seria* (play; *But It's Not Serious*) adapted by Ercole Patti, Mario Soldati, and Mario Camerini; directed by Mario Camerini, starring Vittorio De Sica

Meets with Max Reinhardt in New York about the English sound film *Treatment* of *Six Characters*

Negotiates a contract for the *Treatment* based on *Six Characters* with Hal B. Wallis of Warner Brothers and Max Reinhardt

Irving Thalberg and MGM offer $80,000 for the German *Film-Novelle* of *Six Characters;* to star Pirandello

1936   Collaborates with Max Reinhardt on a proposed revision of the *Treatment* of *Six Characters;* project is described in the Roman periodical *Il Tevere* (7–8 October)

A film treatment for Max Reinhardt of *La nuova colonia* (play; *The New Colony*) is written in German and Italian

Collaborates with Stefano Landi and Corrado Alvaro on the screen adaptation of the play *Pensaci, Giacomino!* (*Better Think Twice About It!*), directed by Gennaro Righelli, starring Angelo Musco

L'homme de nulle part, second French film version of *Il fu Mattia Pascal,* directed by Pierre Chenal, with Isa Miranda and Pierre Blanchar

1936   Dies in Rome on 10 December

« 2 »

Film projects based on Pirandello's works since his death; in some cases negotiations began during his lifetime. Some television films of his plays have been included to indicate continuing activity exclusive of documentaries about Pirandello.

1937   *Der Mann, der nicht nein sagen kann* (The man who couldn't say no), a remake of the 1935 film *Ma non è una cosa seria,* adapted by Mario Camerini and Karl Lerbs, directed by Mario Camerini and Ernst Rechenmacher, produced by Itala Film GmbH

1938   *Terra di nessuno* (No man's land), written by Stefano Landi in collaboration with Corrado Alvaro, directed by Mario Baffico, based on "Requiem aeternam dona eis, Domine!" (Give them eternal rest, Lord!) and "Romolo"

"L'uscita del vedovo" ("The Widower's Exit") optioned for Vittorio De Sica

Film Chronologies

1939   *Cinci* (story; "Cinci"), directed by Michele Gandin for Cine-Guf

1942   *L'esclusa* (novel; The outcast) optioned by Cines

1943   *Enrico IV* (play; *Henry IV*), directed by Giorgio Pàstina, starring Osvaldo Valenti, Enzo Biliotti

Rights sold for two years to Kinofilm for *Il piacere dell'onestà* (*The Pleasure of Honesty*)

Il turno (novel; The turn) optioned by Antonio De Simone

1945   *This Love of Ours* based on play and film *Come prima, meglio di prima* (As before, better than before), directed by William Dieterle, starring Merle Oberon, Charles Korvin, and Claude Rains

Enrico IV (play; *Henry IV*) optioned; Orson Welles to direct and star for London Film Productions

1947–48   *Así te deséo* (This is how I want you), based on the play *Come tu mi vuoi* (*As You Desire Me*) directed by Belisario Garcia Villar; distributed only in Argentina and Uruguay since MGM holds rights for fifty years

1948   *L'uomo, la bestia e la virtù* (play; *Man, Beast and Virtue*) optioned by Lux Film

1951   *La morsa* (The vise), sixth part of the film *Altri tempi* (Other times), directed by Alessandro Blasetti, starring Elisa Cegani and Amedeo Nazzari

Rights to the play *La vita che ti diedi* (*The Life I Gave You*) sold to Daniel Lavengle for Studio des Champs-Elysees di Parigi

1952   *L'uomo, la bestia e la virtù* (play; *Man, Beast and Virtue*), directed by Stefano Vanzina, starring Orson Welles, Viviane Romance, and Totò

1953   *Vestire gli ignudi* (play; *Naked*), directed by Marcello Pagliero, starring Eleonora Rossi Drago, for Cigraf-Roma

Film project: *Il viaggio* (story; "Adriana Takes a Trip"); David Lean to direct Ingrid Bergman

Episodes in the film anthology *Questa è la vita* (That's life) draw on: play and story *La giara* (story; "The Jar"), directed by Giorgio Pàstina; "Il ventaglino" (story; The little fan), directed by Mario Soldati; "Il patente" (story; The license), directed by Luigi Zampa starring Totò; "Marsina stretta" (story; "The Tight Frock-Coat"), directed by Aldo Fabrizi

Proprio cosi (musical comedy libretto; Just like that), originally intended for Broadway; adapted for film by Guido G. Torre. No production record

1955–56   *Never Say Goodbye,* based on play and film; *Come prima, meglio di prima,* a remake of *This Love of Ours.* With Rock Hudson, Cornell Borchers, George Sanders, and Shelley Fabores; directed by Jerry Hopper. Records from various sources conflict

1957   *Todo se para bien* in Spanish, play; based on *Tutto per bene (All for the Best),* directed by Carlos Rinaldi, starring Francisco Petrone, Duilio Marzio, Inda Ledesma, and Susanna Campos

Film project: *Enrico IV* (play; *Henry IV)* to be directed by Burgess Meredith, who will also have the starring role

Film project: *Uno, nessuno, e centomila* (novel; *One, No One, and a Hundred Thousand);* Charlie Chaplin wants to make a film but American politics intervene

1958   Rights to the play *Il giuoco delle parti (The Rules of the Game,)* sold to John Woolf for Romulus Film of London

Of Life and Love, a reissue of the 1953 film anthology *Questa è la vita* for U.S. distribution omitting "Il patente" and substituting "Il cagnolino" (The lapdog), directed by Luciano Visconti, starring Anna Magnani

1961   Film project: "Scialle nero" ("The Black Shawl") with Anna Magnani; American producer unspecified

1962   *Uno, nessuno, e centomila* (novel; *One, No One, and a Hundred Thousand)* optioned by Jean Rossignol

1963   *Liolà* (play), directed by Alessandro Blasetti, starring Anouk Aimee and Ugo Tognazzi

1964   *Ma non è una cosa seria,* based on the story "La Signora Speranza" directed by Gianfranco Bettetini for Radiotelevisione italiana (RAI)

1967   Film project: "Il viaggio" ("Adriana Takes a Trip") to be produced by Dino De Laurentiis and directed by Mauro Bolognini; to star Silvana Mangano

Il mondo di Pirandello (The world of Pirandello), a film anthology drawing on "La cattura" (story; "The Captive"); La lega disciolta" (story; the broken alliance); "La balia" (story; "The Nurse"); *Lumie di Sicilia* (play; *Sicilian Limes*); Il lume dell'altra casa" (story; "The Light Across the Way"); "Marsina stretta" (story; "The Tight Frock-Coat"); "La vita nuda" (story; Naked life); "La giara" (story; "The Jar"); "La fedelta del cane" (story; "Man's Best Friend"); "Quando s'e capito il giuoco" (story; When the game begins). Directed by Luigi Filippo d'Amico, music by Benedetto Ghiglia, produced by Ultra Film for RAI

1970   *La morsa* (play; The vise), directed by Gianfranco Bettetini, starring Silvano Tranquilli and Lea Massari, for RAI

La giara (story and play; "The Jar"), by Iraklij Kvirikadze, for KUVSIN

1973–74   *Il viaggio* (story; "Adriana Takes a Trip"), directed by Vittorio De Sica, starring Sophia Loren and Richard Burton

1977   *I vecchi e i giovani* (novel; *The Old and the Young*), directed by Marco Leto, for RAI

Vestire gli ignudi (play; *Naked*), by Luigi Filippo d'Amico, for RAIUNO

1980   *L'Esclusa* (novel; *The Outcast*), telefilm directed by Piero Schivazappa

1981   *In silenzio* (story; "In Silence"), telefilm directed by Luigi Filippo D'Amico, with Matteo Gazzolo and Sarah Tafuri, for RAI

La fede (story; "Faith"), telefilm directed by Ciriaco Tiso, with Roberto De Angelis and Jobst Crapow, for RAI

Il turno (novel; The turn), directed by Tonino Cervi for United International Pictures, starring Vittorio Gassman, Laura Antonelli, and Paolo Villaggio

1983–84   *Kaos* (Chaos), directed by Paolo and Vittorio Taviano; five episodes based on the "L'altro figlio" ("The Other Son"), "Male di luna" (Moonsickness), "La giara" ("The Jar"), "Colloquio con la madre" (Conversation with mother), "Il corvo di Mizzaro" ("The Crow of Mizzaro"), "Requiem aeternam dona eis, Domine!" (Give them eternal rest, Lord!)

1984–85   *Le due vite di Mattia Pascal* (The two lives of Mattia Pascal) based on the novel *Il fu Mattia Pascal* (*The Late Mattia Pascal*), directed by Mario Monicelli, starring Marcello Mastroianni

Enrico IV (play; *Henry IV*), directed by Marco Bellocchio, starring Marcello Mastroianni and Senta Berger, for Excelsior Cin and RAI

Si gira! (*Shoot!*) by Kra Pictures in Hungarian. No details

1990   "*Fue Mathias Pascal* (novel; *Il fu Mattia Pascal*), in French, directed by L'Herbier. The original film restored by Films Albatros and Cinegraphic; 35-mm black and white and tinted colors, 135 min. Reviewed by *Variety*, May 2, 1990

Film Chronologies

Addendum

Several Pirandello plays have been filmed for television. In Italy the Giorgio De Lullo, Rosella Falk, Romolo Valli, and Elsa Albani Company produced the major plays including *Six Characters* for RAI-TV in the 1960s. Eduardo De Filippo also adapted several short plays for Italian television. In the United States in the 1970s a noteworthy adaptation of *Six Characters* by Paul Avila Mayer was produced for Hollywood Television Theater; it was directed by Stacy Keach, who played the son. It also starred John Houseman as the Director, Andy Griffith as the Father, and Beverly Todd as the Stepdaughter. In Canada, also in the 1970s, Robert Sherrin produced a version of *Six Characters* for the Canadian Broadcasting Company, adapted by Lawrence Mirkin and David Giles, and directed by David Giles. In 1992 Michael Hastings adapted and Simon Curtis produced *Six Characters* for BBC 2's Performance Series. John Hurt played the Father, Brian Cox the Director, and Tara Fitzgerald the Stepdaughter.

CHIEF SOURCES FOR THE CHRONOLOGIES

Francesco Callari, *Pirandello e il cinema*. Venezia: Marsillo Editori, 1991.

Benito Ortolani, ed., *Le lettere di Pirandello a Marta Abba*. 2 vols. (Milano: Mondadori); and *Pirandello's Love Letters to Marta Abba* (Princeton: Princeton University Press, 1994).

Gaspare Giudice, *Pirandello, A Biography.* Translated by A. Hamilton. London: Oxford University Press, 1975.

Frederick May, *Luigi Pirandello: Short Stories*. London and New York: Quartet Books, 1987.

Filmographies and related reference works in special collections of New York Public Library; Cinecitta of Rome; and Museo Biblioteca dell'attore, Genoa. See also Works Cited.

PART ONE

Commentary

ONE

Si gira! (Shoot!)

It often happens that actors do not even know what part they are supposed to be playing, so one hears some actor ask in the middle: "Say, . . . am I the husband or the lover?"[1] Si gira!

S hoot! A film director calls for action – the essence of life. His camera-man, however, rebels at reproducing life on celluloid, a matter of "de-vouring reality" for the sake of a fixed image. "Do you think our souls can be captured by machines," he rails. "Here they are, by bits and mouthfuls, all molded in the same stupid and exact style. . . . You can make a pyramid of the tin boxes holding these lives!" The protest continues like a rhythmic base throughout *Si gira!*[2] Pirandello's avant-garde novel symbolizing filmmaking in 1904 as dehumanizing at best. Three decades later, in 1936, he would be collaborating with Max Reinhardt in New York on a filmscript (the *Treatment*), drawing on his revolutionary play, *Six Characters in Search of an Author.* Bringing a lifelong obsession with the metaphysics of art to consummate form, the projected film was to reveal a hidden Pirandello in a part to be played by himself – the Author Found.[3]

Between the novel and *Treatment* lies the history of Pirandello's contribu-tion to cinema. To a degree, both works resonate those themes long considered synonymous with his name: the interplay of form and flux, the simultane-ous existence of multiple realities, the dilemmas of consciousness and self-consciousness. Pirandello resembles no one so much as himself, at once archi-tect of modernism *and* its satiric critic – aloof, wry, often misunderstood since his perceptions fit no mold. It may be truer to say that his genius was identical to an astigmatic eye that discovered *il contrario* at the base of all things.[4] Especially where cinema was concerned, his enigmatic stance gave rise to apocryphal Pirandellos, either hostile to the medium or simply lured by easy money.[5] Even apart from their obvious reductiveness, neither image quite matches the evidence. Early on he voiced the skepticism shared later by

Duchamp, Leger, Picabia, Cocteau, and others about film's significance, a minor art form waiting on major artists. Possessed by "the demon experiment," as he described his own affliction, however, Pirandello also was among the first to see film's unique resources, to define an aesthetics of cinema, indeed, to write serious works for the medium when writers of his stature were dismissing film as a toy.[6] His witty aside to an interviewer many years later might very well apply to his stance about cinema from the beginning: "I am attracted to film as to a woman; you cannot be a courtier-seducer of her, or of an art medium."[7]

It was not film so much as filmmaking that struck Pirandello in *Si gira!* as the dangerous symptom of a confusing *Zeitgeist:* it crystallized his vision of the self in crisis after the collapse of nineteenth-century traditions. A loss of values and institutions defining experience had left individuals adrift, in need of finding new and stable sources of wholeness and meaning. Runaway technology, however, only exacerbated feelings of dislocation, alienation, and estrangement. Machine-age man was a cog of great wheels, a hand churning a camera and, metaphorically, moving the engine of a culture dazzled by the new, and heedlessly bent on progress without conscience.[8] To the aristocratic man of letters who believed with Nietzsche that identity was recreated "from moment to moment and day to day" (Caputi, 47) with all the skill that continuity, memory, and sheer intelligence might bring to the endeavor, film threatened to reduce individuals to a mass-produced collective, mindless and remote from human scale.[9]

Still, no one remained unaffected by the advent of cinema, whether as mass entertainment or as a racehorse of technology. The new marvel promoted by newspapers and viewed with increasing sophistication by critics exercised a glamorous appeal for writers and intellectuals from Gabriele D'Annunzio to James Joyce.[10] A measure of film's emergence into aesthetic consciousness in Italy can be gathered, for instance, from its impact on the Futurists. The influential group of artists who worshipped the very idea of energy and speed saw film as a trajectory out of the past, an immediate, wholly popular instrument of social awareness that would bring the country into the twentieth century. Pirandello objected strenuously to Futurist polemicism directed at political systems instead of persons; yet his own break with assumptions about continuity and absolute forms in nineteenth-century literature recalls a Futurist sense that fragmentation and simultaneity typify modern experience. Plays by F. T. Marinetti or paintings by Gino Severini either displace or flatly reject conventional subjects and perspectives.[11] So too, as Pirandello's plays clearly indicate, Futurists insisted upon the author's presence in the work, whether allusively in the text or physically on-stage and in film, an especially provocative idea given Pirandello's role in his filmscripts and his self-reference in many works.[12] More immediately, his tour de force, *Si gira!* resembles a Futurist event in the very degree to which his mock hero's camera *creates* the budding culture that he simultaneously deplores as enemy of civilization. Trapped like his author in that double vision echoed by his name, the cameraman Serafino Gubbio represents a reluctant spirit of art embodied in an antic clown who predicts his own ruin.[13]

Conflict, opposites, the other side of the visible, the mask behind the mask, but most of all, the dynamics governing their relationships – these were objects of profound investigation only intimated by Pirandello's more apparent themes, and the territory he wanted to map through film.[14] He came to believe during the 1920s, at the height of his celebrity, that only film could go beyond his startling dramatizations of consciousness to convey the act of creation, a quite different project reaching into ideas about the genesis of art and anticipating much later psychoanalytical formulations about the creative process.[15] His novels and plays had objectified disintegrations of personality and revealed an understanding of interpersonal relations far in advance of theory.[16] But film as film dictated its own separate mission: to visualize imagination *before* language and form, and perhaps satisfy that quest for authenticity which to modernists always lay elsewhere. Had Pirandello found a cinematographer equal to the aims he sketched out in notes and scenarios, he would have set film on a course called "experimental" even now, or "eccentric," or by the politely dismissive term "artfilm," usually alluding to inaccessible works by brooding iconoclasts like, say, Ingmar Bergman.[17] More like Ibsen, Pirandello was ultimately mystical, inward, drawing on himself for knowledge of a psyche always ready to turn on itself with a corrosive wit. Concealed beneath the trite tag "pirandellian" lies his compulsion to know all the names and terrors of making art, even at the risk of seeming a madman.[18] And if madness ordinarily implies some departure from the logic and order ruling an apparent reality, to him it meant the synoptic vision of both reality *and* its appearances, constantly, perhaps schizophrenically, and film was all appearances. It follows that he believed film should lay claim to areas of experience prior to literature and drama since it was more elemental than either.

5

Commentary

In all these senses, Pirandello's split-mindedness about film coincides with his sense of contradiction as the accursed condition of life and art: reason in passion, cruelty in compassion, folly in wisdom, the grimly comic within the existentially true. The mystery of a composite self at once allured and bewildered him: who *was* the role-playing artist, the grand puppeteer who was *one, no one, and a hundred thousand*.[19] Short of protesting like his cameraman that the writer's spirit cannot be "fixed" in words, comment in these pages traces images of Pirandello and film in the light of Pirandello's life and works, of his scenarios for *Six Characters*, of his notes about cinema, and of the infant industry itself – monstrous leviathan, new aesthetic country, and imp of the perverse.

« 1 »

In a large meadow, almost directly beneath Pirandello's house in Rome, stood one of the first cinema companies in Italy. It was organized in 1904, called Film d'Arte Italiana, and owned by the French Pathé. From his windows he could see through the glass-enclosed studio as actors and actresses gesticulated in front of the cameras (fig.1). Then the director's command, "shoot," would reach the writer's observatory.[20] It would have been remarkable had Pirandello remained oblivious to goings-on below. Like other single-camera studios at the time, this was a tall, airy structure resembling a gigantic greenhouse; sunlight poured in through the roof onto small, fixed stages for mounting *tableaux vivant*. Apparently, sets were meager and makeshift – a chair or a kettle might be borrowed from friends – but it was the entire arrangement of such *teatri di posa*, literally, theaters of the pose, that must have intrigued Pirandello. Actors stood poised between reality and illusion in that theatrical limbo of the spirit housing so many of his own characters.

Invited by his friend Lucio D'Ambra, a filmmaker with whom he later collaborated, Pirandello often visited the studio. Its entrepreneurial atmosphere attracted a floating population of hangers-on – financial speculators, circus performers, gentlemen-turned-actors, curiosity seekers – who migrated from lot to lot as well as into the pages of *Si gira!* Indeed, the colorful scene may have inspired the novel as a game that grew more formal as Pirandello learned about cinema production. At least partly in the cause of gathering material for the novel, Pirandello, over the next few years, called in at several studios (including Cines Company, now Cinecitta, as well as Film d'Arte Italiana), jotting down technical jargon about cutting, bathing, winding, and splicing film, and other operations with an eye to their potential

6

utility as metaphors.[21] At one point in the novel, for instance, as his camera-man reviews many frames of a shot before choosing the right one, he waxes rhetorical about "fixing" an image of the actors for eternity. His technically accurate reference to film editing might be the blueprint for Pirandello's ploy, years later, of envisioning his dramatic characters as autonomous, and trapping them in one terrible moment of truth.

Pirandello may have been satirizing one aspect of his studio visiting days in *Si gira!*'s caricature of a highly respectable, philosophical Doctor Cavalena, wise enough about the improvisational style of early filmmaking to carry a scenario with him on his visits to the Kosmograph company. Cavalena's scenario unfailingly included a suicide and unfailingly was rejected, and so the hapless suitor to silent movie fame acquired the nickname "Suicide." Not that Pirandello's submissions to studios were about suicides, but a good many, he remarked drily, were politely rejected as too subtle or arcane for the common run of audiences (*Si gira!* 108). Once, as anecdote would have it, Piran-dello promised to deliver the scenario of a novel by Hippolyte Nievo to his Film d'Arte neighbors "within eight days," a project that never materialized.[22] Lucio D'Ambra, reminiscing in 1937 about his own film career, told his version of the story. A breathless producer had asked him to write a scenario based on Alessandro Manzoni's *I promessi sposi* overnight. Under protest, never having read the novel, he inveigled an extra day for the assignment when Pirandello laughingly made his counteroffer. In fact, D'Ambra says, Il Maestro wisely spent the week writing a new play instead. True or false, D'Ambra's tale captures the combined nonchalance and urgency typifying most projects in those years. If the filming of *I promessi sposi* is any criterion, a scenario might be written in two days, shot in a week, and the related details of business never recorded. Highly expendable as such, a scenario, after all, consisted of a mere plot line divided into groups of major images and linked by brief captions. Only a handful of scenarios survive as testimony to their own sketchiness and to the young industry's insatiable appetite for material.

From 1904, when the first movie house opened its doors in Rome not far from Pirandello's apartment, until 1917, Italy commanded the European in-dustry and the world's notice. The initial center of production in Turin, called Italy's Hollywood by film historians, attracted an influx of workers, techni-cians, and critics whose sheer numbers brought attention to film as a force of modern life. Turin in 1907 produced the first critical essay on film, "La filosofia del cinematografo" (The philosophy of cinema), by Giovanni Papini, which not only examined film's methods and cultural impact but urged a snobbish intelligencia to attend film showings lest they miss an historic phenomenon. Papini predicted that film would develop its own "emotional and moral metaphysics," competing successfully with the more "time consuming, bothersome, and costly theater."[23] Film's greatest advantage, however, was its immediacy, its revolutionary capacity to disseminate a record of events just days after their occurrence. The new medium "gives us the spectacle of contemporary life as lived" (Callari, 22). Pirandello may have read the essay because several of Papini's observations find their way into *Si gira!*

By the following year, a Turin newspaper featured a weekly column on cinema, and shortly thereafter journals on film began to publish regularly.[24] Their advertisements, promotional materials, and feature articles on specific films and performers soon made household names of Pirandello's friends in the industry, Lucio D'Ambra and Arnaldo Frateili. The rapid growth and commercial success of Italian companies can be measured by both their need to hire French and German technicians to meet the demands of expanding markets and their circumvention of American protectionism against foreign imports. From aesthetic perspectives, too, investors like the French Pathé came to Italy to underwrite films whose breadth of approach influenced pioneers like Sergei Eisenstein, especially in the art of mounting spectacle. The Russian declared "that the film-makers to whom he owed most were the pre-1917 Italians" (Leprohan, 60). Indeed Italian costume epics, drawing on the riches of Roman history as well as the national operatic tradition, became the most popular film product of the pre–World War period, employing hundreds of people, and by 1914 regularly filling 3,227 film houses flourishing across Italy.

The golden age of Italian film at its peak in 1914 can be glimpsed in those allusions in *Si gira!* to society people flocking to studios for the fun of participating as extras and because film was "in." Cabarets and cafes buzzed with gossip about prominent members of the film community, from monied backers to stars. Everybody who was anybody tried to hop on film's bandwagon. Pirandello's close friends Arnaldo Frateili, Nino Martoglio, Amleto Palermi, and Carmine Gallone held posts at major film houses;[25] artists and writers not already acquainted through literary channels soon grew familiar with one another's projects, real or anticipated. Excitement was high and so were expectations. Making film deals became the second most important activity in the industry, the most fraught with temperament, the most ephemeral, and far and away the most time consuming, as Pirandello would complain again and again. He grew to resent the demands of meetings, letter writing, and seemingly endless negotiations that often led nowhere. Still, 450 films were made in 1914 alone, representing a huge expenditure of artistic and organizational energy (Leprohan, 63).

Two important events in cinema history further document the year and tell something about the mixed feelings that Pirandello expressed in asides, notes, and conversations. One event was the extraordinary success of Giovanni Pastrone's film *Cabiria*, made in Turin from a thirty-page synopsis to which the literary giant Gabriele D'Annunzio "merely added his signature" (Leprohan, 30). Pastrone spared no effort with technical innovations, from simulating the Alps on the Turin hillsides for location shots of Hannibal's crossing to creating and patenting a camera dolly for effects that impressed D. W. Griffith.[26] His masterstroke, however, was getting D'Annunzio to accept nominal authorship of the film, "an undertaking of the greatest profit with the least bother which would not harm his reputation in any way" (Leprohan, 30). The great man's name, an orchestral score written for the film, extensive advance publicity, an invited list of dignitaries and aristocrats for an opening night comparable to that for the opera – all this turned the film's premiere into what we would call a media event. *Cabiria*'s merits also helped transform film from an entertainment into an art worthy of serious review in a newly developing critical vocabulary. In a word, D'Annunzio legitimized the industry, yet remained wholly aloof, of course. And this largely describes one side of Pirandello's early relation to the many silent films bearing his name. He lent himself to the medium, yet was not of it; he participated when propelled by interest or financial need, yet remained a man of letters rather than of cinema. Many lesser lights adopted a similar stance. Filmmakers on the whole tended to be producers and cameramen, not writers, and decidedly not writers of literary stature.[27]

Still a different event of 1914 reveals the extent to which the medium could and did support significant cinematographic experiment, the sole aspect of the industry that consistently engaged Pirandello's attention. The brilliant Nino Martoglio, at this point head of Morgana Films, located in Catania to escape the clichés of Rome. Martoglio renounced grandiose costume spectacles to introduce a realistic style with his, now classic, lost film, *Sperduti nel buio* (Lost in darkness). Almost immediately successful with the *literati*, it later was imitated throughout Europe and influenced the birth of German social problem films of the 1920s. With scrupulous attention to scenic detail and inventive cross-cutting, Martoglio dramatized class warfare between rich and poor, shooting his film in Naples to capitalize on the city's contrasts between luxurious palaces and ghettolike slums.[28] Documenting the country's problems with meticulous accuracy, he pointed film toward a mission the critic Papini had proposed years before: to reveal the hidden face of Italy to its own people. Martoglio's new realism may have impressed Pirandello more deeply than he realized at the time, since his *Prologo* (*Prologue*) a decade later incorporated a similar realism within a generally expressionistic framework. Whereas he scorned pageants and extravaganzas for their sloppy execution as much as their tiresome subjects, his friend's careful workmanship struck him as an important advance in filmmaking.

By 1914, when the film capital had shifted from Turin to Rome,[29] another innovation was rivaling the popularity of costume epics and exciting Pirandello's interest. Rising directly out of the fantasies of the very class of industrialists and artists involved in financing and producing film, bourgeois drama began a screen career that continues to this day. Beautiful women in exotic settings, displaying both elegant clothing and themselves as well, formed the center of a genre essentially serving up passionate love stories engineered by a femme fatale. Unlike the wicked and destructive vamp of Nordic countries, her Italian cousin represented a minor deity, an unapproachable goddess called "the diva," who ushered in both a personal style of acting and the evils of the star system. Close-ups, stylized gestures, intimate situations designed to frame the glamour of female leads like Pina Menichelli (fig.2), became firmly associated with modern drama's interest in the fortunes of individuals. The industry encouraged the new genre's vogue partly since it cost less than grand pageants that were auguring ill for the future of Italian filmmaking. Yet producers continued, myopically, to do both: they squandered millions on locations and stars while fostering the development of small-scale scripts exploring complex dimensions of personality.

* * *

It was during this golden age of Italian cinema that Pirandello, in urgent need of money and turning out stories at a prodigious rate for sale to magazines, began to pursue film opportunities aggressively. Scattered evidence for at least six projects dated between 1910 and 1913 involved Martoglio, then director of Cines who was still crossing back and forth between stage and film ventures. Pirandello, looking for a financial windfall, described several stories that he might adapt for film as well as many possible scripts he might write. "I already have one," he says in a letter dated May 27, 1913, "called 'Nel segno'" (Bull's eye) (1904). He asked for an advance of 500 lire, saying he "was ready to sign a contract at a decent fee for each film." Apparently this proposal failed since in another letter eight months later, he again offered Martoglio "Nel segno," saying he was desperate for funds. Proposals for his 1902 story *Lontano* (Faraway) met a similar fate, but Martoglio eventually did produce the scenario *I due eroi* (Two heroes), written for the actor Giovanni Grasso but not mentioned among Pirandello's papers. Given the improvisational nature of projects at the time, detail about the shooting of *I due eroi* has disappeared along with the film itself – techniques for film preservation remained primitive or nonexistent until the early thirties. The scenario, however, written in ninety-two highly emotive scenes plus an epilogue, carries recognizable traces of Pirandello's favorite motif of doubling the protagonist(s), who in this case are a schoolmaster, believed to be dead, and his next-door neighbor, a land surveyor, who becomes a hero of the Italian *risorgimento*.[30]

In general, Pirandello's projects during this period took one of three forms: he sold stories to film companies outright; he collaborated with writers and producers on adapting them into scenarios; or he allowed others to write out a scenario after providing them with the main themes. He left several film ideas, for example, sketched out in this fashion for his son, Stefano Landi, to complete. Negotiations for a sale, however, might continue for years in a pattern of proposal, rejoinder, and delay that grew all too familiar. He pursued the idea of a contract for "Nel segno" (Bull's eye), for instance, until 1936 with several companies, ultimately including Universal Pictures. To take a nearer example, correspondence about filming *Si gira!* begins in January 1918 with Anton Giulio Bragaglia, an avant-garde artist of the day who ran a cabaret theater featuring Futurist events; yet nearly ten years later in February 1926 Pirandello was advising Stefano about effecting a contract for the novel with Kra Pictures. *Si gira!* did, in fact, become a Hungarian film in 1985 and a television film in 1987 (fig.3).

Some projects moved swiftly and directly to completion. The first of a series of eight short films, *L'altro figlio* ("The Other Son"), seems to have appeared in 1915 soon after Pirandello signed a contract for a scenario with director Carmine Gallone. The other seven films, made with other directors within the next three years, included *Papà mio, mi piaccion tutti!* (Father dear, they all like me!) on which he collaborated anonymously. One interesting film based on his short story "Il viaggio" ("Adriana Takes a Trip") might have brought Pirandello to the screen in a full-length work relatively early, in 1917, had complications regarding both the rights and censorship not intervened. The well-respected director Gennaro Righelli eventually made *Il viaggio* in 1921, with the sultry Maria Jacobini playing the lead at the moment when dive commanded their own vehicles. (It was remade by De Sica in 1973 with Sophia Loren and Richard Burton). Relative to Jacobini's celebrity, Pirandello resembled his Suicide, Doctor Cavalena, trying to sell his material to highly volatile studio chiefs. Short stories were the ideal vehicles for short films rapidly made, and short-story adaptations were what Pirandello chiefly provided during the period, whether as gentlemanly diversion or as welcome sources of income. Meanwhile, however, Pirandello the novelist was registering cinema's emergence as *the* art of the metropolis and harbinger of a distinctly popular culture.

« 2 »

Written when both high modern novel and film were still inventing themselves, *Si gira!* anticipates the merciless revelations of cinema's dream factory in Nathaniel West's *The Day of the Locust* (1939) and F. Scott Fitzgerald's *The Last Tycoon* (1941). Whereas the structure of these novels brings Hollywood psychology into immediate and brutal focus, Pirandello's tour de force is more distanced by both mirror effects of the hero's acute depersonalization and the work's very scope. A studio romance and a discourse on the making of an adventure film called "The Tiger" filter through the stream-of-consciousness "notebooks" of his comic *archarne*, Serafino Gubbio. Both the notebooks and the film-in-the-making[31] progress along parallel lines – an idea later adapted by Alan Robbe-Grillet – so that technically the work is neither novel nor diary. (More than a dozen years later, the Russian film, *The Man with the Movie Camera,* by Dziga Vertov attempts a similar double structure but ends up being a diary.) Pirandello's unique structure might be called either a cinematic monologue, or a scenario with its filmic design clearly laid out (Nulf, 99), depending upon whether one gives priority to monologue or film. Gubbio registers activity surrounding the film's shooting in disconnected "takes" consisting of scenic openings, captions, theatrical and motion picture elements, scenarios, close-ups, mixed in memories, anxieties, and other synthetic figurations exploiting his first-person narrative (deCastris, 101). These provide not only the fragmentary reality of characters but, more important, the meaning of Gubbio's perspective as he declines from instinctive sympathies, to disgust of these, to an ultimate "stony" deliverance from consciousness.

As may be inferred, structural doubling on a smaller scale applies to Gubbio's split psyche. The observing eye of his camera studies people rushing confidently, he thinks, toward an inevitable doom that he himself ironically exemplifies. Studio "motor cars" dash to and fro, celebrating a cult of speed while he jogs along in his horse-drawn carriage, a Sicilian man of the past, nostalgic for the countryside. That the cameraman creates the film culture he derides, as noted above, becomes a major source of both the novel's bitter comedy and its proleptically structuralist impulse to destroy its own referents. And thus Pirandello, like the surrealists, raises the disturbing issue of how relativism altered definitions of reality. His well-known insistence upon depicting art-in-the-making here corresponds in reverse to Gubbio's "unmaking" as he degenerates into catatonia.

Until then, the hero nicknamed "Shoot" impassively shuttles his celluloid strips of life back and forth between the studio's negative and positive departments, roughly analogous to his disembodied "seraph" self churning a camera and his subjective self writing notebooks to preserve his minimal integrity. He thus plays go-between on both comic and existential levels of meaning. At first Gubbio suffers from his cruel victimization by the engine, which reduces him to a nonlife of mindless motion. Eventually, however, he arrives at an imperturbable detachment that Pirandello equates with the moral void resulting from mechanization.[32] Only Gubbio's hand matters, and someday "they will find a way to make the handle turn by itself" (8). Against that likelihood, he chooses to relinquish the chimera of identity by accepting his servility, renouncing feelings, and shooting pictures automatically, thus knowingly sinking into an abyss of nonbeing as his emotions atrophy. The work ends in a silence marked by the audible ticking of his machine, still operating after his notebooks have stopped "portraying his own absence" – a paradoxical and frightening expression of alienation that Pirandello was to explore again and again.[33]

From the outset, the cast of novel and film burden the diffident Gubbio with secrets, confidences, and messages to be carried back and forth like his film strips. If spliced together, cast and secrets would approximate a Shakespearean comic plot, darkening with the approach of catastrophe. Baron Nuti, a Sicilian gentleman-turned-actor, terrified at having to kill a real tiger, is in love with the femme fatale and star Varia Nesteroff, who baits universal man while living with the histrionic leading man Ferio, who is placed by the harried studio director under Gubbio's watchful eye during a flamboyant crisis of passion. The director sends both men to board with Kosmograph's regular, Dr. Cavalena, his deranged wife, and his innocent daughter, who threatens Gubbio's imperturbability at one point when he becomes dangerously attracted to her and fears he therefore might develop a personality. Treatment of these types shifts between melodrama and farce as jokes and mistakes double back on the jokester – a Sicilian brand of humor especially poignant when Pirandello dips into autobiography.[34] Dr. Cavalena prolongs his studio visits in order to escape the jealous wife who nonetheless follows him, causing scenes that make him ludicrous to the studio crew and humiliating to himself. There is a glimpse here of Pirandello's own sad marriage too clear to be coincidental. More of his life is generalized in the Cavalenas' chaotic domesticity, seen by Gubbio-as-camera when he boards with the family. Pirandello's two alter egos in the novel, "seraph" and doctor, younger and older double, then crowd into one representational space.[35] Does the situation also contain a sly jibe at Il Maestro's ambivalent stance on film, tolerated "in" his life as both paying boarder and invader?

Imbroglios of the nearly incestuous studio family provide occasions sometimes reading like a documentary about backlot bohemia in the days of early film. A socialite, the odd statesmen, a famous scientist, and a distracted scholar stroll in and out of Kosmograph as if at some county fair for the bourgeoisie. The first studio lots did, in fact, resemble fairgrounds with sets and equipment strewn over the area to simulate locations. Any number of acrobats, tumblers, dancers, and refugees from traveling circuses might stop by on their move from lot to lot in quest of a few day's shooting. More important as a sign of the times, studios like Kosmograph became a refuge for persons displaced out of traditional social roles by the flux of modernism. Decaying gentry like Baron Nuti found paid work by miming themselves before the cameras. Varia Nesteroff, "an artiste" born of Russian aristocracy, found the ideal niche as a woman with no resources other than her beauty and a poor speaking voice. Even Cavalena's daughter, a member of the respectable middle class, enlists herself at Kosmograph as a bit-part player. When she worries about her lack of qualification, the director reassures her, "You don't have to know how to do anything, just sit there" (*Si gira!* 72). For her, the studio provides an escape route to independence from the constraints of troubled family life. The phenomenon of emancipated young woman seeking her fortune as budding actress soon became commonplace.

The novel captures this assorted humanity in the process of metamorphosing from person to celluloid illusion – all to the point of Pirandello's credo rejecting permanence in any form as a version of death. One might say with equal justice that the actual circumstances of filming in a circuslike atmosphere probably contributed to his experiments with staging multiple events simultaneously in several locations in the theater, experiments carried on by colleagues and contemporaries later, from Max Reinhardt, to V. Meyerhold, to Russian cineastes.[36] In the novel, of course, Pirandello toys with the paradox of creating art that must die on its own completion. A subtle application of the theory to film is consummately expressed when Gubbio shoots La Nesteroff – as she is sometimes referred to – in an exotic Indian dance sequence. Half-naked and deeply absorbed in her own performance, gyrating and slithering on the floor, La Nesteroff generates extreme eroticism that mesmerizes the men on the set. She, however, remains unaware of every eye but the camera's as she calls to Gubbio in a hoarse whisper, "Is this all right? Is this good?" Sexuality directed solely at the camera expresses an ultimate narcissism, a complete absence of personness and reciprocity as she elicits desire on film for an invisible, eternal audience. In context, the sequence represents an aesthetic appreciation of her sensuality as an irreducible essence of life. And consistent with her characterization, she enacts her narcissistic fantasies as the object of male desire who despises her lovers. But La Nesteroff's eroticism in the void registers a quintessential sense of film playing to itself. Years later in 1966 Michelangelo Antonioni repeats the scene in his *Blow-Up* when a glamorous model writhes slowly on the floor as her photographer goads her suggestively; sexual tension reaches a climax that leaves both slumped and exhausted by mock intimacy that is "all in a day's work."[37]

The camera, "a lying demon," deprives the human presence of its reality. Instead of reflecting a constant interplay between life and its forms, the machine "kills" La Nesteroff in her most intense moment. So, at the close of film-and-novel, form ironically lashes back at life: illusion becomes reality, actor becomes person, and vice versa. In the climactic scene of the tiger's shooting, La Nesteroff's sadistic lover kills her instead of the animal, which then springs and kills the lover before being killed by a quick-thinking bystander suddenly turned actor. Film's simulated violence becomes actual human slaughter, and the implication for natural man engaged in creating artifice could not be clearer. Meanwhile, Gubbio, shooting the entire sequence, becomes a casualty in the melee, losing his voice out of sheer terror. This grand denouement leaves ambiguous whether on a deeper psychological level he willed his disability to some degree, say, out of combined nausea at the moment and the habit of anomie. He rejects a cure, vowing never again to speak. Gubbio's terrible destiny plays itself out with inexorable logic: he has cranked his way to inglorious self-extinction.

* * *

The novel's stance on "film as art form" and "Gubbio as artist" provides glimpses of Pirandello at his most prescient about the medium, long before it became a subject for debate by theoreticians like Siegfried Kracauer or Walter Benjamin. Benjamin's "Das Kunstwerk im Zeitalter seiner technischen Reproduzierbarkeit" ("The Work of Art in the Age of Mechanical Reproduction") turns to the novel with lavish praise to exemplify his own thinking about modernist aesthetics. According to Pirandello's metaphysic, trouble arises since film pretends to distinguish reality from illusion, thereby damning itself as intellectually sophomoric. Only Gubbio, "who has the worm of philosophy gnawing at his brain," is aware that film pictures actors picturing emotions and actions, thus faking the nature of being itself. The result, what film gives back from the process of its making, is extreme, rigid symbols of life's spectacle: gestures, masks, convulsive passions, disjunct thoughts, love, jealousy, escapes into memory, an irrational quality of acts and events issuing from some dark, ancient perdition projected arbitrarily on a screen (deCastris, 100).

Gubbio, in short, sees the chaotic world of relativity and himself after the collapse of history. From his epiphany he learns that film at its simplest involves an interplay of time and illusion, a sophisticated definition shared by few at the time. He ponders, for instance, his act of photographing a young man who will remain perpetually young while the film itself ages and gathers dust (*Si gira!* 320). Since Gubbio's consciousness plays no part in the dynamic between camera eye and actor, subject and object, the medium becomes an instrument of self-division.[38] The insight here in psychological terms is analogous to Pirandello's "humoristic" aesthetic, involving a constant tension between opposites necessary to the making of "true art," and probably the linchpin of all his work.[39] Most of his heroes struggle with conflicting ideas, or perceptions, or opportunities, trapped often enough in Hamlet-like quandaries that bring action to a halt. Gubbio, like the characters Mattia Pascal or Enrico, falls into crisis when compelled to decide between opposites.

More immediately, the myriad ways in which Kosmograph's film falsifies nature and art reveal themselves through the work's ongoing comparisons of film to theater, a wholesale activity among filmmakers, critics, as well as spectators, which continued well into the 1920s. For Pirandello, the genres were superficially alike in employing actors to purvey illusions, and that is where similarity ended. Film was about visual images, as he repeated again and again. Only in the playhouse does a consciousness of drama as enactment exist on both sides of the footlights. Gubbio indicts studio producers and directors for caring nothing about the "reenactment of a truth" by actors on a stage before a living audience.

> They remain here, as on a daylight stage, when they rehearse. For them, opening night never arrives. They never see the public. The machine, *by means of their phantoms,* [emphasis added] is responsible for the performance before the public; and they have to be content with performing only before the machine. When they have acted their parts, their performance is the film. (*Si gira!* 22)

He, of course, speaks as artist manqué with only limited control over his material; that is, he exercises discretion over the speed at which he cranks his handle "making" a film; he positions his camera eye relative to marked spots on a stage; he estimates lighting effects; he assesses the image of the actor while the director cues them into a bit of action, usually without antecedent or sequel. ("Hey, am I the lover or the husband?") In these connections, Gubbio provides a benchmark on the rapid historical evolution of actual cameramen into full-fledged directors and filmmakers (fig.3).

Gubbio's litanies of complaint, however, also strikingly anticipate the dilemma of the absent artist that Pirandello confronts personally, artistically, even obsessively, over the next two decades. "What can they care about me," Gubbio concludes one tirade, alluding to his lack of independent persona. Instead, like his camera, he merely "takes in" characters, so to speak, so that he then consists of their "phantom" imprints on the template of consciousness. The novel's most autobiographical theme may lie in this paradoxical expression of Gubbio's plight, linking filmmaking to the formation of the artist's identity. On a primary level, Gubbio's mechanical conversion of life into art, nature into culture, resonates with the project of high modernism in which authenticity for art and artist remains elusive. Adversarial modernists like Gubbio who are strenuously disaffected, or spiritually estranged from culture, assume that some romantic escape hatch exists leading either beyond or within: to some unspoiled primitivism in Gubbio's Sicily, say, or to an un-colonized unconscious. To the contrary, Pirandello either sees or pretends to see the unconscious as well colonized by the traumas imprisoning most of his dramatic and fictional characters. Still, Gubbio finds no escape as he dwindles into nonexistence, like the Father in *Six Characters* who becomes "less an entity than a non-entity."[40]

Half a century later, theorists will consider the most damaging aspect of Gubbio's dilemma to be shared by all living in a film culture. After stripping him of an absolute self, the "great consciousness industry" refashions Gubbio into a specious natural man; specious, that is, since he represents a sum of disparate self-images mirrored by actors, visitors, director, technicians, and even the tiger, the only genuinely natural creature on Kosmograph's lot.[41] The end of civilization that Gubbio foresees will arrive when disjunct film symbols replace life itself. Pirandello will play variations on the phenomenon in several scenarios. At this stage of his evolving film poetic, the artist as "Suicide" wears the mask of a hollow man, a tragicomic agonist and omniscient angel-clown.

TWO

Variations on a Theme, Fiction to Film

"There is someone living my life and I don't know who he is."[1]

"How can I tell you what Pirandellism is when it exists in its pure form only within my own cranium? It's myself, and what that is nobody will ever know but Luigi Pirandello. But I can tell you definitely what it isn't," he added. "It is not a cerebral or highbrow thing, as critics think. . . . It's all so simple; I find the characters, pull them out of the void, and there they are with beating hearts and wills of their own."[2]

The decade between 1914 and 1924 brought Pirandello personal tragedy and great acclaim. Bold experiments with form revolutionized theater, yet they remained unrealized by his own film company. Brooding preoccupation with the theme of absence found consummate expression in his play *Six Characters,* yet generated as much notoriety as celebrity. That all things were true at once only fostered his ironic view of himself as "other" and his nagging belief in antitheses. Yet, the extent to which Pirandello's terrible personal circumstances enter into all his works has been commented upon many times, as if the one converted neatly into the other. Less often noticed is that alongside his insights into the eroding personality – one result of marriage to a mad wife – there grew a tonic sense of his misery as being at once irremediable and ludicrous. A spirit of buffoonery and farce in the films, stories, novels, and major critical essays, especially those written up to 1919 when his family life completely disintegrated, yes, that humoristic spirit, has yet to be fully appreciated, not only as a force for sanity but as a blueprint for the kind of film he began to envision.

While Serafino Gubbio-as-camera remained poised in an aesthetic distance where ghostly images displaced his own, a tormented Pirandello, who questioned his mental stability, filled his notebooks with a *felt* knowledge of absence.[3] His growing sense of self as a construct of others may anticipate both Jacques Lacan on identity and definitions of split consciousness.[4] But methods for exploiting such insights came slowly, modulating as Pirandello progressed from writing plays, to directing, to taking the spotlight on film himself. As always, a skein of incidents surrounding the evolution of his poetics binds his work to his life.

« 1 »

The poignant line quoted in the epigraph to this chapter and addressed to Pirandello's daughter Lietta alludes to his distressing awareness, beginning in about 1908, that he was existing as a phantom of his wife's tortured imagination. Antonietta Portulano suffered bouts of terrible jealousy and paranoia from the time of her first breakdown in 1899. Thereafter, a pattern of ruptures and reconciliations, increasing desperation over the effect of their chaotic relationship on his three children, and finally despair of Antonietta's recovery consigned Pirandello to bleakness and pessimism. Despite his solicitousness and care, nothing prevented wild outbreaks of Antonietta's persecution complex in which she accused him of adultery with students – he was teaching long hours at the Magistero school for teachers after 1897 – or of secret plots to abandon or murder her.[5] Antonietta constructed a monstrous husband that Pirandello never recognized. Incomprehensible fits of intense phobia during which she barricaded herself in their apartment alternated with occasional oases of calm, all the sweeter for their rarity.

Although advised by doctors to send her to a sanitarium, Pirandello could not bring himself to part with her. He rather grew more aware, if the fiction of the period is any measure, of his dependence on her for the one solace she might give. In Si gira! as in novellas like Suo marito (Her husband) and La realtà del sogno ("The reality of the dream"), Pirandello alludes repeatedly to the humiliating bonds of twisted love in bourgeois marriages very like his own. Indeed, the rancor and perversity of married couples in all three fictions, and especially their "battles of brains," echo Strindberg, whose several husbands find themselves unable to break free of their wives' demonic projections. Nor did Pirandello's considerable study in psychology provide him with a shield of intellectual detachment from his wife's illness.[6] As Antonietta's condition worsened, Pirandello seems instead to have absorbed her feelings of rejection and estrangement, learning to know her illness empathetically. Psychoanalytical readings of the theater plays go so far as to see him suffering a borderline schizophrenia[7] and projecting one of his selves into the characters. If true, the strategy of transforming life into art may have been salutary. His sense of the grotesqueries of madness and the absurdity of trying to reason with unreason deepened his understanding that families consisted in the dynamics of their relations, rather than in the fixed quantities of persons and roles.

Otherwise, Pirandello daily feared for the well-being of his daughter when he left her at home. Neighbors and local shopkeepers might be called in during one of Antonietta's attacks to witness his humiliations, another situation recurring in the fiction and dramatized in the plays *Cosí è (se vi pare)* (*Right You Are [If You Think So]*) and *Vestire gli ignudi* (*Naked*). Conflicting points of view tend to obscure the more profound symptoms of madness, say, of Ersilia in *Vestire gli ignudi* as she retreats from herself into absence, first acting out others' images of her, then committing suicide. By 1913, as Antonietta's fits increased in frequency and intensity, Pirandello no longer could avoid the knowledge that his wife was incurably insane. It was not until February 1919, however, after Antonietta became convinced of his incest with their daughter and Lietta's subsequent suicide attempt, that he committed his wife to an asylum. By then he had developed his own habits of self-estrangement and a nearly clinical facility at applied introspection, for good and ill. When answering a reporter's question about his wife some time later, during an interview about a play he was drafting for Eleanora Duse, he revealed his typical relativism.

> Everybody's a little crazy . . . your thoughts, cara signorina, to you are sane and normal. To me they may appear a little off the high road. My critics see me, a sober, serene man in my own estimation, as something of a mildly raving madman. Who is to set up standards of what is real in a world in which everything, anything, is real only if it exists in someone's mind? This consideration has always occupied me.[8]

Pirandello's deliberate explorations of madness set his work apart from that of other modernists who on the whole either excluded it as a region of study or modified it in themes about alienation. Nor was Pirandello attracted to the madness of cruelty, or sadism, or decadence in the manner of the *fin de siecle* French or Artaud later on. His fascination, rather, is with the power that condemns to madness all those who face the challenges of *deraison*. In such psychological regions, his work becomes something of a Baedeker; even the relentless logic of his most philosophical absent husbands approximates that devilish form of madness underlying farce. The urbane Leone Gala in *Il giuoco delle parti* (*Rules of the Game*) deliberately cultivates absence or apartness as a policy about life; Baldovino in *Il piacere dell'onestà* (*The Pleasure of Honesty*) plays out a husband-in-name only, who in the end turns the tables on the lover in residence. As Pirandello's contact with outsiders diminished, as his sons in school and military service left him more solitary, Pirandello began to live more and more obsessively with a ghostly horde of family, friends, and fictitious characters who visited his writing studio as if awaiting some ideal embodiment. In notes and letters referring to them as materializations of his fancy, he studies their prior existences. Then taking the opposite stance, he recreates them and their mocking author in works reconceiving the phenomenon of their "autonomous" generation from memory and image.[9] About this, however, it is easy to overstate. He records a sense of himself as more than aesthetically possessed by his characters as early as 1904 in a letter to a friend; the relevant lines, however, carry no freight of dangerous psychic splitting and doubling.

> "If material cares and social commitments did not distract me," he wrote, "I think I would remain from morning to night here in my study at the beck and call of the characters of my stories who are struggling within me. Each wants to come to life before the others. They all have a particular misfortune which they want to bring to light." (Giudice, 118)

He rather becomes intrigued with the idea of possession – if that is the term – as his life becomes more inward, well after his ironic treatment of the theme in *Si gira!* and other works anticipating dimensions of both text and filmscript of *Six Characters*. Ghosts, figments of passion, phantoms, and seeds of character (he uses the terms almost interchangeably to get at the essence of feeling or perception prior to its personification) take up residence in his consciousness, potentially deconstituting him while constituting his art. The idea strikes up still other echoes of Strindberg's notions of possession and madness, in his case an obsession with psychic murder, or "soul murder," in which one personality forces itself on another who absorbs its traits. Strindberg sees the phenomenon as a result of incest, an intriguing point given Pirandello's own preoccupation with incest.[10] Pirandello treats the idea more abstractly, examining the relations between possessed and mysterious possessor in works that objectify an individual psyche. Put reductively, this opens the door for autobiographical and psychological interpretations of both his plays and scenarios. His simultaneous interest in the dynamic, that is, quite apart from its content and himself, leads directly to his sense of film's unique power to visualize emotion, memory, dreams, sensation, hallucination, and mental states (Vicentini, 22). Most of his early subjects for cinema feature one-dimensional or "characterless" characters of his stories, swayed by an uncontrollable or incommunicable passion. Such figures expressing, say, grief, desire, or fear lend themselves to the quasiallegorical representations that gave silent film its universal quality.

To take the example of a relatively simple scenario, the first silent film carrying Pirandello's name, *Il lume dell'altra casa* (The light across the way) was a melodrama based on his 1909 tale about the wages of adultery between a married woman and her lover. The unremarkable plot ends with an affecting scene of the lover and disgraced mother confined in a dark room. She peers through a window into a lighted house next door to catch a glimpse of the children she abandoned, living aspects of herself split off and cast at a distance she yearns to cross. (Pirandello's doubling of women often takes the primary figuration of mother and child suffering from their division, a situation with autobiographical echoes of his own closeness to his mother but also of his children's separation from their mother by her illness.) The emotive suggestibility, implied chiaroscuro lighting, and pictorial expressiveness of the deprived mother in the final passages of his novella intimate Pirandello's hope that the film would convey the mother's feelings of grief and loss through inventive imaging. In the scenario, instead, the mother throws herself out of the window and her lover follows, the camera then focusing on his mutilated body and head. Censors suppressed these "bloody" and "suggestive" scenes; substitutes were proposed by the director, the producer, the writers, and nearly everyone connected with the production except Pirandello, who gave up on the film in disgust. He explained years later, "I took no interest in the film because I had a great many family affairs to look after." It seems a clear excuse once the film had sensationalized his theme and ignored its cinematic potentialities.[11]

His experience was not unique. As the English novelist Elinor Glyn put it, "All authors, living or dead, famous or obscure, shared the same fate. Their stories were re-written and completely altered either by the stenographers and continuity girls of the scenario department, or by an assistant director and his lady-love, or by the leading lady, or by anyone else who happened to pass through the studio" (Robinson, 110). Or scenes resembling the original ended up on the cutting room floor. Pirandello was better satisfied by his second film, *Lo scaldino* (The footwarmer), a comedy directed by Augusto Genina and Arnaldo Frateili. Unlike other collaborators, Genina hung on Pirandello's every word. He reported later that they had talked often and at length about a successful Duse film, about cinematography, about a Sicilian dialect play with the great Angelo Musco[12] that they had seen together. Genina appeared to understand Il Maestro's cinematic vision perfectly, though the subject here was far from complex. Still, apart from expressions of mutual graciousness, Pirandello registers obvious delight later in a note to his son Stefano, telling that Genina and company "have flattered me with attention, paid me 4000 lire! and given me a charming footwarmer as a memento. The film has turned out beautifully and they say it will cause a stir" (18 April 1919).[13] Of course, no such stir occurred. The film was not released until 1921, when not even Pirandello's fame could compete with a grave depression in the Italian industry and troubles in the world market.

* * *

Immediately after the war in 1917, Pirandello joined with Frateili, Martoglio, Umberto Fracchia, and others in founding the short-lived Tespi Film, officially serving as literary adviser (fig.4). Tespi hoped to bring the gifts of the country's most innovative artists to filmmaking while Italy still dominated in the field. Filmmakers enjoying the widest possible latitude in choice and treatment of materials would bring the medium into aesthetic maturity. A movement among French Post-Impressionists, Futurists, and Russian artists, subscribed to by Pirandello, already had begun to form against a developing "Hollywood" ideology of film,[14] a term roughly referring to linear narrative films that felt passé even before their technical machinery had fully developed. Tespi produced several films including an adaptation of Pirandello's *La rosa* ("The Rose").[15] He himself collaborated anonymously on *Pantera di neve* ("Snow panther") with Frateili, but "without succeeding in ennobling its content" (Callari, 92), apparently a travesty of banal melodrama aimed at box office sales. The only trace of Pirandello lies in the film's paradoxical title, altered on its release to *Senza amore* (Loveless loves) for promotional purposes since the title echoed his first collection of stories (1891).

Tespi's move to bring Pirandello's prestige and creativity to the medium in any case had little bearing on the larger fact that Italy's film fortunes had been declining steadily after a triumphant first decade. Already inflated by a need to fill those 3,227 cinemas built by 1914, the industry could not weather financial disasters caused by its own excesses and economic failures of the country at large. Italian producers slowly lost their hegemony over international filmmaking and distribution, but not only because they clung to the making of epics and because their star system cost millions. World War I and a Russian revolution had closed off outlets in Central and Eastern Europe, and the United States had seized markets it intended to keep. Meanwhile, unnoticed by beleaguered Italians, their "exaltation of passion and highlighting of adultery" in bourgeois film had been alienating all important Anglo-Saxon markets and the blasé French as well (Leprohan, 49). Censorship became a real obstacle abroad and at home at a time when arbiters of public health were seeking to keep morale high through films with uplifting subjects. The barriers of censorship more generally caused lasting repercussions on the fate of Pirandello's favorite projects, hardly conventional in their treatments of aberrant passion and criminal consequence.

Timing was all wrong for Pirandello and film, with or without Tespi. The brains and energy of the industry began to decamp from Italy early in the 1920s, just when Pirandello achieved international renown. French and German companies that had looked to Italy for jobs as well as inspiration were by the mid-twenties inviting Italian directors and technicians to work for them, and in such numbers that a community of influential Italians formed in Berlin. The city very soon became the center of international filmmaking. Pirandello's friends and colleagues like Gallone, Palermi, and Frateili, who made films of his work, began to shuttle back and forth between Rome, Turin, and Berlin. Germany was competing successfully with Italy for costume films; and the hour of the diva was passing into that of the worldly, mannish heroine of Weimar melodrama.

« 2 »

"When I turned a few years ago from fiction to drama," writes Pirandello, "I found playwriting simple. My characters live in my brain and create their own dramatic situations because life is dramatic."[16]

The history of the Pirandello story *Pensaci, Giacomino!* (*Better Think Twice About It!*) might be a "record in little" of Pirandello's journey through genre, as well as a foreshadowing of the Author's voyeurism in the scenarios for *Six Characters*. The story was rewritten as a play for Angelo Musco at Martoglio's Sicilian art theater in 1916, and then again for a film starring Musco in 1936 (fig.5). Introducing a doubled male in a comic mood this time, the plot centers around the marriage of another philosophical gentleman of a certain age but adds a January-to-May twist to the theme. To summarize briefly, a schoolmaster, Toti, with a young wife agrees to play husband in name only so she can continue a love affair with one Giacomino. The males' split into aloof observer and ardent lover intensifies when the couple's love child, along with forces of respectability, drive Giacomino into hiding and the wife into wretchedness. The schoolmaster, already something of an absent, impotent husband and fond of the child, then comes to resemble the invisible author of voyeuristic plot as he champions the lovers' rights and his to resume their *ménage a trois*. Like the archetypal trickster in the background of many of Pirandello's Sicilian heroes, Toti inverts the social order. He also fools the bureaucracy into providing a pension for his new family despite scandal and gossip. Most important, his honor, that Sicilian iron code, depends on others' knowledge of the ménage remaining tacit rather than public, a situation similar to that in *Il berretto a sonagli* (*Cap and Bells*, 1918). Against all of Pirandello's expectations, this parody of Sicilian marriage was greeted pedantically, even piously, as a "triumph of the individual will over social propriety" (Bassnett-McGuire, 18).[17]

Perhaps the 1936 film exploited the strain of pathology implicit in the theme of a masked man orchestrating his life as other. The film itself perished. Conjecture about such a shift from parody to psychological drama gains credence from two events: Pirandello's drift toward gothic expressionism during the twenties; and a similar shift in the two films of his 1904 modernist romance, *Il fu Mattia Pascal* (*The Late Mattia Pascal*), first in 1925, and then as a sound film in 1936. Again as in *Pensaci, Giacomino!* a husband in name only cares briefly for another man's infant; again his alter ego becomes an ardent lover; but differences between the two fictions matter more. The novel's fine art of doubling concerns a young librarian caught up in existential terrors when he re-creates his identity from randomly chosen names, titles, locations, and the like. At first something of a bystander in his own life victimized by cleverer associates, Mattia Pascal escapes from marriage in a small town to a young woman made pregnant by his rival. He seizes upon a false newspaper report of his drowning and regenerates himself in Rome as one Adriano Meis. Then suffering anguish, anxiety, and yet exhilaration at his phantom life-in-death, Pascal/Meis becomes an early exemplar of modernist disorientation and disintegration, the state of extreme alienation later expressed by Sartre's *Nausee*. He begins to fall in love with a young woman, but like Serafino

Gubbio, threatened with developing a self if loved in return, he "kills" Meis in a futile attempt to reassume Pascal's identity. The convergence of past and present, death and rebirth, sketch out confrontation with mysteries of absence, both Pascal's and those of his women. Pascal's wife, believing him dead, has married his rival other. Pirandello's attachment to his ghost story echoes in the (probably apocryphal) report that during the novel's writing, when his wife was suffering a psychosomatic attack that paralyzed her legs and "fixed" her, he signed a letter "Il fu Luigi Pirandello," a young Sicilian dreaming of escape through death and transfiguration (Kezich, 77). His deeper relation to the work may hinge on a son's rebellion against a father by self-generation,[18] another theme refigured in the scenarios for *Six Characters*.

The novel found its perfect cinematographer in Marcel L'Herbier, already known as a pioneer among surrealists, symbolists, Post-Impressionists, especially cubists, and expressionists; he even became an honorary Futurist since most inner circles in the arts claimed him for their own. His cubist *Don Juan et Faust* (Don Juan and Faust, 1923) and his *L'inhumaine* (The inhuman, 1924) distinguished him among filmmakers playing with accelerated montage, innovative shot formations, split images, simultaneity, and like antinarrative techniques that converted Pirandello into an admirer. (He at first resisted giving the novel to L'Herbier.)[19] Put the other way around, L'Herbier's *Pascal* places Pirandello at the center of debates on film ideology in Italy, France, and Russia. L'Herbier chose the work precisely because its nonlinear structure and imagery pose the problem of finding photogenic equivalents for "metaphysical realism" (Stone, "Cineastes' Texts," 52) and lent themselves to experiment with optical distortions of setting, framing, and stylized acting as well. The performance by the great Ivan Mosjoukine (fig.6) evoked eulogies from many critics, including Leonard Sciascia: "All readers of the novel who have seen the film, perhaps even Pirandello himself, would be unable to remember the character of Pascal except with the figure, movements, and expressions of Mosjoukine."[20] Close-ups of Mosjoukine's exaggerated gestures and staring eyes link the film to supernatural tonalities then in vogue but also to problems of diegesis and subjectivity. We might digress to notice an experimental film shot by Vsevolod D. Pudovkin and colleagues, and famous among cineastes known to Pirandello.[21] The experiment used a close-up of Mosjoukine's face to demonstrate how sequencing and cutting between images could elicit emotional response in an audience. The same static image of his face was followed first by a plate of soup, then by a coffin with a dead woman in it; and finally by a little girl playing with a funny toy bear. The juxtaposition of images aiming to externalize thought and emotion, as well as their content, might well have fascinated the Pirandello of *L'umorismo* (*On Humor*).

Among several shots in Marcel L'Herbier's *Pascal* when poetic image synthesizes meaning, those of Pomino shaking a tree to symbolize the fall of Pascal's gentry house (an echo of the *Cherry Orchard*), or of the funeral cortege for Pascal's mother and baby, lift the film toward tragedy. Settings, however, carried the greatest burden of picturing Pascal's vertiginous experience of freedom while reflecting the deformations current in horror films. "By using heavy shadows and dizzying designs, by distorting plane and surface, he [the designer, Cavalcanti] has underscored the rhythms of this strange, distorted tale of Pirandello's imagining."

> The long lines of windows, abrupt and jagged geometric of the carpet, the heaviness of the gothic arches, the very artificiality of the studio lighting are all used to exaggerate the note of morbid unreality of the drama. The decor is dependent on the lighting and the whims of the camera; the camera, on the mobility of the decor.[22]

Playing off setting against judicious cuts of provincial incident, from grotesque to venal, L'Herbier manages to convey the principle of *il contrario* and to express the mixture of compassion and farce in Pascal's motives. He minimizes Pascal's bourgeois love affair in Rome, expending footage instead on the hero's return to the small town, identified with San Gimignano, and the assorted village types rejecting him.[23]

In a promotional newspaper story, Pirandello cast his high praise for L'Herbier's accomplishment in comparison to the pedestrian quality of his usual collaborators.

> Until now, the rapport between my works and their film versions has been insignificant. . . . In America, a major case in point, they have literally thrown themselves on my books. They offered me a respectable amount of money on the one condition I would permit my story [*Mattia Pascal?*] to be filmed with a modified ending. I too had one essential condition countering their request: my dignity as a writer, which they precisely forbid me, and always will forbid me, by sacrificing my moral interests, my philosophical ideas, and my consciousness to a commercial goal.

Now I enthusiastically give *Mattia Pascal* to L'Herbier, whose character and work I infinitely esteem. He who knew how to film *Don Juan et Faust* will know how to execute the implications [all that's missing] of the romance, and conserve the maximum amount of the original subject's nobility and philosophy. (Callari, 308)

The allusion to *Don Juan et Faust* strikes a particularly resonant chord since treatments of the legend by both L'Herbier and Friedrich Murnau contributed to Pirandello's own growth as a filmmaker.

« 3 »

Ultimately, these and more variations on the theme of absence and self-creation coalesce in *Six Characters*, so pivotal to Pirandello's poetics. Among several forms of the work on its move from fiction, to drama, to film, only one features Pirandello himself as a Character and injects his keen sense of farce into tragic feeling.[24] In "Colloqui coi personaggi" (Conversations with characters, 1915), Pirandello finds his dead mother's ghost among "a visitation of nascent characters during the Author's usual hours of reception."[25] Struck by a painful awareness that her absence deprives him of reality, he confronts an *untransformed* image from his unconscious, recalling Freud on the uncanny, and a splinter of ego formed in response to his desire and grief. Put differently, his apprehension shifts between metaphysical and real territories of conscious and unconscious energy, hitherto untapped in his writings, as he becomes both subject and object of thwarted desire. The experience may have precipitated some of his theater plays' most penetrating insights into *feelings* of lost identity and madness, while advancing his perceptions about the artist's inner world. The story and its autobiographical core, therefore, may represent a turning point in Pirandello's aesthetic, for his twin aspects meet for the first time in writing as if in rehearsal for the film treatments. Throughout the narrative, too, Pirandello renders both the intrinsic theatricality and pictorial quality of the psychological event in sharp detail, both elements exquisitely translated in the film *Kaos* (Chaos, 1986) by the Taviani brothers.

Like the ghost mother, Pirandello's suffering "six characters" emerge from a psychic twilight to meet their everyday counterparts in the daylight of reason. His often quoted letter to Stefano (1917),[26] reporting that his unfinished novel about an importunate and violent family has found its perfect form as a play "in the making," seems plainly to announce a precise correspondence between his characters' rising to his awareness and the play's dramatic conceit. The

29

event resembles dream states, when a sleeping consciousness permits deeply suppressed fantasy to surface into the recognizable and nightmarish, hence rarely welcome forms. Introspection pursued in his quest for authenticity exacted a penalty from Pirandello, as the Author of the scenarios reveals. Complex feelings coincide in the play's representations of women, love, and deprivation; of separation from the mother from the child's perspective; of unstable family relations; of "absent" men and Pirandello's disavowal of his phantoms.

Perhaps the audience on the opening night of *Six Characters* intuited more of these psychological dimensions than has been reported. Certainly, the performance in Rome on May 10, 1921, caused a riot and a scandal.[27] Apart from the play's unconventional opening, its nonlinear form and abstract dialogue elicited catcalls that grew into shouts of derision as the central fantasy of incest between Father and Stepdaughter unfolded. The play reflected a diseased mind (Giudice, 116). Outside the theater, an elegantly dressed audience laughed, whistled, and threw coins at the "poor lunatic" author. Pirandello was badly shaken. At tremendous risk to his integrity, he had drawn on his knowledge of the psyche for universal characters, dramatizing unruly passions from several points of view. Nonetheless, the family's contradictory accounts of tragic betrayals, sibling murder, and suicide struck the audience as evidence of moral flippancy. He had failed miserably in his effort to stage "a public trial of human actions as they truly are," as he phrased it in his speech to the Alexander Volta Congress in 1934, by peeling away every illusion of naturalism. In previous plays, as in subsequent ones of a similar pattern, a group of characters in a framing action interrogate one or more mysterious characters of an inner play whose strange torments arouse suspicion, anger, annoyance, bafflement, fear, and ridicule. Their spectrum of emotions is neither explained nor resolved, thus leaving spectators in acute discomfort. No play before or after, however, cut as close to innate violence or exploited its resistance to reason with such power.

Then in Milan, several months after the disaster in Rome, an audience listened to the play "in a religious silence," signifying a triumph that spread, between 1922 and 1927, to every major city in Europe, to New York, Buenos Aires, and Tokyo. Recognized as the quintessential expression of high modernism and subjectivity, the play is based on a simple premise. A family of six statuesque characters advance into a theater proposing their absolute, autonomous existence. They seek an Author to complete the story of their lives and free them from bondage to the one tormenting moment of near incest shaping their identities. A troupe of professional actors on-stage, rehearsing a play – Pirandello's *Il giuoco delle parti* – when the family arrives, become intrigued by the situation and decide to perform their tales; the Director's frustrated attempts to create a coherent script out of their conflicting reports becomes the dramaturgical work of the play. Two levels of artifice, embodied in the inner group of Characters and outer one of Performers, are thus juxtaposed within the larger artifice of theater itself to explode conventional ideas about mimetic drama. Passionately, comically, tragically, but essentially statically, the family's complicated history unfolds through discontinuous talk, argument, and disquisition, chiefly by the Father. These represent stages in the creation of theatrical illusion and its relation to an absolute reality remaining as elusive as the absent Author. This *is* the play.

Audiences, however, kept waiting in vain for a linear *story* to develop and conclude out of the shocking news that the Father unknowingly had propositioned his own Stepdaughter in a brothel – the Mother had two sets of children, one by the Father, another by his double. One wonders if and to what degree audiences' expectations influenced Pirandello's decisions to develop the family's story realistically in the filmscripts. In the play, while the full story remains firmly suppressed, the Characters enact only their own fragments of the experience: the Mother at the instant she interrupts the brothel scene; the Little Girl at the point of accidentally drowning herself; the Boy, who sees the drowning, in the act of shooting and killing himself; the Stepdaughter hearing about the other children and running away from home. Such melodramatic incident, commonplace in modern drama, remains peripheral to the quest on-stage for one coherent tale, much to the frustration of scores of uncomprehending audiences to this day.

The synopsis of that suppressed story, prepared by Eric Bentley in *The Pirandello Commentaries* and quoted here, reveals the relation of themes to their earlier forms; to interpretations of the film scenarios; and perhaps to problems encountered in many failed attempts to film the work.

A man has a wife and male child. He also has a male secretary. Between the wife and the secretary there arises what the husband considers to be an understanding of a harmless sort. He wants to help them in some way, but whenever he speaks to them they exchange a significant look that seems to ask how they should receive what he says if they are not to annoy him. But this itself annoys him. He ends up firing the secretary. Then he sends the wife after him. In the wife's view, he fairly throws her into the secretary's arms; and the pair set up house together.

The husband, however, does not lose interest in the wife. His continued interest, indeed, though he considers it "pure" (that is, asexual) is a source of embarrassment to the former secretary. When a daughter is born to the lovers the husband is interested in her too – more, perhaps, even than he had been in the wife. And when the daughter becomes a schoolgirl, he waits for school coming out, then on at least one occasion seeks her out, and gives her a present. The girl does not know who the strange gentleman is.

At a certain point the secretary can bear the whole situation no longer, and he takes his family – there are three children by this time – to live somewhere else, out of the stepfather's reach. Subsequently the secretary dies. His family of four are now destitute; they have to sleep all in the same room. And at some point they return to the place where the husband lived. Here the mother gets employment as a kind of seamstress. But her employer's real interest is in employing the daughter, now in her late teens, as a prostitute. The dressmaker's shop is a front for a brothel.

One day, the husband, a client of the establishment, presents himself and would have taken the girl in his arms had not the mother suddenly turned up to cry: "But it's my daughter!" After this encounter, the husband takes his wife back into his home along with his three stepchildren. At the time, he is living with his own son, now in his early twenties. This legitimate son is offended by the presence of the three bastards, and wanders from room to room in his father's house, feeling displaced and desolate. The three bastards react to his hostility. The little girl, aged four, drowns herself in the fountain in the garden. The other child, a fourteen-year-old boy, witnesses the drowning, fails to offer any assistance, then shoots himself.

The mother, who might have been keeping an eye on the young pair, was instead following her twenty-two-year-old son around the house, begging for forgiveness. He rushes out into the garden to escape her, and there comes upon his stepbrother just at the moment the latter watches his sister die, and kills himself. After this debacle, the older girl runs away from home. Left behind are the original father, mother, and son.

Bentley's retelling approximates the play's Ibsenesque trick of disclosing layers of plot in successive revelations. But the Characters' situation, location, background, temporal relation, and all such naturalistic detail, remain as abstract as for medieval moralities, those ancestors of expressionist drama and film. More immediately, Bentley's tale indicates that Pirandello concerns himself principally with the relationships among family members, tantamount to a preoccupation with dynamics and conflicts rather than characters as such. That those relationships reflect primal fantasies (of parental sex, jealousy, and sibling murder) becomes still clearer in psychoanalytical criticism of the scenarios and their reconfigured doubling of Father and Secretary, Mother and Daughter, and the Mother's first and second families. Both story and drama on its own terms anticipated the extent to which psychic experience and the divided self became metaphors for *the* essential drama of the twentieth century, and for role playing as a strategy of survival in an irrational universe.

* * *

It was George Pitoëff's audacious performance of the play in Paris (1923) followed by Max Reinhardt's in Berlin (1924) that launched Pirandello into world fame and presented him with entirely new, and at first objectionable, visions of the work. The productions, nonetheless, contributed to his revisions of the play and his rethinking about its pivotal themes.[28] Pitoëff saw the Characters neither as Pirandello's "living realities" nor as autonomous fugitives from his studio, but as abstract symbols (fig.7). Indeed, Pitoëff saw the entire play as symbolical, a view Pirandello resisted adamantly until he turned to its film scenarios. Persisting with his production plans despite Pirandello's protests, Pitoëff employed a slowly descending elevator, ordinarily used to bring furniture down from the flies, to lower the family from somewhere beyond onto a bare rehearsal stage. In their immobility and restraint they resembled marionettes, a likeness driving Pirandello to reverse his opinion about the production and rethink his own stage directions in the 1925 text of the play.[29] Pitoëff's own "phantom-like aspect" as the Father and his strange diction created a "supraterrestrial" effect (Bishop, "Pirandello's Influence," 34) while the metamorphosis of several other pirandellian themes can be discerned in descriptions of Pitoëff's staging. In all, he succeeded in overwhelming critics and bringing French theater into high modernism with one leap.

Equally though differently critical to Pirandello's evolving poetics, Max Reinhardt's brilliant interpretation exploited psychological interplay between conscious and unconscious forces. He enveloped the stage in an ultra-romantic, nightmarish atmosphere, oscillating between reality and unreality, treating the play as an expressionistic drama of emotional tensions (fig.8). Lighting effects of chiaroscuro so firmly associated with Reinhardt's Kammerspiel theater gave the Characters an unearthly glow, accentuating their nature as splits of imagination and heightening the element of guilt that Pirandello was to develop years later in his film *Treatment*. The most insightful analysis of Reinhardt's 1924 production compares it to the baroque allegorical tradition of seeing the world as a stage, with humans in finite roles and God as Author.[30] Between 1920 and 1926, Reinhardt worked for the Salzburg Festival, collaborating with Hugo von Hofmannsthal to stage his *Jedermann* (*Everyman*, 1911) and also performing an adaptation of Calderon's *Il teatro del mundo* (Great World Theatre). It follows plausibly that the experience might have influenced his giving full faith to Pirandello's original stage directions, assigning fundamental sentiments of "remorse" to the Father, "revenge" to the Stepdaughter, "disdain" to the Son, and "grief" to the Mother.

Still, while Reinhardt's parallel projects matter less to his interpretation of Pirandello than the translations and working scripts he used – more about these in chapter 6 – Reinhardt's vision matters to European theater traditions since his version of the play as a modern parable prevails on German stages to this day. In several ways, too, Reinhardt's production anticipated the Author's role as Creator in Pirandello's film *Film-Novelle* and *Treatment* discussed in chapters 4 and 6 respectively. Rather than doubling the Father in the outer play, Reinhardt's Director overshadowed the Father who dominated in French and Italian productions. His erotic Stepdaughter, while possessed of an exhibitionistic desire to self-display and abandon, retained a residue of middle-class modesty, again contrary to French and Italian versions. Pirandello, absorbed by the superlative resources of German relative to Italian theater, seems to have accepted the liberties Reinhardt took in the course of converting the open-ended play into a closed cosmic system, again like that of Renaissance theater. In any case, Reinhardt repeated his success with more than one hundred productions of the play and initiated a long professional friendship with the playwright who shared his passionate commitment to the drama of the individual as the primary business of the modern stage.

Beyond exposing Pirandello to hidden dimensions of his play, Pitoëff and Reinhardt introduced the playwright to the art of directing, perhaps prompting him to undertake the role himself and bringing him out from behind the dramatist's curtain of objectivity. Certainly, the play's success accelerated the launching of his *Teatro degli undici or dodici* (Theater of the eleven or twelve), referring to the eleven associates involved in its founding (fig.9).[31] He had been nursing the idea of a state theater for some time, but Mussolini's pleasure at the fame Pirandello brought to Italy finally persuaded the government to subsidize a company. While its headquarters remained in Rome, Pirandello also formed a touring company that traveled extensively until 1928 and drove him to discover both the subtleties of theater and his own talents as a performer. He talked often, for instance, about wanting to revive the spontaneity and intelligence of improvisation in the *commedia del arte* tradition, and he encouraged experiment by his actors. As director, however, he also began to appreciate the discretionary impositions of all mediators, including actors, between play and playwright. Staging, for instance, called upon a pictorial sense that he, like Ibsen and Strindberg, had tested as a young man in an occasional painting – albeit none of them painted with distinction. In *Si gira!* he had compared framing shots to painting (266), as if defining his approach to film images *as* images even before he had acquired the experience either of making silent films or staging a dramatic action.

That his eye by the mid-twenties had become as refined a conceptual tool as his ear was evident in the *mise en scene* of his company's productions. Whereas the poet knew words better than action, the director needed words and pictures in an ideal integration.[32] Without emulating the theories of either Konstantin Stanislavsky or Nikolai Nikolaevich Evreinov, whom Pirandello knew and admired, or even of the highly theoretical Erwin Piscator, whom he also met in Berlin, he relied as fledgling director upon his own theatrical instincts.[33] Within the first few months he planned an ambitious season that would stage a series of his own works followed by those of August Strindberg, Frank Wedekind, George Bernard Shaw ("his most revolutionary plays unknown to us"), and Paul Claudel (Tinterri and D'Amico, *Capocomico*, 22). To the extent that he formulated a policy for his company, it aimed first for a clear communication of text to audience, a goal reflecting his judgment of Italian theater as stultified, and also, differently, his considerable gifts as an actor. In this, he ranks with those two other playwrighting giants, Shakespeare and Moliere, who commanded great acting and managerial skills. Friends and colleagues remarked often and volubly on the extraordinary power with which Pirandello "sank into a character" when he instructed actors in the craft by reading works aloud. When he recited *Six Characters*, shortly after completing the manuscript, friends were "shaken" by his ability to enter into each part. "He lived their passions intensely, almost painfully – their love and hate, their joy

35

and pain, their ecstasy and irony" (Giudice, 115). Similar response to Pirandello's gift of projecting himself into characters lends plausibility to his deep psychological engagement in the "reality" of his phantoms. Indeed, Pirandello the actor underscores the claim of Pirandello the playwright that a drama begins with character rather than plot, situation, or philosophy.

Especially important in view of Pirandello's treatment of the unconscious in the scenarios, his London production convinced more than one critic that the great play tapped the unconscious as none had before (Sogliuzzo, *L. P. Director*, 151). One review claimed that the fantastic was omnipresent as a theatrical dream. The family of six in heavy black dress (fig.10) and bathed in red light descended the theater's center aisle and mounted the stage, as if "in a dream," or resembling "spectors from a fable or a fairy tale" (D'Amico and Tinterri, *Capocomico*, 56). Others compared Pirandello's production unfavorably with Reinhardt's, claiming that the ideas of Pirandello the director failed to match those of Pirandello the playwright (Giudice, 176). The gist of criticism seems to be that whereas Reinhardt had given requisite form to the play's psychological depths, Pirandello emphasized a spirit of game playing and a taste for irony and self-parody, warning audiences "not to take things too seriously; events on stage were merely theatrical" (Sogliuzzo, 152).

Perhaps the play's mingling of tragedy and comedy in the spirit of *teatro del grottesco* lost something in his staging; Pirandello only gradually learned the resources of theater. Whereas early on his sets, for instance, tended to be realistic, they in time became increasingly symbolic, especially in their use of lighting effects (Sogliuzzo, 86). But criticism of his early directing to some extent reflects actual abuses of Italian theater in which the self-interest of a *capocomico*, director-producer-manager-(sometimes also)lead actor, reigned supreme.[34] They trained audiences to expect artificial conventions and fostered a cult of personality, so that ensemble acting like that in Pirandello's or Reinhardt's companies scarcely existed. Eleanora Duse herself believed that before Italian "theatre could be reformed all actors must die of the plague" (Sogliuzzo, xxiv). Pirandello instead reserves his wickedest satire in the theater plays for totalitarian *capocomici*. In *Six Characters* the Director resists every possible incursion upon his stage by the spectral family. Later on, in *Questa sera si recita a soggetto* (*Tonight We Improvise*, 1930), another dictatorial director, Dr. Hinkfuss, tries to prevent actors of an inner play about Sicilian jealousies from performing, only to be driven off the stage in the end. Pirandello goes further than in previous theater plays to topple rigid conventions by mixing actors with spectators. By then, however, he obviously had acquired considerable expertise. As a benchmark of the experience he gained after two years of directing, reviews of his *Six Characters* in London (1923) praised its completely fluid, unaffected style, its "threefold power of expression," and the actors' delivery that charmed "the ear like music."

* * *

Given the tight relation during the 1920s between silent film and theater, directing must have refined Pirandello's attention to both the latent imagery and theatricality of his works. Revising the ending of *Six Characters* in its second edition (1923), he attenuates the abrupt ending of the original version with an entirely wordless, cinematic *coup d'teatre*. He backlights the silhouettes of Father, Mother, and Son against a scrim, leaving the Boy's death ambiguous and audiences as perplexed as the Director. Then the Stepdaughter flees the stage into a theatrical limbo situated somewhere between the symbolic family and actual audience. Pirandello made changes to the opening also which appear to stem from a sharpened awareness of the audience as vital participants in a visual experience of the play. Expanded actions of the professional company to make their rehearsal of *Il giuoco delle parti* "feel" more naturalistic, allow audiences to identify with the actors immediately and react with similar astonishment when that nightmarish family of specters invades the stage.

Pirandello also dropped the playwright's mask by including a Preface with the play's 1925 edition, regarded as the equivalent of the director's notes that he first delivered to London audiences after each performance.[35] Even his well-known description of conflict between the Director's desire for form and the Father's ideas about passion belongs as much to criticism of staging as to aesthetics.[36] But the most often quoted passage primarily tells that familiarity never diminished Pirandello's "possession" by his six characters: "One does not give life to a character for nothing. Creatures of my spirit, these six were already living a life which was their own and not mine any more, a life which it was not in my power any more to deny them. . . . At a certain point I actually became obsessed with them."

« 4 »

Perhaps the most poignant result of forming the Teatro d'Arte di Roma concerns Pirandello's devotion to the actress Marta Abba, who became his muse and motive for film. He hired her sight unseen on the strength of glowing praise for her performance in Chekhov's *Seagull* at an amateur theater in Milan.[37] She was slight, physically almost childlike, he says in one of his letters, yet possessed an astonishing ability to embody completely whatever character she played. Reviews of Marta Abba's performance as the Stepdaughter in *Six Characters* and Pirandello's description of the role in his 1925 Preface call on similar vocabulary: she was "disdainful, alluring, treacherous, full of impudence." She seemed to control the part's extreme oscillations between worldliness and vulnerability with ease. If anyone swayed Pirandello from his early view of actors as the theater's necessary evil, it must have been Marta Abba. He admired and enjoyed her, marveled at her skill, wrote plays for her, eventually confided in her as a lover in 552 letters (written between 1929 and 1936 alone), although their relationship remained sexually circumspect. When they met, Pirandello was fifty-one years old, she twenty-three. He looked on her as a beloved second daughter in need of the protection he continued to give freely until he died. As for Abba, she never varied in her respectful response to him, never adopting in her letters the familiar "tu"; "for me, he was like a god" (Ortolani, *Le Lettere*, 5).

For a man whose art and life were inseparable, fondness for and even infatuation with Abba could not help but influence his making of theater and film; but about this, any comment remains guesswork. Colleagues tell that he studied her hypnotic recitals intently, that he even avoided the playhouse when she was not performing (D'Amico and Tinterri, *Capocomico*, 194). Did the man who imagined himself as her father project them both into the revised play? Especially given his elaboration of the Daughter's role in the filmscripts? And more especially given his wife's terrible delusion about incest between him and his daughter Lietta? It would appear, more reliably, that his continuing preoccupation with the psychological split between the essence of character and its expression by an actor shifts over the years of his friendship with Marta Abba toward subtle insight into the dynamic between the actor's persona and the consequences of acting.

One of the late plays written for Abba, *Trovarsi* (*To Find Oneself*, 1932), studies the deleterious effects of the stage on authenticity. Reminiscent of D'Annunzio's novel describing Eleanora Duse, *Il Fuoco* (The fire), the actress Donata of *Trovarsi* must forswear all life except that of her characters. She belongs to the public body and soul, only recognizing the tragic "absence" of her independent persona when she falls in love and sees that her very caresses resemble those she had performed on-stage. Donata never finds her true self through love; life for her represents endless struggle toward an unattainable idea. Redemption for such suffering comes, if it does, only from the life of art. Pirandello's next play, *Quando si è qualcuno* (*When One Is Somebody,* 1933), repeats the theme to show a famous author as no less of a slave to his masks. Both plays come well after Pirandello had been wrestling with the theme in filmscripts.

Finally, as a footnote to Pirandello's travels through genre in this period, the successful stage production of *Enrico IV* (*Henry IV*), which often has been called the twentieth-century *Hamlet,* resulted in the silent film directed in 1925 by another Sicilian friend, Amleto Palermi. The success of L'Herbier's *Feu Mathias Pascal* seems to have persuaded Pirandello to the venture, at least partly since Palermi too shared his film ideology (Giudice, 192). Underwritten jointly by Roman and Berlin companies, the film starred the Reinhardt veteran Conrad Veidt as the wily madman who clings to lunacy as a strategy for survival, then fakes sanity in a world gone insane. Thus emerges the model of modern man as tragic hero, his foundation and imprisonment merely twin masks of madness. Palermi enlisted the technical assistance of Adolf Lantz, the Viennese filmmaker who later collaborated with Pirandello on one of the scenarios.[38] Copious reviews of Veidt's talents include only the most perfunctory remarks about the film by Pirandello – one reviewer equivocated about the film as "dignified, especially considering the difficulty of doing a silent film from this subject."[39] Pirandello's response, nevertheless, may be inferred from the techniques he learned for visualizing madness and absence in the scenarios. *Enrico IV* was the eighth and final silent film made from his works but only the first of several films made of the play.[40] The most recent, in 1983, starred Marcello Mastroianni and is still in circulation.

1. A *teatro di posa* (*Cinema* 23, June 1937).

2. Above: The diva Pirandello
chose to play Varia Nesteroff in a
proposed film of *Si gira!* Courtesy
of the Centro sperimentale di cinematografia, Cineteca nazionale,
Rome.

3. Right: Péter Blaskó as Serafino
Gubbio in *Folog a film* (*Si gira!*) (Kra
Pictures, Hungary, 1985) (*Omaggio
a Pirandello – Almanacco letterario
Bompiani 87*, edited by Leonardo
Sciascia. Milan: Bompiani, 1986).

4. Above: The Tespi Film group (Lucio D'Ambra, "Sette anni di Cinema," *Cinema* 28, August 1937).

5. Right: Pirandello on the set of *Pensaci, Giacomino!* (*Cinema* 4, August 1936).

6. Two film directors' visions of *Il fu Mattia Pascal* (*Cinema* 117, May 1941). Scenes from L'Herbier's production are shown in the left column, Chenal's in the right.

Top: Mattia Pascal.

Middle: L'Herbier's Adriana, Chenal's Luisa.

Bottom: Mattia's wife.

Top: The Mother.

Middle: The medium, Signorina Caporali.

Bottom: Pomino.

6. *continued*

Top: Aunt Scolastica.

Middle: Papiano's brother.

Bottom: The wedding.

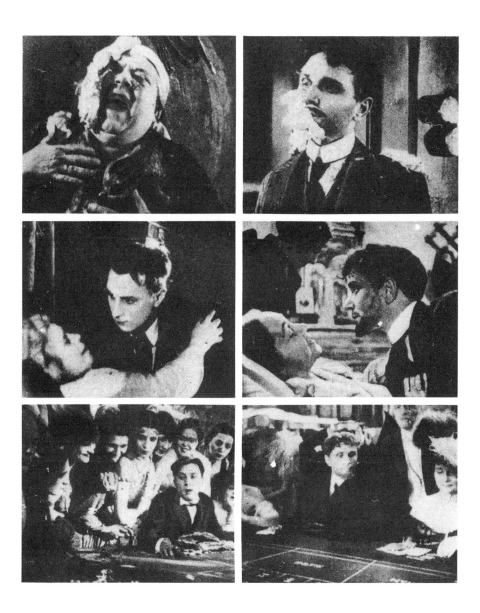

Top: The dough episode.

Middle: The mother's death.

Bottom: Winning at the tables.

6. *continued*

Top: Decision to feign death.

Middle: The doubling of the personality.

Bottom: The idyll comes to flower.

Top: The seance.

Middle: The impossibility of realizing the dream.

Bottom: The last frame.

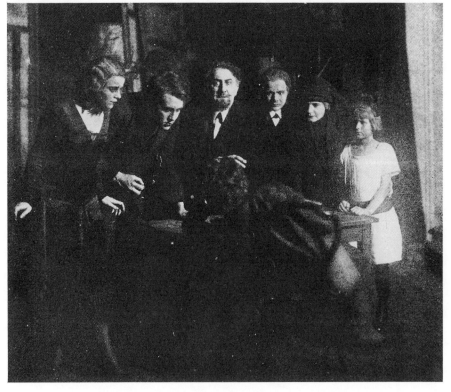

7. Top left: Scene from Pitoëff's staging of *Six Characters in Search of an Author* (*Pirandello Capocomico*). Reproduced courtesy of the Civico Museo Biblioteca dell'Attore, Genoa.

8. Bottom left: Scene from Reinhardt's staging of *Six Characters in Search of an Author* (*Pirandello Capocomico*). Reproduced courtesy of the Civico Museo Biblioteca dell'Attore, Genoa.

9. Above: The Teatro d'Arte di Roma company, 1925 to 1928. Reproduced courtesy of the Billy Rose Theatre Collection, The New York Public Library for the Performing Arts, Astor, Lenox, and Tilden Foundations.

10. Above: Scene from Pirandello's staging of *Six Characters in Search of an Author* for the Teatro d'Arte (*Pirandello Capocomico*). Reproduced courtesy of the Civico Museo Biblioteca dell'Attore, Genoa.

11. Left: Pirandello on the set of Chenal's film, *L'homme de nulle part* (*Il fu Mattia Pascal*) with its stars Isa Miranda and Pierre Blanchar (*Cinema* 11, December 1936, and *Cinema* 120, June 1941).

LUISA - Adriano, non credevo più ~~di~~ rivederti. Avevo capito sai che

non potevi sposarmi, e t'avevo perdonato. Sei ritornato, ~~mio~~

caro, e ora non hai ~~più~~ ~~indre~~ ~~di~~ niente, ~~di~~ nessuno ..?

MATTIA Tu hai creduto che avessi commesso un delitto ?

(Luisa abbassa la testa) *Non sapevo* ...

MATTIA ~~Hai potuto crederpquesto~~ ? No, Luisa, io non sono ~~colpevole~~, *colpevole,*

~~ma ho fatto, con un ... ~~ *soltanto uno spaventoso errore è stato commesso. Le che permesso*

ed ho perduto il mio nome. *Ora non sono più ...*

LUISA ~~e allora...~~ Adriano Meis ?

MATTIA Si, ~~su~~ sui documenti che tu ~~xxxx~~ hai visto, ma sono falsi.

In realtà io sono...io sono il fu Mattia Pascal.

LUISA Che dici ?

MATTIA La verità!

LUISA Tu mi spaventi ...

MATTIA Si, il fu Mattia Pascal, sepolto e cancellato dai vivi.

LUISA Adriano, non ti comprendo, spiegati.

MATTIA Avrò tutta la vita per raccontartelo...

LUISA Io t'amo, ma dimmi subito...

MATTIA ~~xxxxxxxxxxxxxxxxxxxxxxxxxxxxxxxxx~~ Ascolt ..è una strana *così strana*

storia, c'era una volta a Miragno un ragazzo che andava a caccia

di farfalle...

F I N E

12. Filmscript for Chenal's
L'homme de nulle part corrected
in Pirandello's handwriting
(*Cinema* 11, December 1936).

THREE

Prologo (The *Prologue*)

*As I open the door, a cloud of phantoms rise mid-air and enter with me . . . as if
taking on substance from their own inner light: they are Henry IV, Donna Anna
Luna, Signor Ponza and Signora Frola.* Prologue

In 1941 the Italian journal *Cinema*[1] republished Pirandello's précis for a
film version of *Six Characters* along with an article by Giancarlo Beria
entitled "Pirandello and the Surrealists." The article supposes that the
précis, first published in an unnamed journal in 1926, must have been promised to a director connected with the post-war Surrealist Movement. No
director, however, was named. *Cinema's* editor, moreover, calls the précis a
Prologo (*Prologue*), apparently aware that Pirandello also had written a full
film scenario for his play, but disclaims knowing anything about the précis's
provenance.

> We know nothing about the information cited in Beria's article. Whether
> our colleague's ideas, and the hopes he has for the promise of Pirandello's
> cinema are accurate or not, it will be interesting to return to the great
> writer's time and give him a chance to speak for himself. About fifteen
> years ago Pirandello collaborated on a scenario of *Six Characters in Search
> of an Author.* From a newspaper of the time, we are extracting the *Prologo*
> to that scenario, written by Pirandello himself. Is Beria's reasoning cor-
> rect? (*Cinema*, 410)

Precisely when and why the *Prologo* was written, how it found its way into
an unnamed journal in 1926, why it remained unknown to film critics and
historians, how its departures from the play in content and style should be
accounted for given their identical titles are all questions that remained un-
answerable in 1941. The weight of unknowns surely would have precluded
the *Prologo's* publication had it not been written in the first person and signed
by Pirandello. Beria alluded to a collaborator on the *Prologo*, but no traces of a

collaborator existed in available documents, notwithstanding all the writers, producers, and film people with whom Pirandello came in contact. Neither did Pirandello ever mention such a collaborator in any of his papers or interviews. Given the 1926 date of the *Prologo's* first publication and its style, the idea of making a film based on *Six Characters* probably arose some time after the productions by Pitoëff and Reinhardt that emphasized symbolic interpretations. And given the *Prologo's* elaboration of the Stepdaughter's role, it probably was written after he met Marta Abba in February of 1925. But the evidence for even these suppositions remained shrouded in mystery until recent scholarship in film history, along with access to some of Pirandello's private papers and letters, provided a context for a series of educated guesses. The story that emerged reached a climax after Italian film had relinquished its crown to Germany and Pirandello had fled Rome.

« 1 »

By the time the *Prologo* appeared, the Italian film industry had nearly expired. In 1926 not a single film was produced anywhere in the country (Leprohan, 47). Behind the scenes an enterprising distributor, Mario Pittaluga, had been acquiring bankrupt movie houses and production companies until he controlled the last vestiges of the industry. When those 3,227 movie theaters in Italy that showed mainly foreign films were ordered by law in 1926 to include one Italian film for every ten films shown, a ratio that was soon increased to 25 percent, Pittaluga became the official king of Italian filmmaking. When Mussolini instructed him the following year to revive production and distribute films made by the state institute called L.U.C.E (Union of Cinematic Education), the future of film as a tool of fascism was writ large.

L.U.C.E had been founded in response to a government report calling for cinema owners to include scientific and patriotic films in their programs "in an attempt to correct public taste."[2] Reacting to popular melodramas about adultery as well as to "low comedy," the report projected the code of public service and antiseptic family relations associated historically with militant fascist reform. At one point, believing that Pirandello could be lured by state money, if not by patriotism, one of the establishment faithfuls asked him to write a film for L.U.C.E about the glories of work that would stimulate both morale and the sagging economy. Pirandello politely refused. Such a project, he wrote to his son Stefano, would be filled with political dangers. Nor did he spell out his disgust at Pittaluga's effective lockout of filmmakers not in his circle. Politics apart, government support later on managed to keep cinema alive, boosting production at Cinecitta from seven films to eighty-four per year between 1930 and 1939. The company created a film school fostering the work of several gifted directors, Alessandro Blasetti and Augusto Camerini among them. Still, no product sufficiently distinguished to create an international impact appeared until the neorealist movement of the 1940s.

One story of a valiant effort in 1926 to reverse the ebb tide will illustrate the plight of Italian filmmakers. Amleto Palermi announced to the press that he would direct a monumental historical film called *The Last Days of Pompeii*. He rented the largest studio at Cines, where no film had been made for years, hired cameramen at exorbitant fees, signed up stars, filled the Roman sports stadium with 5,000 extras, shot some remarkable scenes with gladiators, lions, and the like, then took the stills to Vienna with the aim of selling the film he had barely begun. Vienna demurred. Then they demanded their own stars; Palermi had to agree. Buyers in Berlin wanted still other actors; again Palermi had to agree. Back in Rome, he had to pay a huge indemnity to his original actors that drove his budget to an astronomical figure and him off on a two-year quest for additional funding. The film, all in all, cost the astounding sum of 7 million lire and was the last important film to be shot in Italy until the industry's post–World War II revival.

Plainly, unequivocally, Pirandello's *Prologo* could not have been written with Italian production in mind. In 1978 the film scholar Francesco Callari found several documents in family archives dating between 1926 and 1928 concerning *Six Characters*. They indicate that a film version was planned to complete a trio of prestigious productions begun in 1925 with Marcel L'Herbier's *Feu Mathias Pascal* and including *Enrico IV* by Palermi and Lantz. The first document was a telegram in August from a Berlin film company that Pirandello received while his Teatro d'Arte troupe stopped over briefly in Rome.[3] The Berlin company informed him that on delivery of a script, and if *Six Characters* was "still free for filming," they would pay 100,000 lire for the film rights and guarantee the Stepdaughter's part to Marta Abba. They obviously did not expect film rights to the play but rather to a yet unwritten scenario and may have seen the *Prologo*.

The second document, a letter from Pirandello in Genoa (10 September 1926) to his son Stefano, reported that Hans Feist, the putative first German translator of Pirandello's plays, had written him on "film business," and that Pirandello had responded with a wire "indicating the minimum sum he had asked for the *La nuova colonia* (*The New Colony*) and *Six Characters*." In another letter from Genoa nine days later, Pirandello reported that "Palermi had telegraphed from Rome offering 5,000 dollars for *Six Characters*. I've telegraphed Feist and await a reply." The two quite separate negotiations with Palermi and Feist indicate that Pirandello was pursuing the most important authors and cinematographers based in Berlin, seeking the best possible arrangement. He continued his theater tour of South America, the company's second, and for about a year says nothing more about filming *Six Characters*, although other film projects proceeded. Then in the spring of 1928, a sense of urgency fills his communications, as if his theater successes have fired him with fresh energy. Pirandello writes Stefano that a proposal from a Brazilian filmmaker, leaving the "strongest possible impression" on him, has rekindled his desire to film *Six Characters*.

At this point, threads of the project's history lead into a web of troubles and ill-will, stretching farther than Pirandello could see from his outposts on tour and ensnaring more than his film interests. He returned that summer from his company's final engagement to find the mood around him in Rome strained and precarious for reasons that might have been predicted by his disdain for power politics at all levels. Like many Sicilian gentry, Pirandello believed that his economically and socially underdeveloped country needed a strong, authoritative government to bring it into the twentieth century.[4] Mussolini at first had appeared to be the right man for the job and so had won Pirandello's support. Essentially, nevertheless, Pirandello was apolitical, deeply conservative, and perhaps naive about government under a dictatorship. Believing idealistically that Mussolini's subsidy of the theater company symbolized a renaissance of the arts, he registered distress, privately and unfortunately publicly, over the inadequate and sporadic funding that led to his company's collapse that summer of 1928, after three years of arduous effort.[5]

Neither did Pirandello anticipate, while abroad, the corrupting effects of state licensing on all public performances and theaters. When Pirandello had returned from his company's first tour in 1927, he confronted a theater syndicate grown strong enough to make bookings at home extremely difficult for him, and antagonistic enough to drive him out on tour again. He returned in 1928 to a still more acute situation. State control had abolished all syndicates but substituted a crippling monopoly of playhouses and theatrical ventures that aggravated mismanagement at all levels of organization. Systematic and de facto personal patronage generated intrigues, jealousies, and rivalry, yet also a kind of paralysis among artists as well as administrators that Pirandello never quite credited as irreversible (Ortolani, 7). Periodically, he seemed convinced, for instance, that a sweeping reform of an inept theater system might "come from above," even after he discovered that the monopoly had been organized by one of Mussolini's appointed czars, Paolo Giordani. "Around Him," [Mussolini] Pirandello wrote Marta Abba, there is "a level of heads which reach just about to his knees and not a finger higher. So everything necessarily remains at a low level, and there is truly nothing but baseness and confusion" (letter 22 September 1928).

A similar myopia kept him from realizing that reports of his open criticism of art in Italy had been ill received at home by both party and colleagues, in theater and film alike. Pirandello had become too great to ignore and too independent to control. Giordani and cohorts, keeping tight reins on their power while also threatened by Pirandello's stature, managed to stir up "unheard of horrors" in the form of cabals against him. In another of his copious letters to Marta late that summer he says, everyone has to bow to "LUI" [Mussolini], and "whenever anyone gains any prominence . . . he is attacked so that he eventually comes back into the fold" (letter 22 September 1928). This, however, Pirandello was not quite ready to do. In extreme disillusionment with friends and country, he saw no alternative but flight into exile in order "to breathe, to work, to regain the sense of one's own personality." His decision, nevertheless, had been more thoroughly engineered than he imagined.

> Yes, I'm leaving. Now that my company has been dissolved I have nothing more to do in Italy. *I shall take refuge in the cinema.* . . . Abroad, in a hotel room, I shall still be able to write. . . . People look at me as though they are reproaching me for the fact that Italy has given the world a writer. But the sequence was different. If I am not mistaken, my greatest fame came from abroad, the best performances of my work are given abroad, the longest and most objective studies of my work are written abroad. So perhaps people should say that the world has given Italy a writer. (Giudice, 183, emphasis added)

Apart from the clue to his attitude about film, the unmistakable bitterness in these words, reported by Lucio D'Ambra, sounded the base note of rancor about Italy echoing through his comments for the remainder of his life. He "had lost every effort to succeed in an Italy where Mussolini systematically destroyed people of worth" (Ortolani, 70). Trying to reverse his friend's decision the night before his departure, D'Ambra wagered that Pirandello would be made a senator in January. A mutual friend, he said, was arranging a meeting about it with Mussolini. Pirandello, nonetheless, remained adamant (letter 25 September 1928). He turned his back on Italy and headed for Berlin, instructing Marta Abba to meet him there. He would find solace in her, and together they would make her a star outshining the brightest "on Broadway" (Ortolani, 6).

"Yes, dear Marta, truly marvelous things can be done with film; I've been convinced for some time; and you'll see that I'll succeed in doing something to astonish everyone, for I have extraordinary things in mind" (letter 12 July 1928). Marta already had conquered the stage wherever the Teatro d'Arte troupe played, and Pirandello never doubted that the world's admiration would follow. Except for business visits or official occasions thereafter, Pirandello quit Rome. "I see no alternative to lifting my feet from this country where unheard of things are happening. . . . It's no longer possible for someone like me to live in Italy. I'll return, if I return, when I no longer need anyone" (letter 12 July 1928). The histrionic tone in his references to theater enemies strikes Ortolani, editor of Pirandello's correspondence, as reminiscent of Sicilian vendettas and as a pathetic evidence of Pirandello's state of mind: aggrieved, wounded, childishly antagonistic (131). Six months later he is still brandishing his fist at "tyrants," promising to "return to Italy after having achieved complete vindication here [in Berlin] in both film and in theatre, with a huge success that will restore all the prestige of my country where already, with the nomination [to the Academy] I have obtained a victory over all enemies" (letter 29 March 1929).

Ironically enough, in approving a performance of Pirandello's *La nuova colonia* immediately after his departure, state censors seem to have misunderstood the play's final cataclysmic ruin symbolizing his disgust with the political road Italy was traveling. Instead, the play was received as a vision of utopia and reviewed by loyal supporters of the regime as "the most hopeful" of all "the master's works," in spite of its ending with a grand tidal wave that sweeps all hopes to oblivion.[6]

« 2 »

Threads of the *Six Characters* project surface again in the fall of 1928 in Milan, where Pirandello stopped on his way north to publicize his plans through a long, detailed interview with Enrico Rocca, then editor of the official fascist newspaper *Il Popolo d'Italia*.[7] At one point, as if clarifying that Italy's eminent son was not merely following the film community out of the country, he said he dreamt of revolutionizing film as he had revolutionized the theater. Perhaps he was reminding Italy of the genius it had lost, perhaps hinting that he would welcome financing from industrialists trying to revive the industry. Given the exorbitant costs of filmmaking and the fragility of supposedly conclusive deals, he at least hoped to use the ear of the press to his advantage.

During the interview, Pirandello alluded to four film contracts for the *La nuova colonia*, *Six Characters*, "La rondinella" (The swallow), and "Nel segno." When Rocca asked if Il Maestro really thought film could translate all "the superb movement of thought" in *Six Characters*, in his opinion the most luminous and original of the master's works, Pirandello launched into a full description of his ideas that began with a paean of praise for the German director, Fredrich Murnau.

> I have the utmost faith in Murnau. Only he would be able to understand me; only with him could I prepare myself to compose and proceed with the work. So thoroughly is this the case that, if I don't get the cooperation of the German house, I will go to America with him where I am sure to connect with other people. And I tell you that if Murnau puts his hand to it [mind to it], *Six Characters* will gain in originality. He knows that I take part in the work as author, the author that I really am. . . . The film will successfully reveal. . . . I will give you an example of how I will work out every detail with Murnau.[8]

And he proceeds to do so. No previous mention of Murnau in this connection exists anywhere among Pirandello's notes and papers. By this time, fifteen years after *Si gira!* his opinions about filmmaking had altered radically. He shared the view of many first-rate artists that the very best Italian directors – from da Genina to Palermi to Righelli – ranked a distant second to Charlie Chaplin, Jean Renoir, Fredrich Murnau, Fritz Lang, or Sergei Eisenstein, who were eliciting something like wonderment at the time. Pirandello's familiarity with and expert judgment about their work is clear from his further comments to the journalist. Singling out Murnau, however, plainly tells that Pirandello expected Murnau would both direct and "put his hand" as collaborator to a yet unwritten scenario (Callari, 41).

Why Murnau in particular? In retrospect, the choice seems self-evident given the men's cultural and artistic affinities. Pirandello had taken his graduate degree in the faculty of philosophy and philology at Bonn; Murnau had taken his degree in the faculty of philosophy and letters at Heidelberg and Berlin. The director had studied music and art history; Pirandello, knowledgeable about both, theorized about their close relation to film in a later critical essay. Finally, Murnau had worked at the university in Berlin under the guidance of the great Max Reinhardt, already Pirandello's well-respected colleague. The German and Italian artists shared both a language and an aesthetic vocabulary. Very probably, they had met when Pirandello's theater company played in Berlin and introduced him to people active in film and theater. Also germain to Pirandello's confidence in Murnau, the director already had translated drama to film successfully. His version of Moliere's *Tartuffe* (1925) added a naturalistic, framing story, a strategy Pirandello uses in all three scenarios for *Six Characters*.

On the internal evidence of the *Prologo* – more of this momentarily – as well as the interview with Enrico Rocca, Pirandello also must have known and admired Murnau's highly reputed films *Nosferatu* (The undead, 1922), *Der letzte Mann* (The last man, 1924), and certainly *Faust* (1926), whose "spirits" Rocca compared to the phantoms in *Six Characters*. The director's genius consisted in the power and composition of his images. Always driven by a strictly functional use of symbols, Murnau attended scrupulously to the effects of chiaroscuro learned from Reinhardt (Eisner, 47). Terror in the lengthening shadows of *Nosferatu*, eroticism in visions of the young Faust, the painterly precision of his shots, their delivery of an intense emotional jolt sometimes by pacing and rhythm alone, these techniques transformed Murnau's films into masterpieces of German expressionism. *Faust* in every sense "deployed all the artifice of the cinema by a man who knew every detail of his craft" (Eisner, 100). The central conflict between good and evil may have been vulgarized in the effort to make the film "a national monument" (Kracauer, 148), but Faust's "angelic apparitions," those shadowy manifestations of his egomaniacal desires, must have outweighed other aspects of the film in Pirandello's eyes. He commented especially to Rocca on the film's "unreal, phantasmagorical glow," originating from unexpected places. Murnau created a sense of dimensionality in the film by adding heightened emotional tonalities to a basic realism, very much the *Prologo*'s intent.

What remains mysterious is Pirandello's apparently serious, almost religious, attraction to the beginnings of a genre that to this day eludes full respectability. Murnau's treatments of dementia, demonism, and vampirism represent a crucial contribution to the origins of horror films, whose appeals, when cast in that light, one might expect to lie beyond Pirandello's purview. Yet the same philosophical bent leading him to formal study in psychology led also to Pirandello's well-documented fascination with occultism, hermeticism, hypnotic trance, Swedenborgism, and like parapsychologies that earlier had captivated Strindberg.[9] One wonders, in short, if Pirandello's deliberate investigations in the irrational would have resulted in more extravagant expressions of the terrain in film, exceeding his typical restraint and wit simply because the medium provided the means to do so. His commitment, for instance, to deforming, depersonalizing, and theatricalizing the experience of passion only begins in his plays to reach the extremes expressed in the scenarios.[10]

Short of positing a Pirandello ready to succumb to the allure of gothic evils, his malefic sprites in the *Prologo* rise from regions of madness excluded by modernism at its most ascetic. Applied introspection in Pirandello's work regularly pivots on a desire to know "unreason" as the way of all things. The underlying question may be Nietzschean. Directly or indirectly, it has led critics to ally Pirandello either with French Surrealists or German Expressionists for lack of a comparable Italian movement more influential and intellectual than *teatro del grotesco* (theater of the grotesque), yet more dangerous than his own theory of opposites in *L'umorismo*. His projected films, however, articulate an Italian equivalent or parallel far from comprehended by the catch-all term pirandellian, as a film of the *Prologo* would have shown. Pirandello's eagerness to work with Murnau, in other words, suggests that his film would have drawn on the visionary dimensions of his interests only hinted at by his experiments with mentalism in other genres. He had written to Marta Abba in July, after all, that he had "thought at length, assiduously, and with every richer result about the cinematography and scenic design of *Six Characters.* I have almost all of it in mind by now."

And then, just as suddenly as Murnau entered into Pirandello's plans, so he suddenly disappeared. Perhaps the absence of the director's name in letters and papers thereafter implies a feigned indifference to what must have been a terrible blow. Pirandello discovered at the eleventh hour, when he arrived in Berlin, that Murnau could not free himself from existing contractual obligations to work on the film. Worldwide success, especially after *Der letzte Mann*, had set his course for Hollywood. According to the interview with Rocca, Pirandello expected that any turning to America, "if Germany failed to cooperate," would include himself. As it happened, the "betrayals" by friends and colleagues that Pirandello sometimes referred to in his letters to Marta might well have applied to such a moment (Ortolani, 5). Yet so too might that stubborn refusal to surrender to circumstance in part underscoring his opportunism about film – what else to call it? According to Callari's reconstruction of events, Pirandello must have been carrying "in his pocket" a contract with the Berlin house of Fellner und Samlo GmbH stipulating that Murnau would direct. He had slanted the interview with Rocca to publicize a partnership that could not help but generate excitement in artistic as well as political circles watching the growth of fascism in Italy and Germany. Yet immediately on arriving in Berlin, Pirandello rescinded the Fellner und Samlo contract, apparently in order to free himself for other possibilities. And to guarantee that he at least had an actual scenario in hand, he contacted Adolf Lantz for help with articulating cinematographic details of a script, booked himself into a hotel, and in five days fleshed out the skeletal *Prologo*.[11]

« 3 »

As may be inferred, even a cursory reading of the *Prologo* confirms Pirandello's otherwise hyperbolic claim to Rocca that his film would vie with the play in originality. The text reveals a conversance with film genres as well as a desire to stretch the limits of the medium in order to realize several specific aims. First was to develop a historical plot including the Author as a seventh character; second, to picture the characters' phantasmal relation to the Author's imagination, thereby exploiting the function of cinema as pure illusion. Then integrating both historical and ahistorical dimensions in corresponding styles, the film would create a third, all-embracing level of representation. Two decades earlier, the image maker Serafino Gubbio had presented the divided self as a recording consciousness; in 1926 the image maker Pirandello not only confronted but imprisoned the divided self in a mind deliberately flirting with pathology.

The opening historical sequence plucks those infamous six characters out of their stage roles as specters of the unconscious and sets them down as a dirt-poor, broken family in the back alleys of Weimar "street film." The genre might have interested Pirandello for several reasons, among them an awareness that film was deriving its greatest impetus during the 1920s from actual social issues. Unlike earlier projects tending to overlook audiences, the *Prologo* seems deliberately to solicit audiences, who by 1926 were associating melodrama and realism alike with political and economic discontents.[12] Both German and Italian films of the period, despite their stylistic variety, were filled with images of proletarian unrest, oppressed workers, hungry children, and exploited youth. Street films especially resembled antibourgeois dreams in which an antirepublic became a new establishment (Kracauer, 159).

In these connections, street film may have responded to a collective need for representations explaining a frightening historical moment that transcended national boundaries. Europe's depression and the upheaval of prewar social traditions had fostered the birth of film subjects and styles in which the city itself focused a character's motivations, deprivations, and necessities. Embryonic in the *Prologo* but fully developed in the *Film-Novelle*, for instance, the Daughter's supposed prostitution, the Son's search for work, the Secretary's love affair – a new element – all will turn on images of the city like those in *Die Strasse* (The street), Karl Grune's film initiating the genre. It featured a rebellious middle-class young man, like the Author's Secretary, who leaves home to follow his passions among an urban underclass but then returns and submits to exigencies of conventional life.[13] Melodramatic depictions of prostitutes, petty thieves, and other habitués of a demimonde further reflected the city as vital, violent, and an apt metaphor for crises of modernism. A typical plot, for instance, involved the protagonist in a sexual or criminal episode, or both, linking the theme of social mobility to the moral corruption of the bourgeoisie (Petro, 163), again like the situation developed in the *Film-Novelle*. Moreover, films like Bruno Rahn's *Dirnen tragödie* (Streetwalker's tragedy, 1927) or Joe May's *Asphalt* (1929), or to a lesser extent G. W. Pabst's *Die Fraudlose Gasse* (The joyless street, 1925), managed to sentimentalize the streets as a refuge of true love and a region harboring virtues that had deserted society at large. So, too, is the *Prologo*'s contrast between the privileged, insulated Author and his Secretary, in love with the Daughter of a derelict family.

Whether seen as mass cultural expressions or as the self-conscious art cinema of an intellectualized community, film in the mode seems to have responded to a desire for immediacy and eroticism after a decade of gaudy spectacles and bourgeois passions.[14] For this reason alone Pirandello may have had "street film" in mind as he expanded the role of his prostitute Stepdaughter. Even briefly sketched, she resembles Weimar's frank hoydens more closely than she does, say, the slum virgins and abandoned women of realistic Italian films like Martoglio's *Sperduti nel buio*. The Berlin genre quite strikingly situated women as sexual commodities and objects of the male gaze, a

role calling for those glamorous, knowing women like Greta Garbo as a night
club dancer in *Die Fraudlose Gasse,* or Marlene Dietrich in *Der blaue Engel* (The
blue angel), both of whom conquered filmmaking on two continents. Pirandello hoped for no lesser fame for Marta Abba.

In heightening story, the projected film also reflects the emergence of narrative techniques in film of the 1920s and the opportunities it provided. Once
moved out of the closed circle of symbolic conflicts in a theatricalized family,
for instance, and set on the streets, the Daughter (Stepdaughter in the play)
may be pursued by the Author himself, no longer a desired principle but an
actual, desiring person. (Considering the intense, daily contact between Pirandello and Abba at the time, one might ask when the scenarist decided that the
famous writer should turn actor and play himself.) In the opening scene, the
Author follows the Daughter down a dark alleyway like a furtive voyeur
brought up short by discovering the girl's mother. She, as a type, resembles
both the strong, despairing, maternal woman in the German genre, as well as
the traditional Italian mother of melodrama, either way a figure designed to
counterpoint the glamorous sirens in bourgeois drama flaunting their sexuality. Also, the Author both sees and remembers Mother and Daughter
embracing, a detail hinting at the emotional values of the projected film and
the style of acting it would employ.

Weaving this historical world into a second, imaginary reality, Pirandello
exploits techniques like dissolve and montage to visualize the Author's struggles with thought and memory, very like those of Murnau's mad Faust,
tormented by devils of consciousness and conscience. At strategic inter-
vals, the Author's ghosts break through narrative in the manner typical of
expressionism.

> The atmosphere is interpolated not as accessory action or reaction, but as
> accessory rhythm, in or out of tempo, as a symbol reinforcing or ampli-
> fying the given facts of the drama: it is reinforced in such a manner, that
> in places, at certain decisive moments, the action is apparently halted
> and can only continue passively, almost secretly by means of an inten-
> sification of the *unwelt* [atmosphere]. (Petro, 32)

The description might apply, for instance, to shots of the Author momentarily
posed or fixed like an illustrative painting to provide a visual summary of the
scene's emotional content. The juxtaposition of realistic action to such tableaux would intercept a spectator's effort to see the film solely as a representa-

tion of either social or psychic realities. Instead, the spectator would be compelled to see the convergence of the two realities, as is typical in romantic
dilemmas fusing external and internal perceptions. The same technique also
underscores the passivity of the Author and his implicit victimization by his
demons, a situation in turn recalling passive male figures in several of Murnau's films, albeit passive for quite diverse reasons.

* * *

In more literary senses, the Author both compares with and represents an
advance over Pirandello's philosophical heroes whose thinking about thinking leads to psychological peril. The irascible Serafino Gubbio likened filmmaking to the "killing" process of thought since it occurs in the abstract, a
devil's game making life unnatural and self-conscious. It aims to catch sight of
the self in mirrors like film that cannot help but reflect someone unknown, or
other, or "absent." And like Gubbio's camera fixing life, so here the thinking
Author absorbs and fixes images of the "real" family of the slums. Giovanni
Moscarda, the protagonist of *Uno, nessuno, e centomila* (*One, No One, and a
Hundred Thousand*), published the same year as the *Prologo*, embodies the
opposite side of the paradox. Playing both client and therapist in a psychoanalytical inquisition of the self, Moscarda's persona steadily deteriorates over
the course of a long, interior dialogue. His many introjected others ultimately
dispossess him of an integrated identity, precisely the risk run by the Author.
Obsessive self-analysis usually coincides in Pirandello's works with the onset
of madness, understood as a specie of disembodiment. An excess of reason
alienates one from "feeling," yet nothing can be known about life through any
other faculty. The self-knowledge gained becomes a mechanized history, like
film itself, extracting life to anatomize and reduce or kill it by means of
technical laws. So too, Moscarda's discourse as a historicizing act deforms his
substance and leads him, like Gubbio, to self-extinction. In both cases, the
novel as history "deforms" itself.[15]

The *Prologo*'s advance beyond the either-or theorem of the novels lies precisely in the "thinking" Author's historical reality. He embodies the polarity
of Gubbio and Moscarda as constant interplay between thought and emotion
bound together on that third level of reality including himself. This sine qua
non making consciousness fully subjective turns the *Prologo* into a projected
work about making art. Notably, for instance, the autonomous phantoms
filling the Author's study and besieging him with their demands include

Commentary

Enrico Signora Frola (from *Così è*), and others, taking on "substance as if from their own inner light," that is, from the light of their prior literary and dramatic forms. Logically, their continued clamoring at the door of his consciousness implies that their earlier forms remained incomplete, or, the other way around, that completed forms had not "killed" them. The Author is bound to them; past and present are one; they testify to his task of continually recreating himself, and therefore them, anew. The wraiths of Enrico and Signora Frola, for that matter, may represent a wry bit of self-parody since the mad Enrico made his film debut in the year of the *Prologo*, and Signora Frola may have believed she was to follow. But by situating itself even to this degree in autobiography, the *Prologo* raises questions about the extent to which the Author's history is Pirandello's, a web involving Sicily, family, philosophy, psychology, literature, drama, and film – in a word, all the life of his mercurial spirit and poetic. Some answers wait on his development of the film projected in his *Film-Novelle*, which reveals depths of personality only thinly disguised by art.

Otherwise the Author demonstrates Pirandello's credo about deconstructing all forms, whether novel, drama, or film. In the final scene, the Author discovers the girl of the streets among his phantoms. As a projection of memory, her ghost represents the second stage of a creative process in which a transformed model returns as an independent other. The girl herself, then, exists in the film's external *and* internal dimensions, whose barriers therefore threaten to collapse. In inexperienced hands, the result would be a chaotic, destabilized film about a personality lacking ego boundaries. The question arises especially since the girl so plainly must "be" Marta, his muse, the beloved with whom he hopes to share the complete work: "the work should be OURS, born from US TWO," the fruit of their love (letter 13 July 1928). Moreover, as if underscoring this amorphousness of limits, Pirandello also assigns her a role akin to the Author's as the film's controlling consciousness; she, too, functions as an aesthetic mediator between worlds. Yet, she remains a model in the *Prologo* of his possession by incubi.

As soon as I lift my hand to my eyes and look around me, it surges toward me from a corner of the study, still evanescent, the ghost of the girl met shortly before in the alley. It is not the same as her reality; she seems already to be infused in an ether of poetry in order to become a phantom of art, as I now see her. . . . [As she reaches the door] she turns to study me, tilting her head as if to arouse in me the temptation to gather these other phantoms of art into myself.

She leads him as muse and temptress, at once a spirit of poetry transforming his own spirit, and a guide who urges him to order the relentless ghosts of his past and future – Donna Ana, Signor Ponza, Signora Frola, and so on. This function of the girl as muse nearly disappears in the *Film-Novelle*. Here, in decomposing her reality, Pirandello reveals the reciprocal dynamic between the self and its mirror reflections, at once constituting the creative spirit and, at its most exacerbated, the schizophrenic madness he set out to dissect.

Finally, then, the Author's role intimates a prescient view of film as both cultural artifact and psychological phenomenon. The difference between the mad Moscarda and the character of the Author makes him an early exemplar of self-reflexiveness in a film culture. Consumed as substitutes for direct experience, film images shape history more powerfully than books or plays, at their most influential, mere artifacts produced by the exceptional for the delight of a few. To the contrary, film creating the culture of its audience is analogous on a minute scale to phantoms creating the Author's consciousness, which re-creates them, and so on in endless and dizzying cycles. The logical absurdity did not escape Pirandello the ironist. Just as *Six Characters* reads as metatheater on theater, so the projected film would read as metafilm that alludes to its own making. Among the many hirelings he enlisted in his art, after all, Pirandello the revolutionary filmmaker included the wit of Pirandello the literary sabateur.

FOUR

Film-Novelle (The *Scenario*)

The mirror clouds over as if some diabolical breath had just blown on the glass. Above this the blurred image of an old satyr appears and immediately begins to grin repulsively and obscenely. Scenario, Take 33

Deprived of their livelihood, threatened with bitter poverty, Mother and Daughter leave Madame Melloni's house. The Daughter implores her mother never to meet the Author again; he has enmeshed her in a web of lies and brought them misfortune. Scenario, Take 82

Disenchanted with their countrymen, high modernist writers chose exile from their homelands: Ibsen in Rome, Strindberg and Joyce in Paris, Shaw in London, and Pirandello in Berlin. The Northerner writers escaped from culturally regressive milieux to cities welcoming the avant-garde. Pirandello's move for similar motives also repeated a different pattern. Beginning with his graduate studies in Bonn, he was following the footsteps of Italian artists, musicians, and intellectuals who had been undertaking the *viaggio in germania* ever since the mid-nineteenth century for mandatory experience of parallel traditions (DiGaetani, xxii). Philosophy and opera gravitated north as often as painting and architecture came south. By 1928, of course, Berlin was not only *the* theater city of Europe and site of Pirandello's triumphs but the capital for international film with a resident Italian colony. Pirandello must have expected an automatic, if not an eager, welcome.

Sojourn in Berlin, nevertheless, ushered in a period of isolation and anguish darker than the collapse of his arrangement with Murnau had foretold. "Pirandello's star had set in Germany too," his biographer says sadly, alluding to reverses in Italy (Giudice, 183). It was the fall of Pirandello's personal hopes, however, that precipitated a crisis from which he never recovered. The jaunty mask of genius spotted in local cafes bore little relation to a deepening depression that lifted only intermittently during the remaining years of his life. Perhaps no reality in Berlin could have fulfilled his expectations of a new Eden where he would be sought after, well-esteemed, amply rewarded financially – his always deplorable economic plight continued unabated[1] – where he would conquer the international film world, and, crucial to the entire fabric of the dream, would begin life anew with Marta Abba tucked firmly under his wing.[2]

Only his letters reveal the degree to which he persevered with filmmaking during this period, out of love for Marta. With the end of the Teatro d'Arte and their daily intimacy, something like panic seems to have gripped him. In one of several extravagant moments before arriving in Berlin, for instance, he anticipated submitting his *Film-Novelle* for *Six Characters* to "her approval," even her "collaboration" (Ortolani, 64). He would realize film earnings of a magnitude obviating any further need of Italy and make her a star abroad, he says, a plan that obviously would compel her to depend solely on him. When she writes that she is learning to drive a car, he envisions her in a "Supercar from a Super-company for the Super-streets of Hoolliwoud [*sic*]." Then his "Queen of all the screens of the world" would return to Italy "as patrona" of the theater (letter 28 September 1925).

In this volatile state of mind, Pirandello installed himself in a small Berlin apartment, established Marta and her sister Cele in an adjoining apartment, and set out to make their fortunes with tireless vigor. Negotiations on works written and planned proceeded at an unbroken pace, at this point including prospects with American companies. His "refuge" in cinema, in fact, involved him even more than before in meetings, correspondence, and conferences with the industry's luminaries on both his own properties and on prospective ones for Marta. Yet, apart from writing a script for Emil Jannings at the insistence of the German director Joe May,[3] and two short films for British International Pictures, proposals to write major film subjects during 1929 led to nothing concrete.[4] Options on *Six Characters* sailed high in proposal, then stalled and died in complexities. He wrote Stefano in November that the Berlin community was polite but essentially unforthcoming: "Here business negotiations are extremely slow and take an infinite amount of time. . . . Nothing yet on *Six Characters*." A month later he complains of his "utter neglect" by the industry, and again of extreme difficulty with negotiations.

Companies want to pay little and are frightened of any subject the least bit intelligent. . . . They find the scenario "too artistic and not adaptable to the mentality of the majority of film audiences. . . . I continue to hear it said, 'beautiful, a work of genius, but not for the masses.' "

The judgment would be repeated many times over the next years. One particularly intricate series of conferences over the *Film-Novelle* led like a hidden labyrinth through German translators, directors, financiers, to Italian state-controlled companies with nominally private officials, each participant linked to conditions set by invisible others whose demands uncoupled the entire chain. A decision to produce a film, moreover, did not automatically guarantee the readiness of others to distribute it.[5]

The blow that unnerved him completely came after five months of frustrating effort to sell himself and Marta. Marta was restless from inactivity, made worse because she spoke no German and saw no one after her sister departed. Her parents were pressuring her since from the first they had disapproved of the great man's "compromising" protection. Without a glimmer on the horizon of a signed contract, Marta Abba decided to return to Italy and get on with her career (Ortolani, 81). The effect on Pirandello was devastating. His already alienated spirits sank into suicidal despondency. At one point he fell into near witlessness, imagining himself dead since all life concentrated itself in her.[6] A vision of Marta's love had sustained him through years of disappointment, reversal, treacheries, and betrayals. Many of his most impassioned letters, idealizing her nearly to the point of idolatry, reveal his desperate and recurrent fantasy of amassing a fortune in Berlin or Hollywood to lavish on a theater company for her and keep her nearby. Given to an existential pessimism, given enormous burdens of responsibility to colleagues and family, including his institutionalized wife, given the torments of writing never offset by his public acclaim, at no time did Pirandello admit that the sentiments of his beloved might differ in nature from his own, at sixty-seven.[7] He was hopelessly enamored, desolate without Marta; temperamental bleakness swept him down into despair. At his lowest point he believed that only Marta's love could save him from death.[8]

Her letters in response, however, often brief, or abrupt and impatient, scolded him for his adoration. Marta was uncomplicated, energetic, an eager young actress inexperienced in the ways of the world, of men, even of herself. "I think that I was rather a timid child," she said of herself before meeting Pirandello.[9] Certainly thereafter she became an adept pupil "in his school of disprizing the life of the senses," for their relations remained perfectly chaste (Ortolani, 83). Fearful of alienating her completely, Pirandello compelled himself to write chatty reports to her of daily minutia: at which restaurant he ate, whom he met, what was said. Becoming father, husband, brother, and mentor in his letters, he advised her about backstage politics in Italy, about which of the managers could be trusted, how to handle contracts, how to approach the few filmmakers still operating under state control, even how to behave so as to disguise her natural timidity. He remained the invisible genii urging her development as an artist, guiding her through negotiations as distant as those years later for playing *Tovarich* in America.

Pirandello circulated word among friends of Marta's availability as an actress, with the result that she may have made several films in Italy.[10] Romantically, Pirandello continued to believe that if the two of them somehow could endure the chaotic state of the arts under fascism, they ultimately would triumph over the government's entrenched bureaucrats. When Marta succeeded in obtaining an audience with Mussolini in February of 1932, after she had played successfully in France and hoped to persuade Il Duce to stabilize theater, Pirandello cued her on topics with which to open and sustain conversation, even on a recommended demeanor.[11] He built up the female part for her in *Acciaio* (Steel) to keep her near him at least during its shooting. If all else failed, certainly his mission to establish himself and her in the international film community would lead them to a paradise of love and art. Even the most inconsequential asides in his letters, however, fail to disguise his utter desolation without her.[12] And in some, his appeals are heartrending. He ends one with the words in double sixed letters underscored, "SONO SOLO, SONO SOLO, SONO SOLO! [I AM ALONE!] May God protect you, my child, from understanding one day the atrocity in this word!" (letter 25 March 1929).

And yet, from the depths of his anguish came a feverish creativity. He completed the final manuscript of *O di uno o di nessuno* (*Either Somebody's or Nobody's*); he wrote *Come tu mi vuoi* (*As You Desire Me*) specifically for Marta;[13] he conceived the vast structure of his mythological work, *I giganti della montagna* (*The Mountain Giants*); he drafted the first ideas for *Quando uno è qualcuno*; he sketched out his final theater play, *Questa sera si recita a soggetto*. By the end of the year, he had been accepted into the prestigious Italian Academy of Letters and received the first hint that he would be nominated for a Nobel prize. Amazingly enough, no sign of his atrocious suffering, or his prodigious output, or his new honors, slipped past the façade of the polite, dapper gentleman photographed (fig.12) while taking coffee with the director, Richard Eichberg, of British International Pictures, or while teaching

Anna May Wong how to twirl spaghetti on a fork.[14] An amusing newspaper article, written by the Chinese star as she was completing a film with Adolf Lantz in Berlin, provides an uncharacteristic glimpse of the public man.

It seems there is a large group of Pirandello admirers in Berlin who follow him about the streets. When he enters a restaurant they go right along, having dinner and sending him the bill, which he gladly pays, for he is a most generous person. When he was asked why he invariably paid everyone's check, he remarked: "If they cannot afford to pay for their own dinners, I'm delighted to accommodate. If they can afford it, then they're insincere and will suffer accordingly. The selfish pleasure of being able to help them is mine in any case."[15]

Pirandello wrote a silent filmscript for Ms. Wong called *Vergine madre* (Virgin Mother) for British International Pictures in 1929 but says it was ill received.[16]

Still another vignette in Berlin situates Pirandello not in "splendid isolation," as Giudice reports, but in the company of distinguished directors and filmmakers.[17] Pirandello apparently met Sergei Eisenstein when the Russian visited Berlin for the premier of the film *Staroie i novie* (Old and new) in August of 1929. According to one account, Eisenstein especially "enjoyed night life and his talks with intellectuals including Bertolt Brecht, Ernst Toller, Fritz Lang, Pirandello, and Alfred Einstein" – one assumes, not all at once (Swallow, 75). After the premier, Eisenstein joined a select group of filmmakers at an international conference held at La Sarraz, Switzerland, the villa of a wealthy patron of the arts; the conference was sponsored by Pirandello, Stefan Zweig, André Gide, and others.[18] The roster of celebrities among sponsors and participants from France, Germany, Italy, Russia, the United States, and Japan probably was chosen by the canny conference organizer, Robert Aron, the French critic-at-large who was familiar with the world of arts and letters. Otherwise, the gathering of literary *and* film figures hints at the state of the medium at the time, still open enough to seek ideas of the most innovative artists in many fields, yet sufficiently defined to discriminate among them.

In the absence of documentation, imaginary conversations at La Sarraz come to mind. Pirandello and Walter Ruttmann might have talked about disentangling film from politics – Ruttmann later directed the documentary film *Acciaio* (*Steel*, 1933), based on *Giuoca, Pietro!* (Play, Peter!). Pirandello and Fritz Lang must have compared the power of shadow images to evoke psychological guilt, a feature of the *Film-Novelle* and Lang's *M*. Perhaps they also talked about Lang's *Metropolis* and its relation to the ideology of street film.[19] But talk between Eisenstein and Pirandello would have ranged over many topics.[20] One conversation might have crystallized their shared vision of theater as inspired by carnival, masking, and antiillusionist abstractions.[21] Another talk might have ruminated on Vselovod Meyerhold, with whom Eisenstein had studied directing, and his efforts to separate character from its traditional stage representations, very much Pirandello's bailiwick.

In still further conversation, Pirandello and Eisenstein may have tread the precarious bridges being constructed between film and theater by many artists. Both men felt strongly that film needed to depart from literature and narrative. Pirandello advocated film's mandatory divorce from words if it was to develop its own vocabulary; Eisenstein applied his theory of constructing film along loosely related "focal points." Working in the prenarrative period when film sequences resembled a "fairground array of disconnected events," Eisenstein had believed in galvanizing an audience's attention through shock effects, rather in the manner of the Futurists. He connected scenes by a "montage of attraction" when other filmmakers in the 1920s were developing narrative strategies that essentially imitated novels or plays. This, he and Pirandello emphatically agreed, drove film in a wrongheaded direction down "Hollywood" avenues. Beyond fancifulness here, Pirandello during these years continued to share the views of French, German, and Russian intellectuals unequivocally opposed to the march of cinema into machine shop commercialism.

« 2 »

The one subject on everyone's mind in and out of Switzerland was the advent of sound: it altered filmmaking completely but in the opinion of many not necessarily for the better. While box office receipts soared by 50 percent between 1927 and 1930, proving the public's enthusiastic response, filmmakers like Charlie Chaplin,[22] René Clair, and Murnau, among others, seemed to be torn between excitement at the potential of the new medium and blank terror.[23] Less extreme, Pirandello and Eisenstein shared a rooted suspicion of the film of natural dialogue. They blamed financial interests for pushing dialogue films into re-creations of Broadway on the screen. And indeed, "plays were transferred to the screen word by word and scene by scene" (Robinson, 166). Words, Pirandello told a reporter, "should be nothing more than the orchestration of a film. They must not be used as other than musical notes, and their importance must not go beyond that of '*drappeggiamento*'" (draping).[24] Eisenstein, writing years later about creating narrative in film through an effective use of subtitles and a narrator's voice, recalled Pirandello's ideas with something more than respect. Cinema, Eisenstein said, still has scarcely touched the potentiality of a narrator's voice to weave elements together dramatically. "The late Pirandello used to dream aloud when we met in Berlin in 1929 of what could be done with that voice. How close is such a voice, intervening in the action from outside the action, to Pirandello's whole concept" of film.[25]

Pirandello's impression of the first "talkie," *The Jazz Singer*, starring "Al Johnson" (*sic*), was dismissive in public, harsh in private.[26] British International Pictures, holding an option on *Six Characters*, had sent him and Adolf Lantz (as interpreter) to the film's London premiere to gather experience for adding a sound track to the *Film-Novelle*. In an interview immediately after seeing the new miracle, Pirandello planted himself against the tide. The film only confirmed his view that "technology would need to improve a great deal before sound represented an advantage rather than a brutal assault on the ears." Speech lent a macabre effect to human figures on the screen since it contradicted their basically mute, spectral quality *as* film images. Instead of emanating logically from a body, usually inside a room, the voice issued from a machine while the screen might be presenting images of forests, mountains, or city streets. On the page, words conveyed imagery to the mind; on the stage, words animated the body; on film, words accomplished neither effect.

In substance, Pirandello justifiably criticized the failure of early sound to synchronize with its sources on the screen. Instead of increasing the inventiveness of the cinematography, the bulkiness of sound technology actually restricted camera movement. Still thinking pragmatically, Pirandello complained that a sound track limited a film's distribution to the country of the language spoken unless it was issued at great cost in several versions simultaneously – as, in fact, became the practice almost immediately. (Films were shot in several languages, and some Hollywood productions, shot abroad to circumvent national quotas, even began to toy with dubbing.[27]) Instead, after seeing *The Jazz Singer*, he wrote Marta that the film's figures resembled "ventriloquist's dummies"; the film was a "horror" that destroyed every illusion and therefore only heralded a rebirth of theater (letter 16 April 1929).

Almost in the next breath, however, Pirandello forgot himself and reported excitedly that "the whole film world is in revolution. It seems the talking film is truly a prodigy. They've succeeded in perfecting the human voice close up, from afar, in the proper timbre for all modes" (letter 22 April 1929). His offhand remark, "Everyone is unsure what to do," probably approximates his swinging pendulum. Within a few days he dashes off the essay "Se il film parlante abolirà il teatro," reporting to Marta on its "humoristic brio"[28]: "Art can emerge from anything, even from human bestiality: satire is the living proof. . . . This devil of an invention, the talking machine, is basically very amusing. It all lies in knowing how to use it" (letter 25 April 1929). And then typically, the demon experimenter afflicted with the spirit of *il contrario* immediately envisions a "talking film against the talking films," reminiscent of Dr. Frankenstein's monster.

> Man has given a voice to the machine, and now [in my film] the machine will speak with a voice of its own, no longer human; like a devil it has entered in the machine and it amuses itself, commenting on the action of a silent film with its moving shadows. It calls out to them, pushes them, freezes them, suggests this or that action to them, tricks them, reveals a secret . . . does anything that it pleases. Only the machine will speak and the ventriloquist's voice no longer will offend because it no longer pretends to be a human voice. . . . The idea is magnificent.

He'll offer the idea to British International who paid for his London trip, he adds generously in his high excitement; he has "many, so many more ideas," more than ever before. But he is not sleeping well he adds, and suspects that "a fire of ideas" is consuming him. His pen has never been lighter; when he writes he is "flying, happy; I should not touch down ever again" (letter 26 April 1929). The frenzied tone in these letters might well have frightened Marta.

In more sober moments, the artist, who transformed every medium he touched, conceived of sound's great contribution through music: not songs embellishing a plot as in *The Jazz Singer*, but music expressing the abstract mental energy that generated images. He called this revolutionary departure "cinemelography," describing it as a union of pure music and pure vision in perfect accord, or cinematic pictures literally expressing sound.[29] "Think what a prodigious mass of images can be aroused by the whole of musical folklore, from an old Spanish Habanera to the Russian Volga Boat Song, or the Pastoral Symphony," he told an interviewer in London. There may be a hint here of his continuing interest in the simultaneous presentation of multiple realities, although he usually saw these as perceptual rather than artistic. One critic sees a resemblance between Pirandello's idea for cinemelography and both Wagner's *Gesamkuntswerk* theories (on the integration of all artistic elements) as well as those of Eisenstein on "vertical montage," ideas Pirandello may have intended to pursue in *Giuoca, Pietro!* (Vittori, 16). More directly, his interest in graphic reproduction of the musical process situates him among French theorists and avant-garde filmmakers of the anti-Hollywood school like Henri Langlois and Jean Epstein, stressing the ideogrammatic nature of film images. Langlois for instance described Epstein's film adaptions of Edgar Allen Poe's "Fall of the House of Usher" and "Ligeia" as "cinematic equivalent(s) of a Debussy creation" (Stone, "Cineastes' Texts," 54). An interest in expressing music graphically became a central tenet of the French cineastes.

Cinemelography, as may be inferred, represents Pirandello's long sought project to re-create mind without words. His quest for artistic authenticity had already led him to explore territory uncolonized by language as discourse: madness, or the "primitive beyond" favored by Impressionist painters, or the state "within" where he sought the "germ" of his characters. Now he wanted film to mirror the artist's imagination at the moment images arise, thereby providing a wordless record of creative activity and its preconscious or unconscious sources. Entries in his *Secret Notebook*, recording experiences that approximate primary process, are all to the point (Giudice, "Ambiguity," 69). The project otherwise suggests its analogy to those gothic demons of the *Prologo* who visualize madness itself rather than mad behavior. Dreams and hallucinatory experiences of one sort or another became favorite subjects of the French cineastes precisely since they invited antinaturalistic styles. (Drawing on similar areas of mental experience, Pirandello at one point sketched out a film in which dreams come true and reality becomes dream.) In the larger context of his work as a whole, cinemelography roughly parallels his invention of antimimetic theater, or *teatro dello specchio* (theater of mirrors), aiming to enact the essence of person or event without the mediation of characterization, plot, exposition, or setting. He would strip film of representation by visualizing an elemental image in its gestation stage, so to speak.

A telling hint that Pirandello continued to ruminate about cinemelography lies in a project he mentioned several times over the years. He tells an interviewer in London in 1935 of a film about Beethoven that has been on his mind a long time. Not the man so much as the fancy of the deaf genius strikes him as the supreme subject for a film visualizing the mysteries of creation purely and immediately. "If I should meet a director who understood this idea," he tells another interviewer, "I should like to bring Beethoven's symphonies to the screen – the *Eroica* and the *Pastorale*. . . . There would be nothing forced about it, and I should do it quite naturally. I do it for myself involuntarily when I hear music, for I am invaded by visions. When the Eroica is played, I always see marching troops go by" (Rousseaux, 513). Presumably, he had approached several elusive directors among the many avant gardists in his acquaintance who probably discouraged cinemelography on purely practical grounds. Undeterred, he reported in a letter to Marta Abba, before their meeting in Berlin, that he had embarked upon preliminary research for the project. Several books on Beethoven, he confided, rendered the "musician's state of mind and spiritual state at various times while in the throes of composition" (letter 11 July 1928). He needed, nevertheless, to hear each of the nine symphonies again, one by one, in order to experience the music anew.

His reading may clarify an otherwise obscure reference in the *Scenario* (Take 43) to an image of Beethoven appearing to the Author among other autonomous wraiths. Certainly, both the *Prologo* and *Film-Novelle* for *Six Characters* reveal his wish to film the creative imagination, with or without sound. And while he continued to invent film modes, an increasingly prosaic industry continued to redefine representation and reportage. The contrast speaks volumes about Pirandello's relative indifference even to his greatest successes. Although often irritated when his film subjects became vehicles for stars, or were distorted by shoddy direction and camerawork, what irked Pirandello more was the lack of a cinematographer of major stature, the Murnau or René Clair, to translate his vision.[30] The unbridgeable gap between his desires and technical exigencies, for instance, may echo in his wistful admission to a journalist many years later.[31] He had been searching, he says, for a means to work with sound film in a manner "completely distinct from the languages I have used thus far to express my experience of life. Dialogue in my dramas always had a greater importance than action." The acknowledgment probably alluded, sotto voce, to unavailing efforts to sell the *Film-Novelle*, although even his most promising option contract for it, with MGM in 1935, had not expected Pirandello to "recompose it as a talkie." An American was to compose a sound track, he told Stefano, while he would "supervise the minimal dialogue" (Callari, 47). That "minimal" may compress both his disappointments and his frustration over the need for compromises, equally audible in his fullest statement on the project.

My drama *Six Characters* will go into production. It may not result in a perfect realization of my wishes; but I am searching for a purely visual manner in which to resolve the problem at the root of my play, although treated there only obscurely. I am struggling to make intelligible, *in this medium*, how the destinies of six characters were conceived in the mind of the author, and then "drunk" on life, how they become independent of him.

Naturally, projecting the problem onto another plane is only a substitution, resulting in a hybrid creature to be found at a distance from the *proper work of cinema*. It [the film] nevertheless will experiment from beginning to end with the author's vision as pure [unformed?] yet reproducible images. (Callari, 126, emphasis added)

« 3 »

Pirandello never divulged a "secret plan" for the *Film-Novelle* that he alluded to while playing cat and mouse with a reporter (Callari, 125) – very likely his intention to play the Author's role himself. That intensified subjectivity, however, invites a reading of the *Film-Novelle* in the light of biography, of the *Prologo*, as well as of parallel trends in filmmaking. Overall, the *Film-Novelle*'s nonlinear form corresponds to Pirandello's thinking about strictly photogenic "narrative." Rather than being carefully motivated, entrances and exits, like abrupt cuts and montage equivalents, allow Pirandello to destroy a continuity of time and space while ignoring any historical development of character that might interrupt the flow of images. The order and unity of the whole instead are achieved by filtering events through the Author's mind. Descriptions of action serve as descriptions of Pirandello's thought processes, both progressing by abrupt shot and scene changes with little or no transition. Dialogue, too, is purely secondary to the shot sequence, so that in all senses pictures render fantasy and reflect Pirandello's cinematic philosophy.

In these connections, the *Film-Novelle* reflects the degree to which filmmaking still was an entrepreneurial adventure rather than either the literary or technological enterprise it later became. Segments of description, for instance, remain open to interpretation by a director and also untranslated into the precise format of a shooting script; or they suggest the blocking action of drama rather than frame sequences. Yet the scenario's manipulation of characters and settings also specifically exploits film's ability to cut rapidly between a number of separate vignettes in differing locations. These and other features of the embryonic cinematography point to an envisioned style for the film consistent with that of the *Prologo:* at once reminiscent of expressionism to the extent directions call for atmospheric effects, and of surrealism to the extent the latter reflects psychological states of mind.

Technical considerations otherwise intimate the range of expertise Pirandello required from his collaborator, Adolf Lantz.[32] Plot elaborations calling upon simultaneity, montage, split screen, or close-up very probably reflect Lantz's hand as he guided Pirandello through the practical vocabulary of filmmaking – his German was literary and conversational rather than technical (Callari, 313). A former theater dramaturg and director turned screenwriter, Lantz had contributed to more than thirty-five films, including Palermi's *Enrico IV,* by the time he collaborated with Pirandello. In addition to handling scripts for silent films like G. W. Pabst's *Abwege* (Crisis, 1928), or Eichberg's *Song* and *Grosstadtschmetterling* (Big city butterfly) with Anna May Wong (1928 and 1929), he also worked with early sound techniques used, for example, on *Rasputin* (1932), starring those veterans of Reinhardt's *Six Characters,* Conrad Veidt and Franziska Kinz.

Lantz also may have added some allusions in the *Film-Novelle* to contemporary German films. To a nearly incestuous degree during that last decade of the silent period, cameramen and directors engaged in a self-contained dialogue by copying, adapting, reinterpreting, punning, and playing variations on one another's subjects and techniques, as commentary below reveals. He had been active when romantic films like *Undine* and *Der Goldene Topf* (The golden pot), or Arthur Robison's *Schatten* (Warning shadows) were experimenting with silhouettes and repeating mirror images very like those in the German scenario. The industry's self-absorption to a degree represents the learning process by which film was evolving from its basic state as "moving pictures" to a medium with its own formal conventions. As if in colloquy, film-on-film in the intellectualized community of Berlin also reflects its relative unawareness of audiences, largely a retrospective concern of later scholars and critics.

It is as a text, however, that the *Film-Novelle* offers a summa of Pirandello's poetics and the "obscure necessities" of his writing.[33] His curious title for the original German manuscript may hint that the script itself had some special significance as a literary work, for example, with film as a novel told through images, in effect elaborating the intermingling of the two genre in *Si gira!* (Nulf, 134). Or he may have envisioned a novel using cinematic techniques as literary devices – say, the novel theorized long afterward by Alan Robbe-Grillet and constituting a "reflection on the puzzles of reality." These conceptual possibilities apart, the scenario unfolds as a wholly unique work, derived from rather than based upon the famous play, taking its point of departure from the Stepdaughter's allusion to phantom characters surrounding the Author and his long deliberation before refusing to adopt them. Dispensing with the professional Actors who failed to bring the Characters to life on-stage, Pirandello the Author plays both sole Actor and central Character. The encompassing theme of the projected film thus responds to the play's premise: why the Author cannot or will not accede to his Characters' demands for artistic completion. In the course of articulating the theme, Pirandello anticipates a sophisticated psychoanalytical theory of creativity not formulated until the 1950s.[34]

Here, a brief summary comparing play and filmscript will be helpful to the detailed analysis that follows. First, the professional stage troupe and Director disappear along with their metaphysical function as "enactors" of "characters" embodying the passions. The complementary role of the Father (and family) as advocates for "characters"-as-the-life-of-art also disappears. The family without the Father now become historical figures, and the original Stepdaughter becomes the Daughter, essentially an innocent victim of circumstance. While this situation precludes the grand scene of abortive incest at the heart of the play, the incest theme remains as a diffuse force with an impact on several significant events including the Daughter's hopeless romance with the Author's Secretary; the Boy's suicide; and the Little Girl's death. The Mother, remaining archetypal, recounts her life story to the Author, while conflicting images of her husbands and two sets of children compete for his judgment of the Mother's truth. His suggestion to her that the Daughter engages in prostitution drives the Mother to the establishment of one Madame Melloni, the play's Mme. Pace. There the Mother breaks in on a scene between the Daughter and a man she believes to be her own first husband, but who turns out to be the Author in a demonic guise repeated in several scenes with new, secondary characters.

The Author's problems with controlling his "live" characters resemble those encountered years later by filmmakers experimenting with *cinema verité*'s use of real people. On a deeper level, however, the device results in his pathological intermingling of actual and imaginary perceptions. Unlike interplay between ambiguous or relative truths in other works – more of this

85

momentarily – here only the Author's truth matters. His obsession with the family whose story he interprets transforms him into a meddling voyeur and cruel instigator of tragedy for his own necessary artistic ends. That is, departing from his disinterested transmutations of reality in, say, *Vestire gli ignudi* or *Ciascuno a suo modo* (*Each in His Own Way*), Pirandello now intensifies the origin, logic, and punitive effects of *his* creative process, the ultimate subject of the *Scenario*.

> In order to complete the work of transforming people into characters, the writer must let himself be possessed by a demon outside of himself, by a force made evident in the flowering of an archetypal image. In this case [of the *Film-Novelle*] that image is the "obscene archetype of the impulse to incest"; he must commit a crime. (Tessari, 13)

The provocative premise here is that the Author considers actuality only insofar as it objectifies his demonic seduction by archetypal images. Put the other way around, prostitution or incest represent mere forms of "an impulse" crucial to a metamorphosis of the "real" through writing, always then an act of violence. In substance, the premise echoes the idea underlying all of Pirandello's autonomous personages who remain incomplete lest he "kill" them. The writer must hesitate at the threshold of his criminal action of making art: an infraction to be condemned though regrettably necessary. And thus evolves the rationale for the play's elusive Author who finally takes responsibility for "soul murder" of these people.[35] In this sense, and by analogy to literary genre, whereas the play redefined tragi-comedy, the scenario's world redefines epic as a vision of constantly and violently modulating outer and inner realities.

Far from augmenting Pirandello's earlier philosophers, then, the Author's characterization differs profoundly not only from the Father or Director in the original play but from *raisonneurs* like Baldovino (*Il piacere dell'onestà*), or Leone Gala (*Giuoco delle parti*), or Toti (*Pensaci, Giacomino!*), or even Serafino Gubbio, his closest relative. These characters enact a principle, or absolute, or truth with relentless (and farcical) logic to prove the folly of divorcing these reasons from life-as-lived. Resembling Henri Bergson's mechanical puppets, they cultivate disinterest and remain outsiders to the extent they stand apart from the very actions they instigate. The scenario's Author, in contrast, who might be expected to embody a dispassionate, absolute Creator, plays outsider *and* insider, a feeling, suffering father-god-artist-creator and destroyer. The concept bears an interesting likeness to Reinhardt's versions of the original play (discussed in chapter 2) and, as we shall find, influences a reading of the filmscript (the *Treatment*) he intended to realize. In all these senses, the scenario represents the most extreme among Pirandello's nonrealistic dramatizations of consciousness, including the theater plays *Trovarsi* and *Sogno (ma forse no)* (I'm dreaming, but maybe not).

Again, taking for granted the readers' familiarity with the play summarized in chapter 2, and with the filmscript in the Documents section of this book, the following list provides an overview of the *Film-Novelle*'s major features. Allusions to German films mean to suggest a referential impulse comparable to the self-reference discernible in Pirandello's other works rather than to imply direct influences on the scenario's unique form. The list's order points toward the scenario's structure and its relation to the *Prologo*.

1. About phantoms and surrealistic atmospherics reaching beyond appearances into imagination and madness. Pirandello plays a subtle game that risks "making a spectacle" of the Author (Tessari, 96), while recalling the mystery and fascination of certain Shakespearean apparitions, like the ghost of King Hamlet, or Macbeth's manifestations of coming disaster. The phantoms' deployments also may express fantasies common to Pirandello's other works and linked by critics to both childhood trauma and sexual predispositions. Whereas Pirandello once contrasted irrational Characters to rational Actors, now the Author embodies a divided self, imprisoned in the equivalent of "a torture chamber" of consciousness, the phrase describing the symbolic setting of plays wherein characters afflict one another with cruel inquisitions.[36]

States of mind as a film subject especially recall Arthur Robison's *Schatten* (1923) and G. W. Pabst's *Geheimnisse einer Seele* (Secrets of a soul). Both films featured a professor's mental anguish visualized in fragmented dream sequences, flashes of biography, and other "remarkable technical devices" used to externalize deeply rooted guilt (Kracauer, 172). Cross-cutting in the German films between historical and psychological realities, along with depictions of therapeutic treatment through quasipsychoanalytical methods of self-scrutiny, corresponds roughly to the *Film-Novelle*'s strategies for depicting both the Author's psychological plight as well as his cure through the "exorcism" of creation. Phantoms forming around him and then "being drawn into his head" make analogy to the German films remarkably apt. Pirandello, however, experimented in other of his own works with depicting perception through destabilized forms of the body as of things; most notably, for example, hands grow and shrink in size, and a mirror becomes a window in *Sogno*

87

Commentary

(ma forse no) and in the scenario, making the works close cousins to one another and to surrealism in these respects.

2. About realistic treatment of the family's history. The Son metamorphoses from the play's shadowy, peripheral Character into a deeply disaffected, suicidal youth. The Mother's version of her life includes references to her first marriage to the Father, then her second marriage to *his* secretary who becomes her lover and protector. The Daughter's role includes overtones of both a femme fatale and a sympathetic elder sister to the Little Girl who drowns. As earlier discussion of the *Prologo* proposed in relation to "street film," the historical dimension of the *Film-Novelle* suggests how filmmakers saw "place" in relation to plot, narrative, and character.

City scenes also represent an advance on Pirandello's earlier strategies for creating the effects of simultaneity. In *Vestire gli ignudi* he carried the world outside an open window into the confines of a bourgeois parlor with its metaphoric resonance of a psychic landscape. Or more pertinently, in the novel of *Six Characters* he described fragmented noises and images surrounding the Man, eyes turned inward, as he walks to Mme. Pace's hat shop. Moreover, whereas the play invented a neutral space for the hat shop scene, somewhere between external and internal reality, the scenario visualizes their interpenetration. Given Pirandello's affinity to Futurists, his inspiration for creating place cinematically, without narrative, recalls F. T. Marinetti's play *Simultaneity* that staged two scenes at once; or more generally recalls Futurists' *"sintesi,"* brief plays consisting solely of scenes or events stripped of plot, dramatic machinery, and all but minimal dialogue, on the whole resembling an embryonic Performance Art. Perhaps the scenario's most purely cinematic place is the amusement park (Takes 83–84) where the Author spies on the lovers. Images of mechanized pleasure palaces with their suggestion of grotesque and frenzied eroticism were to be repeated in many films, especially the film noir of Fritz Lang and Alfred Hitchcock.

3. About the new character, the Author's Secretary. Engaging him in a tragic romance with the girl of the ghetto echoes street film's idealizing of the underclass. Otherwise, paternalism in the relationship between Author and Secretary suggests father-son dramas in "Youth" film, a type of street film stressing the emotional difficulties of juveniles and their "insurgency against the tyranny of insensate authority" (Kracauer, 160), particularly in relation to sexuality. The Author's warning against becoming involved with "a harlot"

drives the Secretary into acute conflict since he "deeply respects" the Author. In Robert Land's youth film *Primanerliebe* (First love, 1927), a college boy, oppressed to the point of suicide by harsh teachers, calls on the girl he loves, finds her about to be raped by a seducer, and shoots the man. Adult culpability for his crime emerges during his trial, the result being the same import of Donald Westhof's trial in *Der Kampf Des Donald Westhof* (The trial of Donald Westhof, 1928). A youth's victimization in all such films by a repressed member of the bourgeoisie leads to tragedy. The similar situation in the *Film-Novelle* leads to the Son's suicide and the Secretary's despair.

4. About doubling and repeating male roles. The actions of the Author, the Secretary, the two imagined husbands, and the Son raise questions about voyeurism, the male gaze, and their erotic implications, as well as about film as film. Played up in sharp contrast to glamorous young women in many Weimar films, the voyeuristic motif pictures the desires of older men as pitiful or grotesque, recalling the extreme antiphonies of *teatro del grotesco*. Similar variations on voyeurism and the January-to-May theme of old man and young lover appear in films featuring intellectualized and essentially passive men, like Murnau's Professor Unrat in *Der blaue Engel,* or Emil Jannings in *Der leztze Mann.* Pirandello's doubles, even as voyeurs, only allude to the suppressed sensuality embodied by the German figures, victimized as much by the perverse eroticism of their own "gaze" as by desirable and unscrupulous women. The gaze in film, of course, always implicates the audience in an endlessly reflexive (and ironically pirandellian) dynamic. As for technical doublings, the Author's vision of twin Fathers, for instance, while listening to the Mother's story recalls Marcel L'Herbier's *Feu Mathias Pascal* with its shots of Mattia's subjective and objective selves sitting side by side in the same frame. In that work, both images are "true"; in the scenario, of course, the Author chooses the true.

To the extent the Author doubles for the original Father, doubling corresponds to the intricate link between the Father's sexual and the Author's imaginary crimes of incest, alluded to above. The Daughter at one point sees the Author reflected in a mirror as a satyr, an image foreshadowing his crime of transforming her into art. (In the late twenties mirrors become an almost obsessional feature of film to create psychological and phantasmagorical effects [Eisner, 129].) Or again, the Mother and Author project contrasting views of an absent Father. Male doubling throughout the script may provide the key to the scenario's deepest meaning (Vittori, 76).

Commentary

5. About the expanded role of Mme. Pace to that of Mme. Melloni, and the original hat shop scene into several episodes of perverse sexuality. The setting in an elegant brothel disguised as a fashion house with models on display intensifies the presentational nature of the film itself and woman as its object. The brothel motif appears in several Pabst films, notably *Die busche der Pandora* (Pandora's box), about a woman driven by insatiable lust.[37] The camera scrutinizes her skimpily dressed person with long, intimately detailed shots that actively create eroticism rather than merely recording it in the manner Pirandello scorned two decades earlier in *Si gira!* (Eisner, 298). At the same time such film, like the scenario, implicitly sees woman as dangerous and evil without addressing sexuality as such: Pirandello typically remains more interested in his film's psychological dynamics. A more straightforward form of voyeurism occurs when Mme. Melloni visits the Author at his invitation and titillates him with pornographic photographs (Take 28). Assuming he wishes to become a discreet client, she sends the Daughter to him. But the Author from the outset sees her in a state of moral degradation that is a result of her profession. He thus replays the role of the incestuous Father, although again the scene's sexual context is displaced by Pirandello's greater concern with its effects on personality.

6. About the film-within-a-film. The device at once distances the Author and draws him closer to the problem of subjectivity in Pirandello's quintessentially theatricalist mode. *After* the Author has interfered in the family's lives and been held responsible for the death of the Son (in the outer film), the Author's phantoms overwhelm him, "sapping all his strength and vitality." He banishes them and then begins writing a play that instantly materializes on screen (the inner film) with the Daughter in the streetwalking guise he has imagined (Takes 100–105). Beyond revealing the machinery of transformation, visualizing the creative process expresses an equivalent of the artist's psychoanalytical exorcism of guilt for having appropriated the family's lives. Like dream-within-a-dream, the outer form disguises by reordering the elements of the inner film. Finally, film-within-a-film becomes a means of realizing an epic, understood as a created world encompassing its Author.

* * *

Addressing any one of these elements in detail leads back to the Author as controlling consciousness. The entirely new subplot, however, involving the Secretary's romance with the Daughter, especially illustrates the projected

90

film's tight structure and the sexual thematics of doubling. After following the girl of the streets, the Author sends his young Secretary to her house with a request that the Mother visit him. The Secretary and the Daughter then fall in love. The next day, the Author *watches* from his studio window as the couple meet and converse on the street below: Mme. Melloni's establishment where the girl works is opposite the Author's house, symbolically an intriguing juxtaposition of professional sex and art. Influenced by *his perceptions* of the Daughter, the Author assumes that she means to ensnare the Secretary and warns him against "foul" women. Romance, nevertheless, flowers and during a visit to the girl's house the Secretary proposes marriage. As they embrace, the Son *spies on them* from the next room, assuming that the Secretary is one of his sister's clients. Deeply shamed, he shoots and kills himself. The horrified Secretary in the next scene accuses the Author of causing the family's tragedy and his own, for the dead boy bars him from the possibility of happiness with the Daughter.

Emphasis on voyeurism ("watches," "his perceptions," "spies on them") increases the sense through the scenario of a powerful dynamic between suppressed male eroticism and culpable, seductive woman. The configuration of dangerous sexuality between the idealistic Secretary and the compromised Daughter repeats in a scene between her and a sexually curious, but passive, Author. (Doubling both the character and situation intensifies the disastrous outcomes.) Not unique to the scenario, the theme reconceives psychological material with vital symbolic significance in all Pirandello's writing, theoretical and imaginative, perhaps referring ultimately to his father (Proser, 156). A tyrannical, wrathful, and physically abusive man, the elder Pirandello casts a long shadow over plots transforming or cancelling out a father's power. Whereas *Il fu Mattia Pascal* may fantasize male re-creation of the self as a form of revolt against a hated father, the scenario's romance allows a doubled Pirandello to play both a victimized Son and a punitive Father-Author who eventually gets his comeuppance. In psychoanalytic terms, through suicide the Son punishes himself first for being unable to control his absent Father's (read, the Author's) sexual aggression against the Mother and her children, and then for his own discovered sexuality as he watches his sister embrace a lover.

Two traumatic experiences perhaps at the root of Pirandello's voyeuristic theme contain almost classic primal content. When a boy of thirteen, Pirandello discovered his father in an affair with an old sweetheart whom he used to meet in the convent parlor of an obliging abbess, who was actually the aunt of both lovers. (The hint of incest in the woman's doubled role intensifies the implicit father-son rivalry.) Young Pirandello went to the convent and confronted the cousin, spitting in her face while his father remained concealed behind a curtain that left only his black shoes exposed. The sight of those black shoes beneath the curtain in turn may have reminded the boy of a more critical event a few years earlier, which may lie at the base of disturbed images linking sex to death in all Pirandello's major works.[38] At the age of nine in Agrigento, Pirandello caught his first secret *look* at a corpse laid out in the room of a tower used by the town as a morgue. From the room's doorway he caught an elongated view of the dead man's feet in black shoes. Then hearing rustling noises next door, he *peeked* into the next room where he saw a man and woman making love. The rustling sound was produced by their movements against the woman's stiffly starched petticoat.

How any childhood experience metamorphoses in the mind of the adult remains pure guesswork: Freud said many events of many orders combine to produce the pleasures and penalties of fantasy. Spying on death and the primal scene, fused in one forbidden moment, may have entered into Pirandello's tendency to characterize women archetypically. Or the experience may in some way have influenced his theory of opposites, in which the fixed pole always resembles death – stasis, rigid art forms, abstract reason, mechanization, Gubbio's camera – against which life and passion continue to struggle. Or again, the childhood traumas may be responsible for displacements of sexuality in his works by obsessive interest in the damaging results of sexual experience. Finally, his powerful vision of sex and death may have permeated his very concept of love, as more than one critic believes.

> In Pirandello's work love always retains a smell of death – not the idea of death, but the physical, putrefying aspect of death. It is either tarnished by madness or poisoned by incomprehension and betrayal. Never do his characters abandon themselves to the emotions and the senses and there is not one woman, however beautiful, to whom the author does not give some more or less repulsive characteristic. (Quoted in Giudice, 10)

As a hypothesis rather than a critical conclusion, this extreme view of Pirandello's love and death theme sheds some light on the *Film-Novelle*'s function as an act of exorcism. First, it may not be death in the abstract but his own death that Pirandello caricatures and mocks in his theories as in his literature – fantasy forms are often protective fictions. Mattia Pascal pretends to kill his first persona; then disempowering a father, he rises again *sui generis* like a comic hero in another identity. The Boy in the original *Six Characters* shoots himself, yet reappears at the back of the stage at the play's end. The schoolmaster, Toti, in *Pensaci, Giacomino!* absents himself from sexual activity, then doubles himself in an active young lover. So, too, with the Author and the Secretary. All the protagonists reconfigure father-son tensions, just as voyeurism in all four works becomes a perverse dimension of self-conscious distancing. Characters written out and "killed off" in one story or play return in the *Prologo* and *Film-Novelle* as importunate phantoms. They originate not in some supernatural world of ghosts, like those Pirandello learned about from his family's superstitious maid, Maria Stella, but from deeply suppressed instinctual aspects of personality contemplated and reshaped by the artist (Giudice, 7).

In short, phantoms may embody fantasy welling up to mask taboo memories and impulses of sex and death, the very process of disassociative splitting Pirandello described in his *Secret Notebook* fictionalized in novels, dramatized in the original play, and finally realized in the *Film-Novelle*. Like other autonomous characters, the Author's phantoms arrive with their own prior stories in forms sharp and compelling enough to compete with and sometimes overpower reality; it was especially during periods of extreme isolation and loneliness that Pirandello resorted for human contact to his chamber of horrors. Yet "his struggles to control his ghostly characters are like re-enactments of the struggles he may have had restraining his passions against his father," or like futile efforts to *control* his father (Hodess, 138). Accidental death and suicide among the siblings in *Six Characters* look very like acts veiling guilt.

If the *Film-Novelle*'s Author *is* Pirandello, he shows himself helpless to prevent the tragedy he causes by projecting his fantasy of doomed sexuality onto the Daughter's reality. He is trapped in the dynamic of materializing and "taking his phantoms back into his head" each time they appear, behavior roughly corresponding to that of his mentally unbalanced wife, who reconstructed reality according to her own paranoid delusions. Still, the Author *is* the Character doubling the role of the play's Father, who tyrannized over his doubled families; Author relates the phenomenon to mysteries of consciousness, and perhaps to Pirandello's psychic warfare over his father. This nexus of unconscious and conscious energies give the incest theme its power as an old, old reflection of the child's primal wish to supplant his parent. In the play, the

Father's abortive incest with the Stepdaughter remains part of the suppressed story generating theatrical confrontations on-stage. That is, the play-within-a-play, consistent with classic psychology, contains the darkest of forbidden wishes that its Author writes out and then disclaims (Kligerman, 734). The *Film-Novelle*, to the contrary, elaborates the incest plot openly, realistically, linking it to the gaze of the Author, Father(s), Son, and Secretary. No longer a hidden source of irrationality, its destructive force can be distributed over several levels of conflict and played out in another register – as a fiction drawing upon Pirandello's traumatic experience of his father, and as an insight into the emotional content of the Author's phantoms.

Finally, then, it is the character of the Author who suggests the scenario's salutary function for Pirandello, even without his experience of acting the role. Psychoanalytical readings of the play, like Kligerman's and Bentley's (referred to in chapter 2), based on the play's dramatizations of Janusian or schizoid thinking, change completely when the Author through doubling accepts the Father he earlier rejected. He now enacts the original Father's persistent, suffering self-justification in which feelings of rejection and deprivation played such a key role. Indeed, both feelings were intensified in the original relationships between Father and Mother, whom he repudiated and sent away; between Father and Stepdaughter deprived of each other; between Mother and Son separated from one another when he is a child. Severed from family and isolated, lacking an identity formed by mirroring from others, the original Father, like Enrico IV, Signor Ponza, and Signora Frola, too, was "talking to live," talking to connect a self precariously structured around a single moment of existence (Hodess, 138). Withdrawal into a singular self-concept was itself an element in Pirandello's creative process since it contradicted his knowledge that a variety of stimuli comprise personality. The Author still calls reality into question, and thereby questions our own. But the Author never questions the reality of his film, a paramount difference to the dynamics in the play.

Many small details of the *Film-Novelle* seem to confirm these probabilities. To take only one example already noted earlier, the Daughter's Father and Stepfather appear together before the Author as *his* phantom reflections in the mirror scene where the Author compares their truths. While their sexuality remains unexpressed in this scene, the omniscient Author "possesses" them both *as* father figures, who in turn "possess" him. As always, Pirandello questions not which image is true but what governs the relation between them. In the 1925 Preface, insisting upon drama's rigorous objectivity, Pirandello adamantly denied that the Father was a mask for himself. The sources of poetry remain distinct from the thing itself. So, too, the scenario maintains its decorum as an epic yet realizes subjectivity as fully as possible, short of mere autobiography. Each work of art, said Goethe, is "a fragment of a long confession." And all art is transformation.

« 4 »

Pirandello decided to publish the *Film-Novelle* (in 1930) to facilitate its distribution among the Berlin film community. Nevertheless a flurry of responses from Otto Kahn, Jesse Lasky, and other notables in Berlin resulted in nothing concrete, partly since amid the rise and fall of options and renegotiations throughout the year, the old obstacle of censorship rose up again to present itself in new, virulent form.[39] The German Censor Board (*Filmprufstelle*) in 1929 demanded cuts to films with scenes of prostitution, rape, bribery, and "protracted depiction of life in a brothel." On these grounds, it removed Pabst's *Tagebuch einer verlorenen* (Diary of a lost girl) from circulation as "morally offensive," claiming that it made prostitution "easy, attractive, comfortable and for that reason desirable."[40] The Board also added ratings to some street film, attaching the phrase *Jugendverbot* to prohibit showings to young audiences. Potential German producers of the *Film-Novelle* remained wary.

After lengthy consideration, British International Pictures along with another film house also decided against risking violation of English censorship restrictions (letter 21 April 1929). Pirandello, of course, had been grappling with the entire issue of censorship, official and unofficial, ever since outcries against the play in Rome on its opening night. In England in 1922 Lord Chamberlain had prohibited public performances of *Six Characters* which "would have been a real scandal." The restriction compelled producers and theater companies, including Pirandello's, to resort either to performance for private societies or to recital in Italian. But the Anglo-Saxon film market consistently shunned depictions of incest and adultery, even during the Italian golden age. The fact that the scenario's most objectionable sequences occur as projections of the Author's mind apparently failed to sway producers and distributors to chance rejection either by regulators or at the box office. Indeed, the contemporary view that all film to some extent expresses collective fantasy remains disputable.

Similar restrictions applied in the American market. From 1915 on, censor-

95

ship of sex and immorality had been exercised by individual states in the form of bans on particular films (Randall, 23). Standards were ill defined and haphazardly invoked against a range of subjects from adultery to specific depiction of crime. By the 1920s, however, the industry began to regulate itself through the Motion Picture Code headed by Will Hays, former postmaster general of the United States. In its first act, the organization passed a resolution to discourage the purchase of questionable books and plays for films, a sufficiently vague edict permitting anyone to evoke it at will. Subsequent attempts to define the code by both a Production Code Administration and a Motion Picture Producers and Distributors organization resulted in no greater clarity. In 1930 Pirandello signed a generous contract with Lasky of Paramount Pictures for four of his works including *Six Characters*. Negotiations broke down nevertheless and excluded the *Film-Novelle* based on Paramount's unwillingness to risk sanction by what Pirandello called "hypocritical" moral restrictions in the newly installed American Production Code. The contract remained a paper trail leading nowhere.

FIVE

Treatments for the Talkies

Meanwhile, both classical theater and the music hall can rest easy in the certainty that they will not be abolished for one simple reason. Theater is not trying to become cinema; cinema is trying to become theater. The greatest success to which film can aspire, one moving itself even farther along the road toward theater, will be that of becoming theater's photographic and mechanical copy, and a bad one at that. Like all copies, it must arouse a desire for the original.[1]

The future of dramatic art and of playwrights is in America – believe it – it's necessary to direct ourselves towards a new artistic expression: the talking film. I was against it; now I am convinced.[2]

In the early 1930s Pirandello was trapped in new forms of contradiction. He took Hollywood by storm, yet *Six Characters* still failed to go before the cameras. Film tycoons paid him huge sums for treatments, yet he constantly feared penury. His novels and plays continued to be seen as exemplars of avant-gardism, yet new works reflected a reactionary mood. While he received the world's acclaim as Nobel prize winner, his health deteriorated and his spirits remained low. Hope deferred maketh a sick heart.

To illustrate, Pirandello played agent and entrepreneur for his work with people who were experts at the game: Lee Shubert, Irving Thalberg, Hal B. Wallis, Rueben Mamoulian, and their counterparts in Europe, each of whom operated with a phalanx of professional staff and advisers in tow.[3] Under those circumstances, the success of any arrangement might depend as much on factors beyond Pirandello's knowledge or control as upon the desirability of his properties. In America, particular writers and directors became far less important than producers and teams of writers, aiming to carry a work to technical perfection and thereby guarantee its acceptance in a shrinking marketplace.[4] (Despite the persistent image in the minds of Europeans that U.S. companies remained healthier economically than their own, by 1933 one-

Commentary

third of U.S. cinemas had closed.) The secretaries, agents, and helpers Pirandello relied upon out of need lacked the experience and acumen to deal with
big business organizations which were growing more complex in the atmosphere of worldwide economic crisis. And Pirandello, whose eye penetrated
the subtle, the abstract, the ambiguous element in any subject, was no busi-
nessman, in spite of his persistent fears of imminent financial ruin. Then, too,
negotiations must sometimes have suffered from his own inconsistencies. For
all his Sicilian canniness he rarely noticed practicalities. He cared about a
work's aesthetic integrity; other considerations tended to fall into a distant
second or third place. His sense of indignation at a marketplace that made
commodities out of art and artists remained strong.

The point applies, for instance, to Italy's cooptation of Pirandello's name for
the first "talkie" it distributed, *La canzone dell'amore* (Song of love, 1930),
inspired by Pirandello's early story "In silenzio" ("In Silence").[5] When the
infamous Pittaluga of Cines decided to bring Italian film into the sound era,
he turned to Gennaro Righelli, knowing that the director held a property
given to him by his friend Pirandello years before. Cines's finished film bears
little or no relation to the original melodrama about a sensitive young man
who rears his mother's love-child in secret after she dies in childbirth. He then
kills himself and the child rather than surrender the child to the father, who
appears years later seeking revenge for the kidnapping and deception. Pirandello's familiar theme of doubled males – displaced father and son – and his
unusual interest in lost or stray children might have been exploited by the
film in a new key.[6] Instead the studio transformed the altruistic protagonist
into a female; concocted a romantic comedy between her and a songwriter
who abandons her, believing the child to be hers, then returns to marry her
after an implausible series of coincidences; and added a final, moralistic sequel. Pirandello agreed to the changes in a contract apparently signed with
more than passing indifference. He rightly suspected that Cines wanted the il-
lustrious member of the Italian Academy to lend his prestige to the project. He
attended the premiere in a Rome "supercinema" (8 October 1930) at Pittaluga's invitation along with several notables including Il Duce, who praised
the film highly. Pirandello, rather, faulted the dialogue, the acting, indeed,
everything about the film except the high quality of Righelli's "marvelous"
photographic images and the music – those elements of cinemelography.

Italy's cavalier disregard of Pirandello's plight as an exile still rankled.
When he signed that generous and ill-fated contract for *Six Characters* with

98

Lasky of Paramount Pictures, they released the news to the United Press; Italian newspapers took not the slightest notice. "Perhaps a ban of silence has been imposed" [on me], Pirandello says drily in a note to Stefano from Berlin. Apart from his bitterness, the letter is worth quoting for its indirect allusion to momentous changes in the industry.

> Anyway, the contract involves me for three months, partly in New York and partly in Hollywood. They will pay my roundtrip voyage plus one thousand dollars per week for my maintenance. The contract covers four works: two are assured and two optioned, with a separate arrangement for *Six Characters*. . . . As if Germany were Italy, the newspapers here regularly report on a film industry which has not known how to avail itself of my presence in Berlin for more than a year; yet now they pretend to reprove the Americans for taking me away. (Letter 15 April 1928)

Hollywood had been encroaching upon Berlin's film supremacy for years. As economic depression following the 1929 crash in America worsened and spread through Europe, international cinema threatened to become a euphemism for American control. Varying sorts of mergers between Berlin and Hollywood initiated during the mid-twenties became formal arrangements by the end of the decade (Murray, 59).[7] Once-flourishing German production companies either consolidated, reduced their size to technical units operating on commission, or left the industry entirely as big money grew tighter and movie attendance dropped. The super company UFA alone controlled seventy-one film-related companies and served thousands of theaters through its distribution network by entering into partnerships with Universal, Paramount, and MGM (Robison, 59). German actors and directors were fleeing to Hollywood in the way Italians once had fled to Berlin. Lubitsch, Murnau, Veidt, Jannings, Lang, Reinhardt, and others whom Pirandello knew well either became regular transatlantic passengers or decamped to America permanently. In all, the resulting impoverishment of the German product may have been greater than gains to the American, with a few exceptions. The shift, for instance, gave birth to new genre like Lubitsch's sophisticated comedy and Lang's film noir that thrived in America. One unexpected consequence of the rise of new genre to Pirandello's projects was a changed attitude to sex. Whether between married people or not, the sexual relation was fun, or daffy, or glamorously escapist, or exciting as in gangster film, rather than

Commentary

guilt-ridden and morally reprehensible. Women "were no longer creatures of menace or mystery, but good companions," with names like Greta Garbo, Claudette Colbert, Katherine Hepburn, and Carole Lombard. Some of the new atmosphere of film as an opiate – the depression was never mentioned in America until 1933 – slipped over to art films; or rather, producers were tempted to blur the line between art films and commercial products.

The view from Berlin obviously differed. Yet, despite deepening gloom, or perhaps because changes generated a panicky rush to reverse a tide, proposals to Pirandello ran high in the late summer and fall of 1930. Ossa Films, looking at short stories, suggested he collaborate on a scenario with Palermi, who later that year optioned the play *Il piacere dell'onestà* for Tonfilm. When Pirandello dallied over a decision, Ossa tried to lure him with the prospect of working with other friends, the respected directors Augusto Genina and Carmine Gallone, both of whom "seriously wanted to make the best films," Pirandello said. (Negotiations resulted a year later in an option contract on two subjects, never filmed.) Or differently, Michael Farley of Paramount invited Pirandello to visit their studios at Joinville, "the new Hollywood" outside of Paris, for a series of exploratory talks. Even Richard Eichberg, formerly of British International and in dubious repute with Pirandello, reappeared as agent to hire him as screenwriter for MGM and Paramount in a joint contract – one never implemented.

Still, against this backdrop of sporadic excitement and uncertainty, Pirandello's daily letters to Marta Abba continued to paint rosy visions of their future. America was never far from mind. The base note of despair in his correspondence, nevertheless, makes painful reading. While he suffered acutely from her absence, Marta Abba responded only with brief notes, or not at all. Pirandello begged for a sign of his importance to her, at one point writing wildly, "Why am I doing all this? America, London, Paris, film, plays, operettas and I want nothing better than to die, to remove myself from this torture that my life has become!" (30 July 1930). By winter, at the bottom of the year without her, his volatility had become histrionic: "You'll see, I'll go to America. And I'll return with a new fortune. Then we'll tour around the world, Europe and America. And then you'll settle, important and happy, [do] some play, and then I'll die. It's not a dream; it's the truth" (31 December 1930).

On the very same day, his extravagant claims to Marta for their partnership seemed finally to be vindicated. Her company premiered with *Come tu mi vuoi* in Turin to great success; and in spite of his dark indifference to offers excluding her, the triumph precipitated a virtual renaissance of interest in him. Requests poured in from the finest companies in Paris, where he had relocated, to stage his plays with the best actors of the day. (The innundation compelled him to lease his rights carefully to avoid overexposure.) One highly problematic proposal engaged him briefly, since it involved Marta as principal actress. The well-known entrepreneur Mario Bellotti of Braunberger Films suggested they form an Italian-French theater company that would tour with two works, one French and one Italian, each translated into the other language.[8] Even the Comédie-Français welcomed Pirandello in 1931, an honor rarely conferred upon a living foreign playwright. As if he were a French national, he then was invited to become a member of the French Dramatists League (in 1932), a great distinction that would allow him to use France instead of Italy as a base of operations. In the same year, he signed a potentially lucrative contract with the agent Desiree Schwartz to handle the republication of works enjoying renewed popularity.

Pirandello's spirits could not help but rally when the success of *Come tu mi vuoi* also attracted Lee Shubert. He and Pirandello signed a contract giving him $4,000 for the rights to four plays to be produced in a pirandellian season in New York: *Come tu mi vuoi* and *Questa sera si recita a soggetto*, as well as *I giganti della montagna* and *Quando si è qualcuno*, both of which were still unfinished. The further possibility of a tour in theaters owned by the Shuberts throughout North and Central America immediately triggered Pirandello's fantasies of reunion with Marta as female lead, either with her film company or a new one. He writes urging her to study languages, to keep her art above all petty concerns of people and politics, and to concentrate on their working together. Since he anticipated a deal with the London producer Charles B. Cochran, similar to that with Shubert, his visions in the letters wax rhapsodic.

The turn in Pirandello's theater fortunes paralleled one in cinema that affected perception of him as a major source of material for the "talkies." He had not changed his mind about dialogue needing to remain minimal and judicious: "If I have to listen to photographic images of actors speaking in strange voices through a mechanically operated machine, then I prefer to go to the theatre, where at least there are real actors speaking with real voices" ("Will Talkies Abolish the Theater?"). To him cinema remained a language of appearances and therefore a potential expression of universal themes rather than particular trite tales. But he increasingly conceded that dialogue had become a necessity, as his observations quoted in the epitaph to this chapter reveal. Years before during his meeting with Irving Thalberg of MGM, when he and Thalberg were both in London seeing *The Jazz Singer,* they had not only discussed the kinds of dialogue that might be appropriate to a sound film of *Six Characters* but had envisioned filming *Come tu mi vuoi,* then in preparation for Marta's theater company. Thalberg, the young genius who began his career as secretary to Carl Laemmle of Universal, had already earned a reputation for imagination and vitality. Also generally regarded as the most cultivated and civilized among Hollywood tycoons, he not only introduced experimental and controversial films at MGM, but he formed its predominant style with escapist melodramas, lavish musicals, and adaptations of novels in glorious settings.

Thalberg continued to pursue his interest in *Come tu mi vuoi* while its successful run for the Shuberts in America the following year attracted several competitive film bids and won rave reviews. With Judith Anderson in the lead, the play earned substantial box office receipts in Chicago, Philadelphia, and then New York, where it filled houses for 143 performances.[9] Thalberg moved quickly from purchase to production, turning the film, *As you Desire Me,* directed by George Fitzmaurice, into an even greater commercial triumph than the play, partly by signing Erich von Stroheim, Melvyn Douglas, and Greta Garbo in the leading roles.[10] Containing a great deal more sentiment than the original text about a young noblewoman's amnesia, the film capitalized on the appeals of the beautiful Garbo who enthralled Hollywood and film critics as well.[11] *The New York Times* found her acting "superior to and more varied than the work of Judith Anderson," suggesting Garbo had far transcended her former label of "supervamp."[12] Pirandello himself praised Garbo's interpretation, and *The Tribune's* reviewer, equally laudatory of Garbo, also hints at Pirandello's reputation in America:

If there were any lingering doubt that Luigi Pirandello's puzzling problem of personalities was adaptable to the film, it was quickly dispatched. . . . The engrossing story was enhanced by several distinguished performances. Pirandello's reputation for metaphysics should not keep away from the Capitol [theater] those who want dramatic stories. There is every quality that full drama demands in his story of the young Italian countess who is swept over and lost in the invasion of northern Italy. (5 June 1932)

On the whole, however, press coverage of Garbo quite overshadowed that of Pirandello – posters in the MGM promotion packet carried Garbo's name in huge type and included a line in small print saying, "based on the play by Luigi Pirandello." Advertising materials, rarely understated, ran from hyperbolic praise for "Sweden's most celebrated actress," to suggestions for local Garbo look-alike contests, essay writing contests, and window displays in local stores on any theme remotely connected to the movie. Bookstores stocking Pirandello's works were encouraged to construct displays using Garbo's name along with Pirandello's, and libraries were urged to distribute bookmarks carrying advertisements for the film. One amusing blurb among publicity materials describes "Hollywood's Italian colony" coming out to act in the film. "Several hundred men, women, and children took part in these scenes," staged on an Italian villa owned by a marble importer, "and the location trip took on the aspect of an Italian picnic with baskets of fruits, meats and long loaves of bread providing a repast for the hungry families."[13]

In spite of voluminous film records, there is a curious lack of evidence about Pirandello's contribution to the actual shooting of this, the sole film produced in the United States during his lifetime. Sources even disagree about his presence on the set, though it would have remained ceremonial if only since his English in his judgment was rudimentary.[14] One perceptive reviewer, noting the differences between stage and screen versions and the substitution of a happy ending, conjectured that Pirandello would receive a "sad blow to his pride when he hears of it," plainly implying his absence. Italian sources to the contrary see him in Hollywood during filming.[15] The point is irrelevant to the obvious success of the film. The bill for the Capitol theater indicates five showings daily, and distribution continued for several years. One enterprising theater producer, planning a month-long festival of thirty Italian classics, intended to mount *Come tu mi vuoi* first, so as to capitalize on its movie fame.[16]

* * *

Exhausted by years of continuous struggle, Pirandello's letters during that winter of 1931 register something like euphoria at the conquest of Broadway and Hollywood as well. His dream of midaslike prosperity at first reemerged with all its promise of freeing him from financial worries and establishing an independent theater for Marta. After the initial excitement subsided, however, he complained that although MGM had paid him $40,000 for the film rights,

Commentary

an extraordinary fee at the time, one-third went to the translator, another third to agents and middlemen, the rest for travel and living expenses, so that in the end he pocketed little. (His arithmetic or his recollection seems exaggerated on all counts.) His outlook, nevertheless, remained sanguine since on the wave of his triumph Pirandello engaged in as many meetings, entertained as many proposals, negotiated as many options, rights agreements, and contracts for plays, films, and publications in Europe and America as in the previous six years – the Chronology lists only major events – a tally ignoring ancillary dealings with translators, lawyers, representatives, and the like, that his productivity entailed. Berlin now pursued him to Paris where projects continued to bloom in an eternal spring. Just before *As You Desire Me* was released, Pirandello told UFA with delight that their request for the film rights to his play came too late. He took similar pleasure in rejecting another German company interested in a "talkie" of *La nuova colonia*, whose American rights he had just sold to Lee Shubert. Offers even came from individuals like the actor Eugen Klopfer, who had played in Reinhardt's production of *Il piacere dell'onestà* and wanted to repeat the role on film. He must have enjoyed refereeing a quarrel between Pitoëff and George Bernard Shaw over staging of *The Apple Cart*: the playwrights agreed that theater managers tyrannized writers; Pitoëff swore that both playwrights were mediocre, "metteurs en scene."[17]

Pirandello's exhilaration reached a high point when he asked MGM for the then astronomical sum of $80,000 for *Six Characters*, double the amount they paid for *Come tu mi vuoi*, to recompense him as both writer and actor – he says MGM's representative appeared unflustered by the request (letter 29 April 1931).[18] If they conclude the deal, his letter continues, he would need this time to pay only some commissions out of the approximately two million "franchi" he would earn for himself. One of several yet unsolved mysteries about the MGM negotiations involves the existence of an anonymous, crude translation into English of the original German *Film-Novelle*. Found recently in the Pirandello archives at the University of California with no accompanying information about its authorship or provenance, the translation probably was commissioned by Thalberg in connection with MGM's plans to produce a film.[19] The document itself carries no indication of having been written as a shooting script; indeed the language suggests it was prepared by a novice translator and might have served as a preliminary rough draft for a film treatment.

It is also surprising that paperwork says nothing about the bogey of American censorship, which was organized more efficiently during the 1930s than previously. Catholic clerics and laymen drafted a manifesto, sponsored by the industry, that became a de facto code for self-regulation some time before its incorporation into the Catholic Legion of Decency code (1934) which threatened the marketing and distribution of rejected films. At the same time, almost as a rebuttal, the industry was forming its own Production Code Administration charged with interpreting the earlier Hays and Motion Picture rules (Randall, 199). Attention to the dicta of any one of these regulatory bodies might have halted negotiations were it not that enforcement remained random. Pirandello, in any case, hedged against the MGM deal's collapse by dickering for a projected film with two French production houses who were to collaborate on underwriting the venture while he would contribute his work. As one of three producers, he would receive one-third of the estimated profit of ten million lire and control the choice of actors. (He had, in fact, demanded control over the actors in MGM's European versions of the film.) The implications here are that Marta would play the (Step)Daughter, no matter who finally produced the film. All the newspapers, he writes her, "talk about it even on the first page: Pirandello is the order of the day in New York too" (letter 29 April 1931).[20]

As always, Pirandello's letters to Marta also shed other light behind the scenes of the industry. "All the internationalization of film is lost and all the American houses want to produce in various languages" (letter 29 April 1931). Pirandello nonetheless feels certain, he says optimistically and against the evidence, that Americans will import the best art from every nation, that is, implicitly, Marta's art. Pirandello in this letter may have had in mind still another project with Thalberg for a series of films, based on subjects of his choosing, for international distribution. But tight money and a shrinking marketplace meant that films by and with stars stood the best chance of competing successfully for production and distribution. In 1932, for instance, when Cines bought *Giuoca, Pietro!* – for a good deal more than they usually paid for subjects – the principals urged Pirandello to use his influence to persuade Eisenstein or Pabst to direct (letters 31 May 1932 and 3 June 1932).[21]

Of course, luring either Eisenstein or Pabst could not have circumvented difficulties that arose over the studio's changes to Pirandello's text, nor could it have prevented the near collapse of the contract over casting Marta, who was not a bright enough star for Cines (letter 6 February 1932). It is not clear whether Pirandello's intention to be present on the set so as to "forestall mismanagement," as he put it, meant he would demand she play the role.[22] By August Pirandello writes that the director, Ruttmann, had decided against casting Marta, but adds that he will fight the decision (letter 11 August 1932). For years he had been reassuring and cautioning her not to "hope for anything from Italy, fallen unfortunately in the hands of those who wish us ill, as for the theater so for film." But they've "condemned themselves to impotence" – all "the worse for them and for the country. . . . They won't achieve anything [good] in either field without me since I'm the only live presence in the nation" (letter 22 May 1931). Exaggeration was not far off the mark. Eventually, Marta's success with *Trovarsi* in Milan and *Come tu mi vuoi* in Paris may have influenced Cines to proceed with the film, retitled *Acciaio* (1933). Whether they took Marta with the property remains unclear.[23]

* * *

More than before, Pirandello's film and theater negotiations seeded one another. When the Shuberts, who already held options on *Questa sera si recita a seggetto* and *Six Characters*, bought the rights to *La nuova colonia* and wanted *Due in uno*, Pirandello enjoyed their contest over the latter play with the Comédie-Français, who were preparing it for the following season. The primary Shubert-Pirandello project in 1931, however, tells a multifaceted and revealing story about the inextricable link between Pirandello's planning and his state of mind concerning Marta. For several months, the Shuberts studied the financing for their projected tour of Pirandello's works through the Americas with Marta Abba and a small Italian company of her choosing. Since Pirandello would be the tour's guest, and since his own quite separate visit to the United States seemed imminent, given the film activity on his properties, he finally had found the concrete occasion that would keep him and Marta together. He regaled her with tales of glory reminiscent of those surrounding Eleanora Duse when introduced to this country by Morris Gaest. With the help of his secretary, Saul Colin, Pirandello tried to supervise every detail of the project, from choosing publicity photos, to estimating expenses for Marta's troupe ($600 per diem), to his own role as visiting author and benevolent genie. He was convinced that the tour would begin as anticipated on October 1, 1931.

Newspaper and publicity announcements of the tour, however, failed to include Marta's name – a minor omission he assured her, which he nevertheless found himself powerless either to explain or to alter. Neither Colin nor European newspaper editors succeeded in correcting the error that persisted through further publicity and communication with the Shuberts. Predictably enough, Marta grew angry and confused. After months of inconclusive correspondence, the Shuberts' lawyers finally told Pirandello that the theater season with *Come tu mi vuoi* had been financially "disastrous." Given the economic depression, any tour in or out of the United States would need to earn profits of at least $11,000 per week to be viable, an unlikely sum to expect.

Where the truth lies no one knows. Pirandello obviously would have withheld any hint to Marta that the Shuberts had balked at the costs of handling a company headed by a little known Italian actress, relative, that is, to costs just for the rights to Pirandello's works with or without the publicity value of his personal appearance. The inference, nonetheless, seems unavoidable – that his negotiations for them as a couple reflected more wishful thinking than hardheaded business sense. Doubtless Pirandello's name opened doors for Marta in Europe – her role in the French production of the farce *L'uomo, la bestia e la virtù* (*Man, Beast and Virtue*) during the winter of 1930 had won good reviews – and he continued to write plays for her.[24] At one point he proposed a series of one-woman shows that he would write for her to take on tour. How she would manage English, however, remained moot. A newspaper interview with her years later, when she played *Tovarich* in New York, revealed that her English was minimal and heavily accented, whereas Pirandello's secretary, Colin, had represented her glowingly as completely fluent.[25] Nor was she as photogenic as American tastes required.

Pirandello's family in Rome, meanwhile, much to his annoyance, approached Marta with fears that his health and sanity were being affected by his and Marta's problematic relationship (letter 17 March 1931). Certainly, Pirandello's wildest letters to Marta from Berlin and Paris might substantiate the family's fears; and certainly his impassioned appeals ignore the import of her unresponsiveness. Generously, he seizes every opportunity to minimize the disparity between her and himself, simple actress and celebrated writer, often enough presenting his work as the product of her inspiration. And perhaps some of it was. He says he will reject an (unspecified) film deal, for instance, that would take him to America for three months if her proposed tour with the Shuberts cannot be arranged to coincide with his. In another letter he dismisses with one line rival offers from UFA and MGM for filming *Six Characters* (letter 21 March 1931), his dearest desire, yet expends himself on long pages of irritation and indignation when an interview with Marta (in the French Journal *Comoedia*) carries a photograph of them together rather than of her alone (letter 22 July 1931). This minor incident receives equal attention in the letter with his report that Carl Laemmle of Universal would film an Italian version of *Come prima, meglio di prima* (*As before, better than before*) starring Marta, but only after they complete an American version; in plainer words therefore, a distant prospect.[26] As before, whenever cinema is concerned, Pirandello's letters rarely dwell on obstacles to a future hovering glorious before them.

« 2 »

In the spring of 1932, a business visit to Rome turned into a welcome of Italy's prodigal son. Cines wanted to discuss several properties; Pirandello's friend Ruggero Ruggeri owned a new theater company that wanted to produce *Quando si è qualcuno* and *Il giuoco delle parti*; the composer Gian Francesco Malipiero was eager to write music for Pirandello's play and story *La favola del figlio cambiato* (The changeling). Family and friends gathered, Italian theater appeared genial, and colleagues cheered him with visits. Pirandello's spirits rose, too, on unexpected signs of good will from Il Duce during a meeting on March 13, 1932, that opened with excessive cordiality. "Oh, Pirandello, finally we see you again. I'm pleased too to find you sharper and younger than ever" (letter 14 May 1932). Speaking as a member of the august Italian Academy of Letters and laden with honors from France, Pirandello presented Mussolini with a plan to reorganize regional theaters.[27] He intended to follow up with hard evidence of the project's feasibility, he said, aiming to forestall protests from the theater czar Paolo Giordani. All good reasons seeming to conspire, Pirandello spent the summer at Stefano's villa in Castiglioncello, enjoying long missed friends in the evenings and working to complete theater and film pieces waiting on uninterrupted quiet.[28]

Still, pressured and overextended professionally, Pirandello experienced a brief but frightening cardiac incident that prompted him for the first time in three years to consider remaining near family in Rome permanently (Ortolani, 671). The moment passed but not its effects on Pirandello's depressed state of mind, intensified that fall by another brief meeting with Mussolini. The leader revealed that Italy's terrible economic plight would worsen and that a "frightful world war threatened."[29] Obviously, theater and film were peripheral concerns. Pirandello fought against pessimism by reminding himself of his mission as an artist. He mustered enthusiasm for an extremely successful premiere of *Quando si è qualcuno* in Buenos Aires,[30] which welcomed him with the utmost respect, and he appeared at several major conferences over the next few years.[31] He also struggled to ignore the devils of professional animosity and jealousy ever ready to surround him in Italy by retreating again to Paris.

* * *

In several real senses, exile had failed to protect Pirandello from the evils of theater and film politics that he had fled. If anything, his distinction kept his name current among enemies currying state favor, while his information about activities at any one time remained partial.[32] An accretion of disappointments and personal troubles, however, began to silence his once vocal antagonisms; he grew more cautious yet resentful of the necessity. For example, although a major international conference on theater in 1932 was unthinkable without his presence, he declined to attend such a one in Berlin. He explained in letters to Marta that he tired of factions in Italy "commenting in the press on his comments" while he was abroad. The Berlin conference leaders' insistence that he speak about current conditions in Italian theater and film would have compelled him to tell the truth: that the state "strangled" its artists by intimidation and manipulation, and this with the full compliance of the Italian Society of Authors.

Since he could not bring himself to damn his country from a pulpit, he chose silence. His only regret, he added lightly, was disappointing Jean Giradoux with whom he had planned to travel (letter 11 March 1931). Hints of continuing surveillance from afar over Pirandello's movements also can be gleaned from his asides. He tells Marta that Hugo Bernsteil, a producer for UFA, was annoyed by rumors that Pirandello would act in a German film of *Six Characters.*[33] Such a film inevitably would attract international attention and overshadow any future negotiations with Pirandello for a project based in Italy. Of course, Bernsteil had stumbled blind onto thorny territory. Responding immediately to Bernsteil's consternation, Pirandello coolly assured him that no contract yet had been signed and that he remained open to a proposal from UFA. At that, of course, dialogue ceased.

By the end of 1932, for all these reasons and more, Pirandello reestablished himself in a small apartment near family in Rome and decided to curtail his traveling. Although a wealth of documentation on his last, most public years shows him active and influential in Rome, Milan, London, Paris, and New

York, he grew even more inward than before and somewhat eccentric, as if engaged in a kind of soul searching and rethinking of some of his strongest convictions.[34] As Giudice (195) points out, his last play, *Non si sa come* (*No One Knows How*), tackled the issue of moral responsibility in a distinctly Catholic vein that branded him as "a reactionary rather than a precursor" in the arts. Pirandello defended the work as a culmination of his thought but convinced no one of its importance. We might digress to notice that his libretto for *La favola* fared no better with reviewers. The operetta, at first well received, was banned in Germany where Chancellor Hitler attended a performance, and was hissed off the stage of the opera house in Rome.[35] By all accounts, the music was undistinguished and the story line heavy with political portent, although the degree to which the performance reflected his original intentions remains unclear.

Pirandello's folk tale, which hinges on his favorite doubling motif, involves a beautiful but weak infant boy, stolen in the night and replaced by an ugly one who grows up an idiot. The golden boy reared as a prince eventually meets the sad mother and flourishes in her love and the warmth of simple village people; instead of returning him to court when royal messengers come for him, the village sends off the idiot boy to be king. It would have been difficult to prove that no barb was intended about a congenitally defective ruler, even though Pirandello's short stories contain many similar themes. The idea of a missing son, for instance, may hark back to *L'altro figlio*, one of his first films, and reappears in the elegantly made contemporary film called *Kaos* after Pirandello's birthplace. The film assembles six Sicilian tales about ordinary incident and superstition among ignorant peasants, or about buffoons whose tricks backfire. Apart from class conflicts between rich and poor, North and South, political implications in such stories never develop into specific programs that might, say, have predicted Fascist antipathy to *La favola*. In their general resistance to legal or moral authority, many tales rather dip into that river of anticlericalism and antiestablishment sentiment running through so much of Sicilian literature.[36]

* * *

The Fourth Volta Congress on the subject of dramatic art, over which Pirandello presided, echoes with the contradictions of these years in several ways. His inaugural address reiterated his convictions about theater being vital to civilized life, but his view of the stage as a "mirror of moral values ... entering into the life of a nation" strikes a new note.[37] In the great plays and novels, moral issues arise, when they do, as dimensions of larger psychological or philosophical concerns. Pirandello otherwise had alluded to the subject of public morality scornfully as, say, a bone of false contention among self-righteous drama critics, or a hypocritical curb on filmmaking. He was no respecter of institutionalized authority. His address also elaborates on his earlier comparisons of theater and film as spoken and silent forms respectively. Now he remarks astutely on the function of cinema as mass entertainment in an evolving "performance society."

> At other times people were drawn to performances on the occasion of major feasts and great religious festivals. Now that no longer happens, and people go on a daily basis, drawn by habit that has become a need, which is a sign of developing civilization. . . . Only the cinema has succeeded in satisfying this daily hunger for performances that is now so widespread.

He amplified the perception later in an interview, observing that "cinema might again become universal, as it was in its silent days, were it not subject to the mob, which is always particularist" (Rousseaux, 514). The point seems commonplace today, when a sociology of cinema has formulated definitions of its cultural role. At the time of the Volta Congress, however, Pirandello, like many artists, distinguished between film's social impact and its lagging steps toward finding its own "artistic expression." Film and theater are not equal in function, he repeats, going on to show that a decline in theater going was a temporary sign of economic hard times rather than evidence of competition with cinema. Turning practical, one of his diplomatic strategies, he finally proposed that "film showings be limited to one a night at a fixed time," so that the two arts need not vie for a dwindling audience.

« 3 »

The Nobel prize at the end of 1934 brought Pirandello the world's tribute yet no formal honors from Italy. Deluged by invitations, ceremonies, and theater celebrations throughout Europe, he seemed not to mind Italy's official neglect. According to Giudice (198), Pirandello appeared to be happy yet sunk in himself, afflicted by an inner anxiety, sometimes distracted and speaking in random, ironic asides. The event that pleased him most was a gala performance in Paris of *Questa sera si recita a soggetto* at the Theatre des Mathurins,

followed by an extraordinary homage by Pitoëff and all the actors of Pirandello's plays. When the director, Gaston Baty, announced Pirandello's award,
each actor filed past in character, wearing the makeup of a particular role and
pronouncing the appropriate lines (Giudice, 199).

Thereafter, while his fame resounded, while journalists and columnists
reported on his personality, his tastes, his dress, his smallest idiosyncracy,
while the strain of mandatory travel aggravated his physical debility – he
suffered periodic attacks of angina – film offers and requests flooded his mail.
Five American film studios asked his New York agents for subjects; Alexander
Korda wanted a subject for his London film company (letter 29 May 1934),
Pitoëff produced *Questa sera si recita* in Paris, and Mario Camerini bought the
play *Ma non è una cosa seria* (*But It's Not Serious*) for a sound film starring
Vittorio De Sica (released in 1936). Camerini's project was part of a move
after the Nobel prize to republish Pirandello. Camerini's brother, Augusto,
had made a silent film of the play in 1920 in collaboration with Arnaldo
Frateili. Details about that version, however, seem to have disappeared along
with the film itself.[38]

The most provocative of such projects was the French director Pierre Chenal's remake of *Il fu Mattia Pascal*, for which Pirandello supposedly edited the
script.[39] Photos of him on the set with the film's stars, Isa Miranda and Pierre
Blanchar, probably served publicity purposes (fig.11). But a photo of the
script's final page, corrected in Pirandello's handwriting, raises more questions than it answers (fig.12). Whereas the groundbreaking 1904 novel ends
with Pascal's existential crisis when he returns from "death" to find his role as
husband taken by a rival, Chenal provided a happy ending. Pascal secures
false documents authenticating his "false" persona, Adriano Meis, and marries his new love, Adriana, renamed Luisa in the film. No longer a young
drifter of about thirty who becomes a husband and victim of modernism by
happenstance, the new Pascal is a charismatic forty-year-old model of nobility in decline. The early chapters of the novel with their cast of local
grotesques disappear – the witchlike mother-in-law, the manipulative town
official (Malagna), the clown Pomino, Pascal's distraught mother, all given
full play in L'Herbier's 1925 version of the film. Chenal's more naturalistic
emphasis falls on Pascal's new life in Rome after a big windfall at Monte Carlo
prompts him to turn the accident of his official death into a deliberate experiment. Secondary characters change accordingly. The timid, unimportant wife
becomes slightly mad and provocative, presumably to provide Pascal with a

realistic motive for flight; Malagna becomes a Fascist mayor; Adriana-Luisa becomes a cool socialite; and the austere elegance of the whole creates a sense of the bizarre, when it does, through a controlled, surrealistic heightening of the familiar.

A good deal was written in Italy about the two Mattia Pascal films; an article in *Cinema* as late as 1941 included an extraordinary double-page spread of stills comparing L'Herbier's and Chenal's versions, laid out scene by scene to show their differing styles (fig.6). Still more criticism appeared after a 1985 version with Marcello Mastroianni, not distributed outside of Italy.[40] Most reviewers agree that L'Herbier's silent film captured the pathology in Pirandello's subject more effectively than did Chenal's, although the novel's narrative richness offers sufficient material for widely differing cinematic visions. L'Herbier's film had hinted at pirandellian grotesquerie, which appeared for the first time in the novel and recurred in later works. He had emphasized doubling in the twins born to Pascal's wife, in a "good" mother whose spirit remains influential on Pascal even after she dies, and a wicked mother-in-law remarkably like Madam Pace of *Six Characters*; he likened a doty old librarian, addicted to the printed word, to Pirandello's philosophers; and he highlighted a spiritualist's seance in Rome that may represent Pirandello's first literary encounter with phantoms. Chenal's film, to the contrary, saw a class-conscious novel dominated less by Pascal's manic imposture than by peripheral events. A cool, logical surface manages to rationalize the mystery of doubled personalities, and thereby the novel's central *raison*, by padding the theme with additional explanatory scenes. After his mother's death, for instance, and while wandering around the countryside in grief, Pascal sees one drunken vagabond kill a second one, assume the dead man's identity, and later on confess his crime in lengthy detail during "his own funeral."

Preoccupied with visual stylishness at some expense of metaphor and symbol, Chenal's film version seems to have approximated a linear costume drama, too icy for romance and too shorn of ambiguity to be Pirandello's. The disengaged hero of the novel may have anticipated Camus's *L'etranger*; the hero of Chenal's film rather resembles a kind of "Jean de la Lune": an absent-minded "butterfly catcher" attached to his mother. Yet one admiring critic describes the impact on him of a single frame early in the film that left him "thunderstruck" and eager to discover the novel. Blanchar, as Pascal in shirt-sleeves, rests an elbow against a chest of drawers in front of a framed photograph of himself. The eyes of the picture gaze on emptiness; those of the character look straight at us. The critic asks, "What was he trying to tell us, that perplexed man risen from the dead, an unequivocal symbol of transfixation? From what race of zombies did he come with open eyes?" (Kezich, 80).

If Pirandello, in fact, edited Chenal's entire script instead of merely approving it from afar and allowing a random page in his handwriting to be photographed, he departed almost completely from his novel's premise of quixotic madness and the tormented opportunism of his deluded hero. He also departed from his credo that cinema's role was to suggest: adapting literary works for the screen only made them banal. Only short stories, he claimed, weathered their translation into film as into drama since these were synthetic forms. "Remember," he pointed out to one interviewer, querying him about his 365 short stories, "all Shakespeare's plays were drawn from Italian short stories."[41] In any case, the virtues of Chenal's film ultimately may derive not from its cinematic merits but from its reminders of Pirandello's original work once again revived and transformed (Campassi, 305). Indeed Pascal's ghost seems to have become quite thoroughly autonomous, for the theme of the double certainly acquired a life of its own on the twentieth-century screen: whether in antic form like Woody Allen's spoof of Six Characters, entitled The Purple Rose of Cairo (1985), or in farcical form like The Captain's Paradise (1953), drawn from L'uomo, la bestia e la virtù (1919).[42] The latter play features still another version of displaced paternal sexuality, the theme reaching back through Il fu Mattia Pascal and down a long history of traditional satire. In the film, the comic actor Totò, famous for his deadpan style, played the cynical lover Paolino, who administers an aphrodisiac to Orson Welles, the bigamist captain of voracious appetites, so as to induce him to sire his pregnant wife's child after the fact. More psychologically provocative, Michelangelo Antonioni's Professione: Reporter (1975) returned to Pascal's dramatic irony. Antonioni cast Jack Nicholson in the role of a television journalist who substitutes for an army merchant felled by a heart attack in an African hotel. To obliterate his identity, Nicholson sinks himself into the personality of the dead man until he himself assumes the same extreme risk of heart failure.

Small wonder that Reinhardt was a household name among Berlin theater and film audiences, rich and poor, who compared notes on performances as avidly as professionals. During his sojourn in Berlin, Pirandello memorialized the revered director in his witty theater play, *Questa sera si recita* (1930). The plot's director, Dr. Hinkfuss, bullies his rebellious actors into improvising on a melodramatic story line without a script, in *commedia dell'arte* fashion. Through his imprecations, disquisitions, cajolery, and outright tyranny, a play-within-a-play is almost performed and an actress falls dead in the effort.

For at least six months Pirandello laid careful plans to insure the play's success, banking on it to end that terrible period of his isolation and to renew interest in him in Germany and abroad. Over one of several dinners (letter 20 September 1929), he and Reinhardt thrashed out how to manage without Max Pallenberg as producer if neither he nor Reinhardt could be freed from engagements; whether to schedule the opening in Frankfurt or Hamburg instead of Berlin; whether to postpone entirely; which theaters offered the best technical resources; and so on. By April 1930 an "excellent" cast was assembled and music for the cabaret scene by Ralph Benaski, a well-respected talent, proceeded into rehearsals that amounted to about fifty in number (letter 15 April 1930). Initial performances, finally staged in Konisberg, augured well: "The work has already been optioned in most of the world." Pirandello says; "unlike *Six Characters*, it's amusing and it plays very well" (letter 15 April 1930). Thereafter, however, for two months Pirandello worried, doubted, and spent entire days at the theater, struggling to explain the difference between the German and the Italian "nature" or "temperament," so crucial to the idea of improvisation. Finally he described it as an absence in the German sensibility of a tempo and rhythm that he envisioned as a Tiepolo fresco: "Alive, as though moved by the wind, and capricious." Instead the German director Hans Hartung attended to every line and word like a miniaturist, getting lost in details, losing breadth and imagination, creating a "pretentious and pedantic interpretation" that might please the Germans. Pirandello conceded, but it did not please him (Abba, 24). He nevertheless counseled himself to compromise. Newspapers including the *New York Times* began to run bulletins and feature stories. "I confess," he writes to Marta on the eve of the premiere, "that I am very nervous. . . . This is due to the bitter realization that I have become a stranger to my own country and that I therefore shall have to win another home for my art" (Abba, 23). Then the Berlin opening, on June 1, 1930, turned into a "tempestuous" riot by a "gang of rascals" that reminded Pirandello of nothing so much as the disastrous Roman premiere of *Six Characters*.[2] Letters to Marta Abba, pieced together with newspaper accounts, reveal an incredible conspiracy among Reinhardt acolytes and supporters, that was calculated to undermine, if not wholly discredit, the play, the production, and the playwright as well.

Apparently, a Reinhardt faction led by Pirandello's first German translator, Hans Feist, not only disrupted the opening night performance with outcries and protests but managed to suppress all but damning reviews the following day. Feist had become an enemy during the Berlin year, even bringing Pirandello to court for breach of contract over Feist's right to translate works written after *Six Characters*.[3] Before the performance of *Questa sera si recita a soggetto* Feist had given out that the character Dr. Hinkfuss was a caricature of Reinhardt; fans, therefore, saw insults to their idol in each circumstance surrounding the play as well as in the play itself. For one, opening night coincided with the banquet night of a Reinhardt Jubilee already in progress; then, too, the director Hartung, hired in Reinhardt's place, fell far beneath him in talent. Reinhardt enthusiasts even found cause for complaint in the play's dedication to him – a wholly mystifying piece of the puzzle. Pirandello recognized that Hartung's misreading of the text and overall weak production contributed to the debacle. While he reported to Marta that three-quarters of the opening night audience paid no notice to outcries and disruptions, and gave him and the leading actress a standing ovation, newspapers reported to the contrary that a majority of the audience had joined in the disturbances. Reviews damned the performance as "flaccid, messy and incoherent . . . stupidly directed . . . in short a fiasco" (Bassnett-McGuire, 69).

Henchmen from the Reinhardt camp attacked Pirandello's concept of theater with so humiliating and savage a fury that they managed to generate a defense of the playwright in newspapers around the country within a few days. Flowers, wires, letters from leading German writers, including Thomas Mann, poured in, reassuring Pirandello of their continued respect and keeping his helper Adolf Lantz busy writing responses. Neither these endorsements, however, nor the fact that subsequent performances played to outstanding notices affected the disheartened playwright. Sometime afterward, Pirandello also learned that entirely unbeknown to Reinhardt, the riotous opening night had been engineered by supporters who were seeking an opportunity to repay critics for poor reviews, weeks earlier, of one of Reinhardt's productions.[4] Apparently, Lantz had known trouble was brewing but had declined to upset

Il Maestro over a fuss that he was certain "would come to nothing." He was convinced, in any case, that the play's success in Konisberg promised to be repeated in Berlin. But the damage was done: the "fiasco" drove a faultline in Pirandello's friendship with Reinhardt and dashed his hopes for a revival of interest in him in Berlin. He found it incredible that such manipulation and enmity could prevail in so cosmopolitan a climate. His premonitions and worries had been justified. "Last night I was back in Italy. Everywhere I am pursued by hatred . . . annihilated by the incomprehension of idiots." The "catcalls of enemies" would not hurt him, he said, if his spirit were still what it used to be. But he had lost even the pride of his isolation (Abba, 25). "I won't set foot again in Germany, where something this monstrous could have taken place," he wrote to Marta in a letter on June 6, and he shifted his residence-in-exile to Paris.

* * *

When Reinhardt two years later restaged *Six Characters* to great acclaim in Vienna (February 1931) and then in Berlin (March 1931), he laid to rest any lingering doubts in Pirandello's mind about the director's complicity in the horrendous reception of *Questa sera si recita a soggetto*. The depressed Pirandello instead treated his play's clamorous reception as a sign of his renewed importance to German theater. Writer and director renewed their friendship again the following year in Rome when *Il piacere dell'onestà* was performed successfully during an International Theater Congress (21 April 1932). When the curtain came down, Reinhardt was the first to present himself at Pirandello's box with "the warmest congratulations." Equally flattering, Reinhardt wanted to produce *Come tu mi vuoi* with his wife, Helen Thimig, in the lead. But if the inception of a project ever can be dated so precisely, the artists' rapprochement might have generated their momentous decision to work together on a film based on *Six Characters*. The plan took on a life of its own, resulting in a fresh manuscript written specifically for Reinhardt, and a meeting in New York in 1935 to negotiate the project with backers.

Of course, Reinhardt and Pirandello may have advanced the idea over the course of several documented meetings and letters well before 1935, say, when Reinhardt wanted to perform *Six Characters* with his Viennese company at the Volta Congress in 1934. (Pirandello rejected the offer because he felt that preference for a German production might arouse jealousy among participants, especially the French (letter 2 March 1934). Playwright and director also may have discussed details later that spring in Milan. Reinhardt cabled Pirandello in an "exceptionally gracious tone," asking him to attend his performance of the play on May 4 (letter 4 May 1934).[5] In all senses, however, and especially in view of their mutual respect and previous successes, the film project seemed at once golden and self-evident. Reinhardt had staged more than one hundred performances of *Six Characters*, most of them before the film *Treatment* was written. Both men had committed themselves to their absolute belief that modern theater should reveal the "great game of life" by using the stage as its picture, frame, and very essence, set on a plane somewhere between reality and dream (Callari, 53). More to the point, both men understood theater and film as two separate arts and shared similar ideas about film's untapped aesthetic potentiality; as the more static of the two forms, film should represent fantasy and realms of imagination. Reinhardt's still classic film of *A Midsummer Night's Dream* for Warner Brothers (released in 1935) had set out in that direction, and the studio, according to report, was eager to continue their happy association.[6]

* * *

In all records of the project, both playwright and director expected to work at Warner Brothers with Hal B. Wallis, the man whose reputation for discipline, drive, and well-made scenarios had lifted the company into a charmed circle of backers.[7] Pirandello told a World Telegram reporter in Paris in December 1934 that he was going to Hollywood where his current project would give "modern films a new impulse, making the idea supreme over material superficialities."[8] Yet when he arrived in New York on July 20, 1935, to meet Reinhardt, his statement to television, radio, and newspaper reporters only generalized his intentions – "to set some film projects in motion, the first of which would be that of *Six Characters*. He preferred Hollywood actors to Italian stars for the project. . . . He believed the play would be even better as a film because . . . the screen can portray illusion so much more effectively than the stage." He completely avoided using the name of Reinhardt or any actors at all.

Several equally plausible reasons may apply. First, stating a preference for Hollywood actors may have been a diplomatic ploy since bringing Marta Abba to America was never far from his mind. He also needed to step clear of continuing negotiations with Thalberg and MGM for a sound film based on the *Film-Novelle*. Even though those talks had excluded Marta Abba's participation, to name any names might have jeopardized ongoing relations (Callari, 50). Perhaps most important, Pirandello certainly knew that his politics augured ill for business in America. Reporters were quick to question him on his arrival about his fascism, by this date a part of his legend. They asked if he had traveled on the Italian liner the *Conte di Savoia* by choice or on government instruction. They printed his "blunt and frank defense of Italy's Ethiopian policy," purportedly compared by him to American attempts to civilize "the barbaric nation" of its native "Indians."[9] The rude words belong to his English translator and secretary Saul Colin, who, judging from other evidence, might have been cavalier in paraphrasing Pirandello's remarks. Colin, after all, often tended to overplay his hand, or bask in Pirandello's borrowed light.[10] Neither can the accuracy of interviews be verified. Since Pirandello's theater and lecture tour in 1923, American journalists in Europe had been filing stories at whim, quoting or misquoting his admiration for and attraction to the United States.[11]

My trip to your country showed me many wonderful things – your great, rushing cities with their towering buildings, your overpowering strength and wealth, your adaptation to everyday life of all the latest scientific discoveries. . . . But what interested me most of all, what fascinated me was the American psychology. That's what I want to write about some day . . . a study of the American soul.[12]

Diplomacy apart, throughout the summer and early fall Pirandello fielded movie ideas with Paramount, RKO, Fox, and Universal from his suite at the Waldorf Astoria in New York. Agents for Marlene Dietrich wanted to film *Trovarsi*, while Pemberton, the Theatre Guild; Herman Shumling; Judith Anderson; and others approached him with theater projects. Rueben Mamoulian at that point expressed an interest in *L'esclusa* and *Six Characters*. Needing to keep all avenues open, and debating whether to go out to Hollywood himself, Pirandello followed Mamoulian's advice about placing his affairs in the hands of his agent rather than setting foot in California and risking uncomfortable questions about either his politics or his works' scandalous themes. To interviewers, he vacillated cleverly between the specific and the general. He expected to spend a few weeks in New York and then two months in Hollywood; hoped to contribute new ideas to the studios; and wanted to write original stories for the screen. Cinema was of greater social significance than the stage, he temporized in one conversation, adding his familiar comment about the stage being related closely to novels and literature, the cinema to music and painting. As for his disinterested observance of the social scene, why reporters neglected to record his reactions to a New York Police Department Headquarters lineup visited out of curiosity is all our loss.[13]

After a brief meeting with Reinhardt, Pirandello spent three months on the forty-first floor of the Waldorf Astoria in New York working on the *Treatment* for *Six Characters* with Saul Colin. He accepted few social invitations – one visit with Albert Einstein at Lyme, Connecticut, confirms an otherwise apocryphal tale about the mutual respect of the two architects "of relativity," astronomical and literary. (The physicist years before supposedly had greeted the author backstage after a performance of *Six Characters* with the words, "We are kindred spirits.") Pirandello saw as many plays and films as possible in the evenings, especially remarking on those of Frank Capra, Ernest Lubitsch, and King Vidor. He writes Marta, however, that his other impressions of the moment at once "tired him and filled him with disgust" (letter 13 August 1935). Not only the tensions about politics and censorship – ultimately "not important" to art – but the steep ups and downs of movie negotiations struck him as useless for additional reasons.

They admire me too much, you understand? They hold my art in too high esteem and fear that it can't be brought low enough for the mediocre level of the "mass's understanding." They themselves are distressed at what they say they're forced to do and therefore you can't argue with them. So here it's like everywhere else and perhaps worse. If you could see the theatres, the plays which are the most successful! And the films they see! (letter 30 August 1935)

* * *

Weary of delays in concluding a workable contract with Warner Brothers, Pirandello returned to Italy in October, exhausted, and suffered another cardiac incident in November. He left Saul Colin to finish translating the *Treatment* according to ideas initiated with Reinhardt and to represent him in other projects. Apparently, sometime between July and October, Warner declined to pursue their arrangement with Reinhardt, perhaps out of some anticipated revulsion against the taint of Nazism in all things German, perhaps for artistic reasons. Callari says the delay remains mysterious. In all, there were three sets of offers and replies involving three versions of a manuscript, each one recording an increased fee for rights. Callari reconstructs the events following

Commentary

Pirandello's arrival in New York from correspondence in the estate archives and from two interviews published during 1936. The first of these in Turin in February, with *The People's Gazette*, confirms that Pirandello left "his personal secretary Colline [*sic*]" in New York to reach an agreement with Warner Brothers and to represent him on several theatrical projects. (This probably included *Trovarsi*, which Colin was negotiating separately for Marta Abba.) The pertinent letter to Pirandello from Colin, dated New York, March 6, 1936, says "Reinhardt and Warner Brothers love the idea and the new form of the scenario and Reinhardt has accepted it entirely." Pirandello's Paris adminis-trator, Umberto Mauri, then replies to Colin from Milan on April 25.[14] "Il Maestro has read the subject [an amplification of *Treatment?*] you prepared and in his opinion it could be developed a lot more. He however is not disposed to perform this new work unless on the basis of a contract with Reinhardt and Warner Brothers." The second interview with a Berlin corre-spondent for *Il Tevere* in Rome, on October 7–8, 1936, reports that Pirandello "also spoke of the film of *Six Characters* that Reinhardt will direct for Warner Brothers." A lengthy description of the script's outline, reported in direct quotation, concludes with the statement: "Reinhardt will do the rest and certainly will do something great and beautiful."[15]

To summarize here for the sake of clarity: Warner Brothers accepted the *Treatment* in its rough state sometime near the end of 1935 or the beginning of 1936. Pirandello completed his work during the summer of 1936 in New York. In October he reports on a concluded agreement with Warner Brothers to a journalist in Berlin, where he was attending an international conference of playwrights and composers. Conclusion: Hal Wallis of Warner had edged Thalberg and MGM out of the field. The official signing of the Warner Brothers contract was scheduled for January 1937. Pirandello died in Rome on Decem-ber 10. The rest is "if only's."

« 2 »

Written in English and prepared according to its inscription with Saul Colin, the *Treatment* is a curious document in several respects. In substance, it repre-sents a rough translation of the original German scenario, condensing the action severely and summarizing rather than dramatizing the basic plot. In the typical style of film treatments, dialogue is omitted and the six Characters are generalized: the Stepdaughter of the play becomes "a young girl," the younger children are merely alluded to, and the Father only mentioned as relevant to the action. The *Treatment* also omits the many atmospheric and

122

cinematographic indications in the *Film-Novelle,* while adding long opening and closing scenes placing the Author more firmly in the context of his film-within-a-film. The scenes also accomplish two other goals in somewhat perfunctory fashion: they establish firm links to the stage production of *Six Characters* in progress as the (projected) film ends; and they tighten connections to the historical family that inspires the film's Characters. The increased amount of doubling and simultaneity evident in both of these changes probably indicates Pirandello's responsiveness to Reinhardt's ideas, since from the outset of the planning the director wanted their film to incorporate many more scenes from the play than it eventually did.

But the changes primarily reflect the increasing boldness of Pirandello's theatricalism in the decade following his 1921 play. Simulated audience participation in the *Treatment* may culminate strategies, dating from his earliest plays, to break the "fourth wall" of nineteenth-century theater. By the time of *Questa sera si recita a soggetto* (1930), Pirandello had called for simultaneous actions on-stage, in the audience, and in the theater lobby. Still greater fluidity between "real" persons, actors, and characters can be measured in the *Treatment*'s reconception of the once static Mother. Her "real" persona now confronts and condemns the "real" Author responsible for the family's tragedy, driving him to end his interference in their lives.

> While . . . the actress playing the mother is on stage . . . the mother herself runs hysterically in front of the stage and tries to stop the rehearsal. . . . And when the mother discovers the author, she runs toward him screaming, "do you want to kill my little girl, too." . . . The Author is profoundly moved. . . . Soon afterward, a broken man, he sees an image of the dead little girl and decides to stop the play. (*Treatment,* 145)

In heightening the contrasts between these three aesthetic levels, which have developed through the *Prologo* and *Film-Novelle,* Pirandello demonstrates his perfect accord with Reinhardt's complementary flair for theatrical spectacle.

* * *

Reinhardt's prompt-book and director's notes for his 1924 and 1934 productions of the play, in Berlin and Vienna respectively, offer some indications of what the projected film for Warner Brothers might have accomplished.[16] As comment in chapter 2 indicated, Reinhardt's version of the text for his 1924 productions taught Pirandello to German audiences.[17] He substituted *Il piacere dell'onestà* for the original rehearsal piece in Act One of *Il giuoco delle parti* probably to advertise its inclusion in his company's season. But he also elaborated on the actors' improvisations, the element Pirandello deliberately had left open to a director's imagination, so that incidental talk on-stage establishes an immediate link with the audience.

More substantively, cutting lines from the Father's philosophical disquisitions and interjecting dialogue results in a sharper distinction between Actors and Characters, such that the Characters resemble allegorical representations of human fate on earth – an interpretation accentuating the baroque view of theater as cosmos discussed above in chapter 2. The responsibility then falls to the Director, even more heavily than in Pirandello's original text, to balance the comic world of the stage with the tragic one of the Characters. The Director dominates over the Father in their contest, thereby becoming the play's virtual protagonist and functioning as the desired author-creator: he must provide an ending for the play, even a tragic one if necessary. While Pirandello's Characters as imaginary creatures merely seek a form of incarnation, Reinhardt's become souls in Purgatory who seek an equivalent of salvation through an end to their painful story.

The second act includes two startling changes which appear against all logic to anticipate the diabolic aspect of the Author's characterization in the film scenarios. Reinhardt may have read both the *Prologo* (1926) and *Film-Novelle* (1928) before his 1934 productions, but the major changes under discussion here all occur in his 1924 text for the play. The only possible explanation, and more interesting as guesswork, reverses cause and effect: that Pirandello acquired a slant on his Author as godlike Creator from Reinhardt's cosmic view of the "world as stage" and the "text as morality play." For example, Reinhardt's scene between the Stepdaughter and two young children introduces the Author as an evil force who has consigned the children to their destinies "for his own pleasure and for that of others." (Other gods? The perverse impulses of an audience of others?) The most theatrical change occurs in the act's closing scene. Instead of a scream from the Mother prompting the Director to cry out "Curtain!" as in Pirandello's original, the Mother pleads with the Father to stop demanding and justifying a reenactment of their tale. Suddenly, mid-sentence, the curtain falls *on the Father*, "burying" and "wounding" him both physically and psychically, rendering him unable to continue. Punitive Author indeed.

Act III, therefore, begins from an entirely different premise, with a more humanized Father *and* Son resisting the re-creation of their drama now being called for by the Director. The invisible Author thus assumes a far greater importance than in the original play. The word "creator" used over and again in this act signifies both Author and God in the German, leading to a discussion of blame for the Characters' suffering. Responding to the Director's question about culpability, the Father says,

> "We are all responsible, all of us. We've all harmed our neighbor. But it is He who made us this way! Our Creator shaped our characters like this. We could not have behaved in any other way. In the end, every creature is innocent."
>
> Director: "But your Creator didn't finish your drama. So, leaving a certain limit to your free will . . . your responsibility begins here, my man."

Reinhardt's principal focus on the theater's metaphysical role casts the world in the image of humankind rather than in the image of God. Whereas Pirandello confronts the notion of an objective reality constantly changing with eternal reality, Reinhardt symbolizes theater-as-reality (Rossner, 48). In this effort, Reinhardt omits the original ending in which the Boy, on witnessing his sister's drowning, is driven to shoot himself. Instead, as one of the many liberties he takes with the text, Reinhardt invents a less traumatic scene of a quarrel amongst Father, Mother, and the Son who refuses to cooperate in the enactment for the Director of the family's tragedy. Reinhardt then cleverly positions the Boy so that he watches and overhears the family from a distance, then calls out fearfully to the Mother at several junctures: "Mother! Mother!" Caught up in the argument, the Mother fails to reply to the Boy. And so, as the Son accuses her of "disavowing her children," a shot is heard. At that point, new stage directions (in faulty English) read as follows:

> NOTE: FATHER, MOTHER, STEP-DAUGHTER, AND SON, as always, so now, live throughout the tragedy as though it happened for the first time. The theatre people, rather used to stage shots, by no means realize the accident at once as such, but as the already previously announced discharge of a prop pistol. Gradually, however, is developing the atmosphere typical for the occurrence of an unforeseen, serious working accident – with scanty noise – while at the end is dominating the ghost-likeness and unsolved mysteriousness of the whole event.

The Stepdaughter soon runs off to the back of the stage, followed by the Mother and Son, then the Father last; their disappearance again emphasizes

Commentary

their spectral quality, whereas in Pirandello's text and scenarios the Step-daughter runs into the audience, thus emphasizing her human quality. Fi-nally, in the Renaissance spirit of epilogues, Reinhardt's Director comes for-ward to dismiss the audience and appeal for applause. "Excuse us, Ladies and Gentlemen, but I must ask you now to leave us alone while we rehearse; when we've finished I'll call you back." Reinhardt thus transforms Pirandello's play-in-the-making into a play concluded: "a theatre parable of baroque ancestry conceived by Reinhardt (and in part the translator) and activated by Piran-dello, a mix, so to speak between Pirandello and Calderon" (Rossner, 52).

Why Pirandello never complained about Reinhardt's reconception of the play remains a mystery. He certainly voiced his indignation regularly, vocif-erously, irascibly over interference of any sort between art and artist. Whether he was more concerned in 1924 that the play be produced at all; or failed to notice because, as he said, his German had grown rusty with disuse until his Berlin sojourn; or had distanced himself from the play's productions because his interests after 1928 lay with film rather than stage versions; or whether he simply enjoyed Reinhardt's version as a separate theater event, his relative quiet still amazes. In comparison, in a long letter to Marta (18 April 1930) after seeing a German production at the Klosterstrasse Theatre, he had com-plained at length that the work had been "mutilated" (was "*monco*"). Not only was the company using the text's first edition (1921), "without the new ending," they "have another way of interpreting, another sensibility; they phrase or highlight lines differently." With him at the performance, Lantz reassured Pirandello that the German staging had a "powerful efficacy," and the matter was dropped.[18] In any case, the depredation of Pirandello's Author as Creator in the filmscripts differs so profoundly from Reinhardt's view of the play's Author as to make his version irrelevant.

Otherwise, Reinhardt's ideas for the film seem to minimize the very meta-physical and psychological aspects he had emphasized on-stage, although he keeps his focus on Actors. In arguing for incorporating more scenes from the stage play to increase movement between "levels of action," for instance, he questioned the *Treatment*'s "overemphasis on incest," the element he had turned into "nightmarish suggestion" on-stage. (The powerful American Pro-duction Code would have prohibited a film on those grounds alone.) He apparently liked the *Treatment*'s new closing scenes, which situated the ele-gantly dressed Girl and her elderly gentleman courtier first at Mme. Melloni's and then at a box in the theater. They add a decorous and bourgeois tone which counterbalances the girl's parallel, titillating scene at Mme. Melloni's with that other elderly gentleman, the Author. So, too, the *Treatment* stresses the girl's upward mobility and correspondingly diminishes the grotesque tone of the January to May theme exaggerated in the more gothic *Film-Novelle*.

Quite apart from Reinhardt's influence on Pirandello's projected film, if there was influence, and apart from some added description to its summary of the German scenario, the *Treatment* most remarkably eliminates the Author's phantoms. Except for a "long shadow of the Author" in one paragraph, no trace remains of his tormenting ghosts. While a film treatment by definition only summarizes, and while Pirandello may have expected this dimension of the film would be "written in" by Reinhardt, a spirit of logic and realism seems to pervade the entire text. For example, in the *Film-Novelle* the Boy's visit disturbs the Author's process of transforming the family into art; in the *Treatment* the Boy's anxiety during the visit excites the Author's sympathy. Also, the Little Girl's drowning disappears along with any sense of providential disaster, as is true of Reinhardt's text. Instead, seeing his sister playing near the duck pond in the Author's garden, the Boy runs to his sister in time to prevent her tragedy. His suicide by shooting remains; so does the Secretary's condemnation of the Author; and consciousness of these still trigger the composition of the Author's play. Thereafter, however, rehearsal scenes in the theater expand, as if compensating for the missing interplay between characters and actors that Reinhardt had written into the opening of his 1924 stage version, and that he kept trying to add to the filmscript. Perhaps a cue to the *Treatment*'s flat tone is encapsulated in extremely condensed lines near the end describing the inner play's opening night. "The theater is crowded. The author cannot escape his characters, and the poor mother's family cannot escape its fate. The author, backstage, is nervous."

« 3 »

As for Saul Colin's role in producing the *Treatment*, from the day he stepped into Pirandello's life as secretary, at the age of twenty, he elected the role of Il Maestro's manager and protector against unscrupulous wheelers and dealers.[19] They met late in 1930 in Paris, where Colin worked as a scenario editor for Paramount Pictures and as a representative of Ossa Films, a French film production house interested in Pirandello's work. Colin presented himself to Pirandello as a "comer" in the industry, "enthusiastic" about his stories as film subjects.[20] At first Pirandello remarked that Colin was "unusually reticent for a Frenchman" (a misperception since Colin was Hungarian) and wondered about his business acumen. Soon afterward there began a six-year-long complaint in his letters to Marta of Colin's impetuousness and "mismanagement." Colin spent other people's money too easily; he assumed too much too quickly; he seemed unable to learn all the details of a negotiation before rushing ahead to a closing. More than once, it seems, a deal collapsed because Colin neglected to send pertinent information to Pirandello and instead handled it on his own.

Still, each time Pirandello remonstrated with Colin, the young man protested his good intentions. A farcical element entered their stormy relationship when Pirandello threatened to dismiss the young man but then complained of being unable to "wrest records away from Colin," who swore of his deep caring and devotion (letter 25 February 1933). The letters also suggest that at one point during his tenure with Pirandello, Colin chose short stories for film projects, a significant responsibility whether assumed with or without Pirandello's instructions. Yet other sources indicate that Colin functioned chiefly as English language translator until 1935, when his position officially ended. His inexperience in artistic matters but eagerness at public relations implies that Pirandello valued him chiefly as a contact person to the industry. The probability gains from hindsight since Colin later served as chief executive for Continental Productions Inc., and as executive director of New York's Drama Workshop.

The truth may lie somewhere in between Colin and his employer's reflections. Pirandello, after all, often chafed at his need to rely on collaborators, translators, and agents to advance his interests, complaining sometimes unreasonably about their intellectual limitations – as if anyone could have fit themselves inside his thought – and often about their inefficiency. He vented his irritation to Marta more than once about both Colin's and Lantz's prodigality with his money, though his own improvidence just as often landed him into financial difficulties. Whereas Lantz elicited his sympathy, Colin apparently did not. At one point during the depression years in Berlin, Pirandello supported "the good and affectionate" Lantz as secretary, though he never learned Italian or any other language. Lantz earned a salary (2,000 lire monthly) plus lunches, dinners, gifts, and regular outlays for cafe bills.[21] "It pains me to see him so devoid of means . . . with a mother to maintain, and a mother-in-law, and a wife, and a son in school who grows by the minute, and a big dog, and the house, and the telephone for which he'd need a patrimony a day" (letter 1 May 1930).

Obviously generous to a fault, Pirandello ruled by affection and ranted in private. He footed the bill for Colin and for Marta in London in 1935 so that she could learn English; and then for both of them in New York in 1936 after he had left so that they could conclude a deal with Gilbert Miller for Marta to play *Tovarich*.[22] Yet three years earlier he had determined to entrust no serious money matters to Colin. A blowup in which he called the young man "a perfect imbecile," incapable of managing deals (letter 2 June 1932); followed by another crisis a month later when he worried that no one in the industry "took Colin seriously" (letter 2 September 1932); followed by two years of fulmination that Colin was "absolutely ineffectual" in business. All this still did not result in an actual break between them. Even if Pirandello's epistolary excess is discounted, his relationship to Colin remains suspect. Colin's failure (in 1933) to send Pirandello a contract he had concluded for *Trovarsi* resulted in its double sale by his American agent and a horrendous threat of legal action only barely averted.[23] Yet through all Colin's mismanagement up to the day he concluded the deal for Marta, Pirandello urged her to suspend her misgivings about him: out of loyalty to Pirandello for six years, he told her, Colin would defend her against manipulators in the great outside world. Perhaps the final word goes to Colin's entrepreneurial talents, since he managed to open his own literary agency in 1936 based on earnings from his work for Pirandello and Marta Abba.

« 4 »

Reinhardt continued to nurture expectations of a Hollywood film based on *Six Characters* until a few years before his death. In January 1937, after the opening of *The Eternal Road,* an interviewer asked if Reinhardt might want a change of pace from the huge scale of that film. Reinhardt "smiled quizzically." Meyer G. Weisgal, the producer, present during the interview added, "That's what I want, too. Simple. I'm looking now for a play with six characters – six characters in search of a producer."[24] As late as 1940, Reinhardt hoped to engage the cast of his celebrated Hollywood Actors Studio, which had staged the play to rave reviews with Robert Ryan playing the Father and Nanette Fabray the Stepdaughter.[25] A copy of the working script based on Reinhardt's 1934 text shows several emendations initiated when Reinhardt mounted the play at the Josefstadt theater in Vienna.[26] Playbills and programs for productions thereafter, like those for the Hollywood Studio, referred to Reinhardt's "famous Vienna version, which was originally created with the collaboration of Pirandello himself." What that may mean is anyone's guess since beyond trimming the length of his 1924 script, Reinhardt added the Director's new desire to find a "happy ending" to the Characters' story, hardly a pirandellian impulse. (The idea also echoes with irony given Reinhardt's break with Warner Brothers in the following year.) Otherwise, compared to the scope of his changes to the 1924 text, the later ones are peripheral. Altered lines increase the colloquialism of the framing play and the Hat Shop scene, while also naturalizing byplay between Persons, Actors, and the Director. The setting, for instance, remains a middle-class world in which the Characters supposedly appeared as "blurred photographs" (Rossner, 51).

The Hollywood Studio productions generated their own legends and anecdotes tending to exaggerate not merely the liberties Reinhardt took with Pirandello's text but the degree to which his intervention influenced the play's success. In a conversation on the subject between Reinhardt's son Gottfried, his wife, and S. N. Behrman, for example, Gottfried said: "Even though my father practically took the play apart – something he almost never did – and put it together again his own way, Pirandello was overjoyed." Behrman replied: "I hear that Pirandello's enthusiasm was not shared by New York audiences." To which Mrs. Reinhardt said: "*Six Characters* wasn't really a success anywhere except with Reinhardt" (Reinhardt, 378). Well. So much for memory. Another recollection of Reinhardt rehearsing the "Characters" suggests their resemblance not to Pirandello's specters but to tragic figures pushed to intolerable extremes of passion. He supposedly taught Robert Ryan "to collapse after the discovery of his daughter in a brothel . . . to fold up like a jackknife and to exit, his torso bent, [to a] horizontal, a *destroyed human being*" (Reinhardt, 307 emphasis added). Jackknifed or not, the Father in all scripts collapses completely, not in the discovery scene but after the Boy's suicide. As with most anecdotes, their heat registers more than their content.

Reinhardt's Studio productions in 1939 and 1940 succeeded in enlisting Josef von Sternberg's enthusiastic agreement to make a film using the Studio cast and based on the *Treatment* as rewritten by Pirandello's son Stefano Landi.[27] According to von Sternberg, Reinhardt intended to play the role of the Director himself, an homage to Pirandello that would have delivered a witty surprise to audiences. "I told him that I would like to film this classic with his help, and that no one but he could play the part of the director . . . and he agreed instantly" (von Sternberg, 48). A precedent for the production's actual director to play the role had been established with *Six Characters'* first performance in Rome by Dario Niccodemi and repeated in 1930 by Hans

Soltinger in Berlin (letter 17 April 1930). (So too, for one Studio production of *Questa sera si recita a soggetto*, Max Pallenberg was scheduled to play the expanded part of the Director made up to look like Max Reinhardt – a result that would have presented theater-within-theater-within-theater *en abyme*.) But obviously no precedent applied to Reinhardt's playing the role in a *Six Characters* film. That this project, too, failed to materialize should be blamed, said von Sternberg later, on "the man [the Pirandello estate] who sat on this property and demanded a huge sum of money from us, impossible to raise." The most significant among relevant documents is a letter written in German to Colin from Reinhardt dated November 25, 1940, and signed by him and von Sternberg.[28] The letter also represents incontrovertible evidence that Colin remained the contact person on the *Treatment*, no matter how else his collaboration is assessed. He also was to handle distribution of the projected film through Continental, the company he headed at the time.

My dear Dr. Colin,

I have received your letter and enclosed contract. It took deplorably long. The first inquiries in this matter were directed to you at the end of August. Your agreement in principle is dated Oct. 3. Now we're at the end of November. Nevertheless there would still be time today to carry out our plan and to begin work at once if we, as I had hoped, really had a contract in hand. It is however only a "tentative contract" which you are sending, and you mention in your accompanying letter that you must obtain the signature of the Pirandello heirs. It seems clear to me that the unpleasant and also unfortunately questionable delay lies in this circumstance. Yet, it is equally clear that before the contract has been finally, legally concluded, we can begin neither the artistic work nor the complicated technical, organizational, and financial preparations. I include here a statement in which Joseph von Sternberg himself formulates his point of view explicitly, and I shall therefore have this letter signed by him also, so that you at least will deal with a completely clear situation.

"Immediately after acquisition of the rights for filming the subject *Six Characters*, legal applications will be filed for the establishment of a company for cinematographic production. At the same time, practical arrangements shall be made for filming. The direction, photography, and the administration of the company shall be provided by von Sternberg and Reinhardt without immediate reimbursement. The actors, too, will be supplied by the Reinhardt ensemble on a profit sharing or mini-

mum wage basis. The film rights, which can be resold by Dr. Colin to
whomever he wishes a year after the experiment is produced, shall be
compensated at 10% of the total earnings of the company to be established with the acquisition of the rights. The sum earned by a 10% share
is a large one relative to the other shares. After filming and not before,
the plan is to distribute the finished product through the usual distributors. The distributor must then assume the costs of copying and advertising, which costs usually are in the range of 100 thousand dollars.

"All the income earned by our group after repayment of small cash
advances shall be used to satisfy every shareholder [or participant] so
that filmrights shall be paid at the same time as all other forms of
participation or investment.

"Giving preferential treatment to the reimbursement of small cash
advances is necessary since otherwise money would have to be raised at
50% participation – but the intention is not to allow profit to become in
any way important to the enterprise, a fact that is in the interest of all the
participants. We commit ourselves to start production within six months
after the acquisition of the rights."

These stipulations are in line, as you know, with our correspondence
to this point; they are fair, justified by the facts, and doubtless in the
interests of all the participants, and therefore also of the Pirandello heirs.
You meanwhile will have convinced yourself that no other offer exists,
and that no film house will, wants to, and can, risk this experiment.

Apart from the general depression and uncertainty and the alarming
contraction of the market, it is the enormous overheads and understand-
ably cautious attitude of capital investors at this time which exclude
artistic experiments today even more than before. The contract addi-
tionally guarantees you the right to make use of a conceivably better
time, and to accept a possible offer from the big studios, for which our
experiment can only help to clear the way. I personally believe, with von
Sternberg, that it is to experiments like ours, based upon fairer profit
sharing by all participants, that the future belongs. They are in accord
with the irresistible progress in the social restructuring of the world
economy, and they will favor purer values than those which flow from
the canals lying between Wall Street and Hollywood. Only one proviso:
if the assent of the heirs can *not* be achieved, as you announce, in the
shortest time (by cable), I shall consider the matter decided in the nega-

tive. You know how in the life of the theater, the moment rules. And film is only a branch, if a mighty one, on the age old trunk. What today is still desirable and possible can tomorrow, through a political, economic, or cultural gust of wind, be blown away forever, even in the intentions of the artist, who is, as we know, an especially sensitive instrument of his age. Our days present us so abundantly with upheavals altering the face of the earth that I need not say any more about it.

The chance of a successful student production is what gave one of the foremost artists of the screen (there are only a few) the idea for the plan. Von Sternberg is a painter in the narrowest and broadest senses of the word, and he was born into the medium of film. He is convinced, as am I, that the screen makes possible a more obvious distinction between real and fictive worlds, and that the cinematic closeup permits psychological and mental events to dominate, while the world around us with its distractions simply excludes them at will. Thanks to this, new and decisive values can be gained for the work.

That I as a born man of the theater can direct the stage atmosphere of the piece and the actors has been proved by innumerable performances. We have furthermore a cast of the best young forces of the American theater who all come from my school, have completed their studies, and are experienced actors. Several of them are bound by contracts with the studios here. This is another reason why the time element is such a determining problem.

In short: all conditions promise the success of the experiment and I summarize them again not in order to convince you, since I have not the least doubt on this point, but only to supply you with material for your communications with the poet's heirs, which perhaps may be desirable for you. The enthusiastic dedication of all the participants, which usually only grows with difficulty in the courtyards of this sunny factory town, and the readily measurable fact of what the result of this experiment means for von Sternberg and me, offer you a weightier guarantee than could be offered by any producer no matter how many zeros he had trailing after him.

In conclusion, one more word about the *Treatment*. The scenario which you sketched out with Pirandello is poetically valuable and exceptionally interesting artistically. But it leads even deeper and more subjectively into the complex creative process of the author, and removes the work still further from reality as generally understood. We should in no case give up the milieu of the theater whose romantic and comic effects have been reliably tested. We must take the general public into account, and must not remove from the work those existing structures which have supported it until now everywhere in the world.

The single essential change (every art form requires certain appropriate adjustments) which I consider desirable is to exclude the threefold incest. In any case, it is only presented as a suggestion, but the relatively few who understand it are mostly shocked, and the many others are confused. Both reactions are superfluous, detrimental, and easily avoidable. There still remains enough of the obscure, daring, and profound which is indispensable, and which requires the compensation of the comic.

Von Sternberg as I have already emphasized is against every invasive alteration on principle, which, as a sign of opposition to the general formulas (recipes) current in this country, is easily understandable. I am less papal because as a man of the theater I know that the adaptation of plays has always been, in all times, a legitimate component of theatrical vitality, and that we owe its strongest values to such continuous renovations. Yet in these slopkitchens here (in this country) von Sternberg's principle is an incomparable bit of luck and a most promising augury.

May I expect the favor of an immediate response to this detailed letter, and [expect] that you will not keep us waiting longer for a decision we have been hoping for far too long, and which will decide so much that is essential for all of us.

Cordially,

« 5 »

Since 1936 innumerable attempts have been made to realize a film of Pirandello's great play. The roster of proposers to the writer's estate reads like a who's who of theater and cinema luminaries, among them: the group around Piscator, Preston Sturges, and Marcel Pagnol; Vittorio De Sica, Anna Magnani, Vittorio Gassman, and Eduardo De Filippo; Jean-Luc Godard, François Truffaut, and Michelangelo Antonioni; Otto Preminger, who enlisted Fred Zinneman, David Lean, William Wyler, and Ingmar Bergman, who offered his own proposals as well.[29] Reasons for their failures to create a film may vary from clumsy dealings with the Pirandello estate, to hesitancy regarding the incest theme, to the industry's sheer lack of vision. Perhaps a mistake by all parties lay in imagining a film that looked backward in homage to the great play as a monument of the twentieth century. The film scenarios instead invite us to look forward to their Author, still far ahead of us, still an unfinished tragi-comic character. The man who toppled all forms so as to live in the moment reinvented himself in the end through a film-in-the-making. Perhaps then, since this book has been a "ghost story," the availability of the scenarios might even free the Author's ghost to "possess" a new filmmaker with the spirit of *il contrario* – demonic, tormented, mocking, and sad. Pirandello never wrote out his aesthetics of film in a single, formal essay. As is true for the novels and plays, the work and the man are one.

PART TWO

Documents

The *Prologue*

to a screen adaptation of *Six Characters*

Translated by Jana O'Keefe Bazzoni

Signed by Luigi Pirandello and originally published circa 1926 in an unnamed periodical; referred to and reprinted by Cinema, *15 June 1941, as an appendix to the article by Giancarlo Beria, "Pirandello e i surrealisti."*

Late at night, a deserted alley, barely lit by a weak streetlight. I'm going through it as it is the shortest way home. At a certain point, as I approach the streetlight, I see a young woman, about sixteen years old, creep up alongside me beside the wall. She is dressed in black, as if in mourning, but in an equivocal fashion. In passing, she looks at me obliquely. Curious, I follow her. A bit further down, in front of the dirty door of an old house on the same alley, I can see in the shadow a poor mother in a black woolen dress, waiting in the night. Suddenly, the young woman, crying convulsively, runs into the Mother's arms; then both Mother and Daughter disappear inside the filthy door. Deeply disturbed by what I have seen, I stop for a moment in front of the door; I lift my eyes to examine the windows of the old house.

* * *

One of those windows is lighted. I can see the light coming through the shutters of the Venetian blinds. A small dim room, just big enough for a bed placed lengthwise across it, and an old straw chair next to the bed. The room is lit by the light in the next room rather than from the door's being ajar. A pale Youth, all eyes and hair, awakened by the sudden reflection of light, gets up from the bed; he listens to the noise and then calls, "Mamma." The Mother, hearing the voice, detaches herself from the Daughter's embrace and listens.

The room is bare: a sewing machine, fine cloth ready to be worked on, two small beds. On one of the beds, a beautiful, blond, four-year-old girl is asleep. The Mother goes to the open door and calls to the Youth in the other room: "Hush! Go to sleep," and she closes the door.

In the alley, having looked through the lighted window, I lower my head and set myself off again toward my house, still some distance away.

The Mother now approaches the Daughter who has thrown herself on the other bed, burying her face in the pillows: she shakes her – the Daughter rises halfway, allowing her Mother to see her eyes which are full of tears, yet lit with a desperate and terrible anger. The Daughter opens her purse with shaky hands; she takes out three 100-lira bills, crumples them, and throws them on the bed with disgust; she buries her face in the pillows. The Mother looks at the dirty, crumpled money and hides her face in her hands.

In the meantime, I come out of that alley into a vast boulevard lit by the moon, with large trees and a long line of streetlights in the middle. But I still have the scene of that alley in my mind; it is as if that alley with its filthy walls is following me: here is the light that barely breaks the darkness, and again the young woman, passing by, looks at me obliquely. And over there, the Mother in her black wool dress in front of the door, and the young woman, running and throwing herself into her Mother's arms, and both of them disappear inside that door. The vision fades away. I keep walking along the boulevard, troubled. While walking I observe now the movements of the two shadows of my body on the ground: one longer and thinner, generated by the moonlight; the other shorter and denser, generated by the electric lights; they move around me. Who of we three is more shadow? In the bedroom, now lit only by a votive candle in front of a holy image, the Mother has gotten into bed; she is crying. Next to her, where the Little Girl sleeps, the Young Woman is about to lie down. The Little Girl wakes up, smiles at her older sister who is undressing and gestures toward her sister with open arms. Horrified, the Young Woman moves away so as to prevent those pure hands from touching her contaminated body; sobbing she collapses on the floor beside the bed.

* * *

I am at the gates of my house, which just inside is guarded by two giant pine trees. Over the two pines, in the sky, the arc of the moon hangs like a sling hanging from a star. I open the gate, I enter and close it again. An old wrought-iron lamp is lit at the corner of the house on the stairs that I am now climbing. The light from the lamp creates a strange grayish-purple dazzling light on the landing, a thin fog of vague apparitions, diaphonous and changing in form. Incubus of infinite sadness, not unlike madness; it is there each time I come to the entrance of my deserted and solitary house. As I open the door, this fog of phantoms, vaporizing, enters with me. In the dark, before I can put the lights on, the specters become more definite, as though lit by the weak light of their own substance. They are Enrico IV, Donna Anna Luna (*The Life I Gave You*), Signor Ponza and Signora Frola (*Right You Are [If You Think So]*), a gentleman, very dignified but with crazed eyes, who is pushing a little dog by her hind legs, as if the dog was a pushcart, the wretched "contessa," poised like a statuette on the hand of one of the Mountain Giants – characters whom I have in mind but who, now, as soon as I light the lamp, run down the hall of my house and through the door of my very large studio.

The pushcart man comes and throws the dog between my legs. Enrico IV is pushing me from one side; Donna Anna Luna pushes me from the other, and from behind, the Mountain Giant is so irreverent as to put the statue of the wretched contessa on my head. Once there, the agitated contessa rebels, incapable of suffering such indignity, and wants to return to the Giant's hand; he, on his part, is laughing a wild and ferocious laugh.

Here I am now in my studio, leaning against my large writing desk, besieged by these petulant phantoms who are asking me to give them life. I rouse myself with a long breath; I pass my hand over my forehead and eyes; the phantoms disappear. But as soon as I take my hands away from my eyes and stare before me, I see arising on the corner of my desk the still evanescent ghost of the Young Woman whom I met earlier in the alley. She is not the same as the real one: she appears already diffused in a halo of poetry, ready to become a phantom of art; as I now indeed see her, a possible character to whom I can give life. Although for now, she cannot offer me any other action but that of throwing herself into the arms of the Mother, who suddenly comes up beside her. She, too, is transfigured, although she is not yet defined.

I rouse myself, shaking my head as though to tear myself away from the temptation to welcome these phantoms of art within me.

Film-Novelle: Sechs Personen suchen einen Autor

LUIGI PIRANDELLO & ADOLF LANTZ

This scenario for a silent film based on Six Characters *was written in 1928–29 and published in Berlin by Reimar Hobbing in 1930 with the additional line on the title page,* Nach dem gleichnamigen Theaterstuck von Pirandello *(based on the Pirandello play with the same title). The booklet included Pirandello's 1925* Preface *to the play as a guide to readers, pp.5–30.*

Three translations of the German scenario have been published. A French translation by E. Goldey was published in La Revue du Cinema *in May 1930. Two Italian translations apparently rely on the French rather than on the German original: (1) by Antonio Illiano and Giovanni Bussino, "Pirandello: progetti filmici sui* Sei personaggi" *in* Forum Italicum *16 (1982): 119–46; and (2) by Roberto Tessari,* Il trattamento cinematografico dei *Sei personaggi,* testo inedito di Luigi Pirandello, *edited by Rossano Vittori. Florence: Liberoscambio, 1984.*

Der Dichter Luigi Pirandello sitzt in seinem Arbeitszimmer am Schreibtisch.
Er übergibt seinem jungen Sekretär Briefschaften und ein Konvolut von Papieren. Der Sekretär verläßt das Zimmer nach respektvoller Verbeugung; flüchtig, aber freundlich hat ihm der Dichter die Hand gereicht.

Jetzt tritt er ans Fenster und sieht hinaus.

Abenddämmerung liegt über der Villenvorstadt.

Der Dichter tritt ins Zimmer zurück, geht auf und ab, wie in Gedanken versinkend.

Dann setzt er sich.

Das Zimmer füllt sich mit Nebel, in welchem verschwommen Gestalten sichtbar werden, unklare, veränderliche, phantastische Schattengebilde. Sie dringen auf ihn ein und scheinen auf ihm wie ein Albdruck, eine unbestimmte Traurigkeit zu lasten.

Die Gestalten beginnen ein wenig im Dunkel zu leuchten.

In gebeugter Haltung, gestützt auf seinen großen Schreibtisch, gleichsam belagert von der Unbändigkeit jener Gespenster, sitzt der Dichter.

Vor dem Hause – es ist bereits dunkel – wird eine Laterne angezündet.

In das Zimmer, in dem noch die phantastischen Nebel um den Dichter schweben, fällt plötzlich das Licht der Laterne von draußen herein.

Die Nebel weichen wie verscheucht von diesem Licht und verschwinden in den Ecken.

Die Gestalt des Dichters richtet sich auf, wie vom Albdruck befreit. Er zündet die Tischlampe an. Sein Gesicht hat einen übermüdeten Ausdruck.

Er steht auf, sicht durch das Fenster und geht dann aus dem Raum.

Der Dichter tritt aus der Villa, in Hut und Mantel. Sowie er die Tür öffnet und auf das Gittertor, das er aufschließt, zugeht, dringt aus dem Hause, zerflatternd in alle Winde, jener phantastische Nebel.

Der Dichter kommt durch eine öde Gasse, die von einer trüben Laterne schwach erleuchtet ist. Hinter ihm zerflattern die Nebel.

Als er sich der Laterne nähert, erblickt er ein junges Mädchen, das an einer Mauer entlang schleicht. Es ist in junger Trauer schwarz gekleidet und sieht ihn scheu im Vorbeigehen an.

Der Blick, der ihn getroffen, hat ihn aufmerksam gemacht: war der Blick dieses noch sehr jungen Mädchens zweideutig?

Etwas weiter in der Gasse, vor dem Tore eines schmutzigen alten Hauses, steht eine abgehärmte Frau in Trauer. Sie wartet in die Nacht hinein. Es ist die Mutter des Mädchens.

Der Dichter sieht das junge Mädchen zur Mutter eilen. Es fällt ihr um den Hals. Mutter und Tochter umarmen sich. Beide gehen in das Haus, verschwinden in dem schmutzigen Tor.

Der Dichter ist verwirrt von allem, was er gesehen hat. Er bleibt einen Augenblick vor dem Tor stehen. Er schaut nach den Fenstern des alten Hauses.

Eines der Fenster wird hell. Licht schimmert durch die Jalousie. Der Dichter versucht durch die Spalten einen Blick zu gewinnen.

Er sieht in eine armselige Stube, die kaum Platz für ein Bett und einen alten Korbsessel hat. Das Stübchen ist erhellt durch den Lichtschein, der durch die halboffene Tür aus dem Nachbarzimmer kommt. In diesem Lichtreflex erscheint plötzlich ein bleicher Jüngling, der Bruder des Mädchens. Er hat in dem Korbsessel gesessen, springt jetzt auf, als hörte er jemand ins Nebenzimmer treten und ruft: „Mutter!"

Die Mutter löst sich im Nebenzimmer aus den Armen der Tochter und lauscht. Armselig ist auch dieser Raum: eine Nähmaschine, allerlei Stoffe in Arbeit, zwei Betten. In dem einen der Betten schläft ein schönes blondes Kind von fünf Jahren, das Schwesterchen des Mädchens.

Die Mutter erscheint in der halboffenen Tür des Stübchens und bedeutet dem auf dem Bett sitzenden Knaben „Still! Schlafe!" und schließt die Tür.

Der Dichter kann in dem dunklen Stübchen nichts mehr erkennen. Er entfernt sich langsam und nachdenklich.

In der Kammer entnimmt das Mädchen einer kleinen Börse Geld und schüttet es der Mutter auf den Tisch hin. Die Mutter nimmt es. Traurig blickt das Mädchen hinter ihr her, als sie das Geld im Schrank verwahrt.

Der Dichter geht wieder durch die öde Gasse und gelangt auf einen vom Mond erhellten Boulevard mit großen Bäumen und einem Lichtersaum elektrischer Lampen.

Während er unter den Bäumen des Boulevards weitergeht, hat er immer noch eine Vision von jener Gasse, als verfolge sie ihn mit der Enge ihrer schmutzigen Mauern:

da ist die Laterne mit ihrem matten Licht, da jenes schwarz gekleidete Mädchen, das an der Wand entlang schleicht und ihn von der Seite ansieht, und da die Mutter in Trauer von dem Tor, und das Mädchen, das sich ihr um den Hals wirft, da die beiden, die sich umarmen und in dem Tor verschwinden.

Diese Visionen sind hinter ihm her und zerfließen.

Der Dichter kommt vor seiner Villa an. Er sieht seinen Schatten, der auf dem Pflaster immer länger wird. Der Dichter betrachtet seinen Schatten. Der richtet sich auf, wird er selbst.

Der Dichter dreht sich um, wie auf der Suche: Ist es sein Schatten?

Und wieder, während er die Gartentür aufschließt, drängt hinter ihm her, nebelhaft, die Erscheinung jenes Mädchens, im matten Licht der Laterne an der Mauer jener Gasse entlang schleichend.

Die Erscheinung verschwindet. Er dreht sich um: sein Schatten ist wieder vor ihm.

Der Dichter tritt in seinen Garten.

Da stehen, gleichsam als Wächter, zwei riesige Pinien.

Über den Bäumen Vision am Himmel: die Mondsichel, die wie eine Schleuder an einem Stern hängt.

Das Licht der Laterne fällt auf den Absatz der Freitreppe, die er hinaufgeht, wie ein seltsames schwüles Blendwerk halb grau, halb veilchenblau.

Ein dünner Nebel unklarer und phantastischer Gebilde dringt an der Schwelle wieder auf ihn ein und schleicht sich mit ihm ins Haus.

Ehe er in der Vorhalle Licht macht, beginnen im Dunkel die schemenhaften Gestalten wieder zu leuchten.

Beim aufflammenden Licht schweben die Gestalten vor ihm als Nebeldunst durch die offene Tür in sein Arbeitszimmer.

Noch brennt die Lampe auf dem Tisch. Der Nebel schwebt durch den Raum.

Der Dichter atmet tief, legt seine Hand auf Stirn und Augen.

Dann sieht er scharf und durchdringend in die Ecke des Zimmers: Da erscheint verschwommen und bald wieder verschwindend das Bild des jungen Mädchens, dem er kurz zuvor in der Gasse begegnet war. Schon trägt es eine Art Heiligenschein: die Gloriole der Dichtung. Als wäre es zu einem Bild der Kunst geworden, so wie er es jetzt sieht, zu einer Person, der er zwangsweise Leben geben muß. Doch im Augenblick kann er ihr keine andere Geste einhauchen als die, der Mutter um den Hals zu fallen.

Auch die ist, wenn auch noch in unbestimmter Weise, verwandelt.

Der Dichter zuckt zusammen, als wollte er die Gesichte seiner Phantasie abschütteln.

Er tritt ins Licht der Schreibtischlampe und greift nach einer Zigarette. Dann setzt er sich. Papier liegt vor ihm.

Seine Hand spielt mit der Feder.

* * *

In der Kammer steht das Mädchen vor dem Bett, in dem das Schwesterchen liegt.

Das Kind wird wach und lächelt der großen Schwester zu, die im Begriff ist, sich auszukleiden. Es kniet in seinem Bettchen und streckt die Hände der Schwester entgegen. Die Schwester schließt das Kind in ihre Arme. Die Mutter legt ein eben fertig genähtes Kleid in einen Karton.

* * *

Klarer, schöner Tag.

Ein Privatauto hält vor dem Gitter der Villa des Dichters.

Der Chauffeur öffnet die Wagentür. Eine sehr elegante Dame steigt aus. Der Chauffeur klingelt. Ein Diener kommt und gibt auf eine Frage Antwort: „Madame Melloni wohnt dort drüben!"

Er weist auf ein anderes Haus mit einem Schild: Maison Melloni, Robes et Manteaux I. Etage.

Die Dame dankt, stellt noch eine Frage. Der Diener sagt: „Hier wohnt Herr Pirandello!" Die Dame ist hocherfreut: „Ah, der Schriftsteller? Gibt er Autogramme?!" Dabei greift sie in ihre Börse. Der Diener lehnt ab: „Gnädige Frau werden schon selbst einen Weg finden müssen, ein Autogramm von ihm zu erhalten."

Die Dame nickt nur mit dem Kopf, dann deutet sie dem Chauffeur an, er solle warten, und geht in das Haus hinüber.

Sie geht bis zur I. Etage, tritt durch eine Tür mit mattgeschliffenen Scheiben mit der Aufschrift: Maison Melloni.

Ein reiches Atelier, verschiedene Zimmer von Madame Melloni. Zwei elegante Salons, durch einen Bogen getrennt, der auf beiden Seiten mit Vorhängen verkleidet ist. Eine mit Teppichen belegte Stufe.

Junge Mädchen, Mannequins, gehen ein und aus, um den Damen, die in den Salons sitzen, die Modelle und Kleider vorzuführen.

Sie steigen von der Stufe herab, gehen zunächst in den einen Salon, dann in den andern, mit jenen Schritten und Bewegungen, die Mannequins eigen sind.

Eine von ihnen ist jenes junge Mädchen, das der Dichter schwarz gekleidet in der Gasse und später in der armseligen Wohnung mit der Mutter gesehen hat. Da steht es auf der Stufe, gerade in dem Augenblick, als die Dame aus dem Auto den Salon betritt und sich zu den anderen Damen setzt, vor denen der Rundgang der Mannequins stattfindet.

Gleichzeitig erscheint Madame Melloni im Salon. Eine charakteristische Erscheinung: sehr zweideutig, dick, halb Spanierin, halb Italienerin, geschwätzig gestikulierend.

Sie nähert sich beflissen der Dame aus dem Auto, stellt sich hinter den Sessel, lobt die Eleganz des Pariser Modells, welches das Mädchen aus der Gasse vorführt.

Und weil das Mädchen einen Volant als Schärpe auf der Brust nicht vorteilhaft genug zur Geltung bringt, macht sie ihm bittere Vorwürfe und zeigt ihm, wie man die Schärpe am wirksamsten trägt.

Das Mädchen wird ganz gedrückt bei diesem Tadel, setzt seinen Rundgang fort und tritt ab.

Die Dame hat sich erhoben und plaudert mit der Besitzerin. Sie wünscht von dem Dichter dort drüben ein Autogramm. Madame Melloni, dienstbeflissen, eine Frau, die alles erledigen kann, sagt ihr sofort: „Lassen Sie das meine Sorge sein. Ich werde Ihnen das Autogramm verschaffen!"

Sie bittet die Dame zu warten, setzt einen charakteristischen großen, frechen Hut auf, läßt sich von der Dame ihr kleines Notizbuch für das Autogramm reichen und geht.

Trotz ihrer korpulenten Figur steigt sie flink die Treppe hinab.

Der Dichter arbeitet an seinem Schreibtisch.

Der Diener tritt ein und meldet den Besuch.

Der Dichter liest erstaunt die Karte und nimmt den Besuch an.

Madame Melloni tritt sehr zeremoniell ein, in gut gespielter Verwirrung. Sie trägt ihre Bitte vor, gibt ihm das Notizbuch.

Er lächelt, schreibt auf eine Seite sein Autogramm.

Madame Melloni dankt und empfiehlt sich. Dabei gleitet ihr die Tasche aus der Hand. Photographien schöner und sympathischer junger Mädchen fallen heraus.

Madame Melloni spielt die Erschrokkene, sammelt die Photographien vom Boden auf.

Während sie sich aufrichtet, lächelt sie gemein und maliziös.

Sie spielt mit den Photographien, breitet sie fächerartig aus, um sie dem Dichter zu zeigen, und blinzelt schlau: eine raffinierte Kupplerin.

Er betrachtet lächelnd die fächerartig ausgebreiteten Photographien.

Da plötzlich packt ihn ein Bild. Es ist das Bild jenes Mädchens, dem er, als er durch jene Gasse ging, begegnet ist.

Er nimmt das Bild in seine Hände. Ja, sie ist es!

Madame Melloni wird durch seine Aufmerksamkeit irregeführt. Sie wittert ein Kupplergeschäft. „Ein Mannequin aus meinem Salon!"

Er erwidert: „Ich möchte mit diesem Mädchen sprechen!"

Ein vieldeutiges Lächeln von Madame Melloni und die Antwort: „Ich werde es sofort zu Ihnen schicken!" –

Das Zimmer, in dem die Mannequins sich umkleiden, um andere Modelle anzuziehen.

Jenes Mädchen in Kombination.

Madame Melloni kommt herein, ist voll heuchlerischer Liebenswürdigkeit. Sie klopft dem Mädchen auf die Wange und sagt: „Ein älterer Herr möchte dich gern sprechen!" und deutet auf das Haus gegenüber.

Das Mädchen weigert sich.

Madame Mellonis Gesicht wird hart. Sie wendet sich brüsk ab, geht an einen Schrank. Nimmt den Karton mit dem von der Mutter genähten Kleid, tritt zu dem Mädchen zurück und sagt: „Ich kann die Näharbeit deiner Mutter nicht mehr gebrauchen. Auch dafür zahle ich kein Geld mehr!"

Und geht hinaus.

Traurig steht das Mädchen da, kleidet sich langsam an.

Madame Melloni kommt zurück und sagt energisch: „Gehst du nun hinüber, ja oder nein?"

Das Mädchen senkt den Kopf wie bejahend, worauf Madame Melloni befriedigt das Kleid aufnimmt und in den Schrank zurückschließt.

Der junge Sekretär tritt mit Briefen zu dem Dichter an den Schreibtisch.

Von seiner Arbeit abgelenkt, sieht der Dichter ihn zunächst ärgerlich an. Als er aber bemerkt, welchen Eindruck dies auf den jungen Mann macht, der ergeben untertänig und respektvoll dasteht, wie in beständiger Furcht vor der Überlegenheit dieses Mannes, lächelt er ihm zu und läßt sich die Post vorlegen.

Im Ankleidezimmer der Mannequins steht das Mädchen im Trauerkleid, das so merkwürdig zweideutig wirkt, vor dem Spiegel, setzt sich den Hut zurecht.

Der Spiegel wird trübe, gleichsam von einem teuflischen Odem angehaucht und das undeutliche Bild eines alten Satyrs, der sofort widerlich obszön zu grinsen beginnt, erscheint im Spiegel.

Das Mädchen senkt den Kopf und hält die Hände vor die Augen –

In der Vorhalle empfängt der junge Sekretär das junge Mädchen.

Er führt es in das Arbeitszimmer.

Der Dichter bietet dem Mädchen Platz an in einem der großen Ledersessel, die vor dem Tisch stehen. Das Mädchen ist zunächst befangen. Er fragt: „Sie arbeiten als Schneiderin?" Das Mädchen schüttelt den Kopf: „Nein, als Mannequin! Meine Mutter näht für Madame Melloni!"

Das Mädchen gibt sich sichtlich nach einem inneren Kampf einen Ruck, setzt sich, wie lockend und eine vorgeschriebene Pflicht erfüllend, auf die Armlehne des Sessels, in dem der Dichter sitzt, als illustriere es den Sinn der Worte: „Wir sind von ihr abhängig!"

Dabei macht es den Versuch, ihn zu umarmen. Aber so, daß man deutlich erkennt, wie völlig ungeübt es in Dirnenkünsten ist.

Der Dichter entzieht sich diesem Versuch, indem er aufsteht und sagt: „Ich habe Sie nicht aus diesem Grunde zu mir gebeten!"

Das Mädchen macht ein ungläubigerstauntes Gesicht und antwortet: „Ich bin aus diesem Grunde zu Ihnen geschickt!"

Und wendet sich ab, so daß der Dichter den Gesichtsausdruck, der tief unglücklich ist, nicht sehen kann.

Von der ganzen Situation peinlich berührt, verabschiedet er das Mädchen, blickt ihm versonnen nach. Aber an der Tür hält er das Mädchen zurück, sieht ihm ins Gesicht, lange und prüfend, und sagt: „Ich könnte Sie liebgewinnen wie meine eigene Schöpfung!"

Das Mädchen versteht ihn nicht und schlüpft fluchtartig hinaus.

Versonnen bleibt der Dichter zurück. Er überlegt. Er geht langsam zu seinem Sessel, setzt sich. Die hohe Rückenlehne verdeckt ihn dem Zuschauer.

Der Rauch seiner Zigarette steigt auf und vermengt sich mit dem Nebel, der das Zimmer wieder erfüllt. Die Gestalt des Mädchens mit dirnenhaften Bewegungen wird sichtbar, wie sie auf den Sessel zugeht und sich anbietet.

* * *

Es ist Abend.

Vor dem Haus in der engen Gasse, wo das Mädchen wohnt, erscheint der Sekretär des Dichters mit Blumen.

Er überzeugt sich von der Richtigkeit der Hausnummer und geht hinein.

In der Kammer sitzen die Mutter und das Mädchen und nähen.

Das kleine Kind spielt zu ihren Füßen.

Der Sekretär tritt ein.

Das Mädchen blickt verlegen auf die Blumen, in innerer Erwartung.

Aber da wendet sich der Sekretär der Mutter zu, stellt sich vor, überreicht ihr die Blumen und sagt: „Herr Pirandello bittet Sie, ihn zu besuchen!" Er deutet an, daß er sie gleich erwarte und sie mitgehen möge.

Die Mutter gerät in Aufregung. So wie sie gekleidet ist, kann sie keinen Besuch machen. Sie geht in die Kammer.

Der Sekretär und das junge Mädchen bleiben mit dem Kind allein.

Beide sehen sich etwas verlegen an, dann beschäftigen sie sich mit dem Kind.

Zwischen beiden ist ein gewisses Interesse füreinander vom ersten Moment an sichtbar.

Das Kind greift nach den Blumen, zieht verspielt eine aus dem Strauß heraus und legt sie dem Mädchen in den Schoß. Das Mädchen will sie zurücklegen, aber der Sekretär, bittet, diese Blume für sich zu behalten. Ein innigdankbarer Blick des Mädchens trifft ihn.

Sie plaudern lebhaft –

* * *

Die Mutter kommt, vom Sekretär geleitet, zum Dichter.

Der Dichter fordert sie auf, ihm ihre Lebensgeschichte zu erzählen.

Die Mutter, die dem Dichter dankbar ist, daß er sich für ihre Tochter interessiert, schüttet ihm ihr Herz aus und erzählt: „Ich stamme aus gutem, aber armem Hause. Ein reicher, sehr absonderlicher Mann heiratete mich. Wunderlich lebte er mit seinen Büchern"....

Großaufnahme des Kopfes der Mutter, die erzählt.

Hineinkopiert erscheint: der erste Mann der Mutter, so wie sie ihn in ihrer Erinnerung hat.

Er ist der Typ eines geistigen Herrenmenschen, mit grüblerischem Gesichtsausdruck (etwa Beethoven-Maske). Zwischen Büchern sitzend, studiert er den Totenschädel eines – Kindes.

In Großaufnahme erscheint der Kopf des Dichters. Aufmerksam hört er der Mutter zu.

Der Kopf verblaßt, bleibt aber nebelhaft sichtbar. In den Kopf einkopiert erscheint der erste Mann der Mutter, so wie er aus der Erzählung der Mutter vom Dichter in seiner Phantasie gesehen wird: ein Mann von körperlichem Format, Professorentyp, also im Gegensatz zur Wirklichkeit, die wir eben aus dem Bild der Mutter-Erzählung gesehen haben, im Gegensatz zu dem Mann mit der Beethoven-Maske. Der grinsende Totenschädel, den er studiert, ist der eines – erwachsenen Menschen.

Die Mutter erzählt weiter.

Aus ihrem sprechenden Gesicht blendet das Bild nach dem Titel: „Wir hatten einen kleinen Knaben ..." über in: ihren Mann (Beethoven-Maske) am Schreibtisch, zu dem jetzt ein etwa dreijähriger Knabe gelaufen kommt, der ihn in der Arbeit stört. Die Händchen greifen nach dem Kindertotenschädel.

Und wieder verwandelt sich das Bild in das Gesicht des zuhörenden Dichters, in das jetzt seine Vorstellung dieser häuslichen Szene und ihrer Fortsetzung hineinblendet: der Mann (Professorentyp) hat das Kind auf seinen Schoß gesetzt; er dreht den Totenschädel wie einen Globus und entdeckt visionell, mit tastendem Finger darüber gleitend, in den Flächen, Furchen, Erhöhungen und Buchten, in diesem Mikrokosmos – das Antlitz der Welt.

Der Kopf der erzählenden Mutter taucht auf, die Realität der Vergangenheit blendet in ihn ein.

Der Vater (Beethoven-Maske) und der Knabe spielen mit dem Kindertotenschädel Ball.

In das Zimmer tritt die Mutter, ist entsetzt über das Spielzeug, nimmt es dem Kind fort. Das Kind weint. Der Vater stellt sie ärgerlich zur Rede.

Sie, die ihn nicht versteht, widerspricht.

Er wird immer gereizter, bis zum Wutausbruch.

Mit einem Konvolut von Manuskripten und Papieren kommt der Sekretär des Vaters in diese Szene hinein, bleibt bestürzt und respektvoll an der Tür stehen, wirft einen mitleidigen Blick auf die Mutter.

Das Kind läuft auf ihn zu, heult sich bei ihm aus.

Auch die Mutter sucht bei ihm Schutz.

Der Vater wendet sich ärgerlich ab, setzt sich an seinen Schreibtisch.

Die Mutter will mit dem Kind hinausgehen, es dem Sekretär sanft entziehen. Beide sind um das weinende Kind bemüht.

Der Vater steht auf, tritt zu der Gruppe, sieht mit scharf beobachtenden Blicken beide an, lächelt spöttisch, als wollte er sagen: Ihr versteht euch ausgezeichnet! Er hält ihre Köpfe zusammen, um anzudeuten, daß sie beide ein schönes Paar abgeben würden, und hat eine zynische Freude an ihrer Verlegenheit.

Er schiebt die beiden zur Tür hinaus und behält das Kind bei sich.

Erregt erzählt die Mutter, von der Erinnerung gepackt: „Sein Wille war es, daß ich mit seinem Sekretär eine neue Ehe schloß! Das Kind gab er zur Erziehung aufs Land!"

Der Dichter fragt: „Was ist aus den beiden geworden?"

Die Mutter antwortet: „Ich habe nie wieder von ihnen gehört. Ich weiß nicht, ob sie noch am Leben sind!"

Der Dichter sieht durch sie hindurch, gleichsam von den Möglichkeiten, die ihr Schicksal in seiner Phantasie anregt, beherrscht.

Die Mutter beendet: „Vor einem halben Jahr ist mein zweiter Mann gestorben – nun lebe ich mit den drei Kindern aus meiner zweiten Ehe in Armut!"

Das Bild des Wohnzimmers blendet in ihren Kopf ein:

Sie arbeitet an der Nähmaschine. Die Tochter ist angekleidet und nimmt ein Paket mit einem Kleide, das wir aus der Szene mit Madame Melloni kennen, unter den Arm, um zu gehen. Das fünfjährige Schwesterchen wird von ihr beim Abschied zärtlich geliebkost. Der vierzehnjährige Junge liest, den Kopf mit dem wirren Haar in die Hände gestützt, in einem Buch.

Nun erscheinen Mutter und Dichter zusammen:

Sie hat ihre Erzählung beendet; der Dichter sitzt nachdenklich, unter der Einwirkung der Erzählung. Plötzlich hebt er den Kopf und sagt:

„Wissen Sie, worin die Dienste bestehen, für die Ihre Tochter von Madame Melloni bezahlt wird?"

Er sieht sie mit einem Gesichtsausdruck an, aus dem die Mutter zum erstenmal erschrocken den Verdacht schöpft, was Madame Melloni von ihrem Kinde verlangt. Unter der blitzartigen, entsetzlichen Erkenntnis, die plötzlich über sie hereinbricht, stockt ihr Pulsschlag. Ihr Blick wird irr.

Der Dichter arbeitet sich immer mehr in das Schicksal der Personen, wie er es in seiner Phantasie sieht, hinein: „Und wenn Ihr erster Mann noch lebte? Wenn er eines Tages zu Madame Melloni käme, seiner Stieftochter begegnete, ohne zu ahnen, wer sie ist?"

In den Kopf des Dichters blendet der erste Mann der Mutter (Professorentyp), in einem Lehnstuhl sitzend, so wie der Dichter vorher beim Besuch des Mädchens.

Das Mädchen setzt sich lockend auf den Armstuhl und beginnt mit den gelernten Zärtlichkeiten der Dirne. Und der Stiefvater genießt die Situation, die er sich im Hause der Madame Melloni gekauft hat.

Die Mutter verbirgt verzweifelt den Kopf in ihren Händen. Die Gedanken, die der Dichter ihr eingepflanzt hat, fassen von ihr Besitz. *Das Bild, das der Dichter eben gesehen, blendet in ihren Kopf ein. Aber mit dem Unterschied, daß jetzt der Mann mit der Beethoven-Maske im Sessel sitzt.*

Aufgewühlt verläßt die Mutter das Haus.

Der Dichter sieht ihr tragisch-bewegt nach.

Das Zimmer füllt sich wieder mit dem uns schon bekannten Nebel, und in ihm erscheint der Gespensterreigen der sechs Personen, nämlich: das Mädchen, die Mutter, der vierzehnjährige Sohn, das fünfjährige Schwesterchen, der Vater, wie ihn der Dichter sieht, also der Professorentyp, und Madame Melloni. Die Figuren wachsen schemenhaft ins Überlebensgroße und umtanzen, immer kleiner werdend und in ein geisterhaftes Licht getaucht, den Dichter und sammeln sich schließlich

auf einer ungeheuren Hand – der Hand des Dichters.

Die Hand des Dichters erhebt sich, sie regiert die Geister und indem sie sich hebt, wird sie ganz langsam normal.

Und schließlich ruht sie auf der Stirn des Dichters, in die sie die sechs Personen hineingehen läßt.

Und jetzt erscheint der ganze Kopf des Dichters mit der Hand, die sich langsam von der Stirn abhebt, dann die ganze Gestalt des Dichters, an den Schreibtisch gelehnt, immer noch mit der Hand vor der Stirn.

Der Sekretär tritt ein.

Der Dichter wird in die Wirklichkeit zurückgerissen und sagt: „Ich wünsche, daß Sie sich um das Mädchen und ihre Familie kümmern. Ich habe lebhaftes Interesse für diese Menschen!"

Der Sekretär verneigt sich schweigend.

Die Mutter irrt von Angst und Verzweiflung gejagt durch die Straßen nach Hause.

Eine Dirne, die einen Mann anlockt, hält sie für ihre Tochter.

Durch winklige Gassen eilt sie dem Paar nach, um endlich erlöst zu erkennen, daß sie sich getäuscht hat.

Und dort dieser Mann, der mit dem Rücken zu ihr irgendwo im Schatten steht, ist es nicht ihr erster Mann? Und der junge, schlanke, elegante Mensch, der jenem vor dem Haus begegnet, ist es nicht vielleicht ihr Sohn aus erster Ehe, den sie seit seiner Kindheit nie wieder gesehen hat?

Und wieder muß sie erkennen, daß ihre Sinne sie getäuscht haben, daß die Gedanken des Dichters, die er ihren Gedanken aufgezwungen hat, sie hinter Phantomen hertreibt, die ihre Seele ängstigen.

Sie kommt nach Hause.

Da liegt ihre Tochter mit dem fünfjährigen Schwesterchen friedlich schlafend im Bett.

In der Kammer wacht der vierzehnjährige Junge.

Erschöpft und zerquält sinkt die Mutter auf dem Sessel an der Nähmaschine zusammen.

Eine unruhige Bewegung des kleinen Mädchens läßt sie aufblicken.

Und wie von dem Gedanken plötzlich beherrscht, daß dieses reine Kind nicht neben der Schwester schlafen soll, von der sie befürchtet, daß sie in Schande lebt, nimmt sie das Kind aus dem Bett, hüllt es ein und setzt sich mit ihm abseits.

Die Tochter erwacht und beobachtet noch im Halbschlaf die Mutter.

Jetzt richtet sie sich auf und fragt mit entsetzten Augen die sich abwendende Mutter, der die Tränen aus den Augen stürzen, was das zu bedeuten habe.

In der Kammer horcht der vierzehnjährige Junge mit großen, fiebrigen Augen auf das Gespräch nebenan.

Die Tochter steht in einem Überwurf vor der Mutter, die ihr ihre Anklagen ins Gesicht schleudert.

Verwirrung erfaßt den Jungen in der Kammer. Man sieht, wie er leidet, man sieht, wie er dem Vorwurf glaubt, den die Mutter gegen die Tochter erhebt.

Die Tochter ist verzweifelt. Sie beschwört und beteuert bei der Madonna, daß die Mutter sich irre, daß jemand sie verleumdet haben müsse, daß sie den Versuchungen im Hause der Madame Melloni nicht erlegen sei.

Diesen Beteuerungen schenkt die Mutter langsam Glauben.

Die Tochter legt das Schwesterchen wieder ins Bett zurück.

Jetzt birgt sie, mit der Mutter versöhnt, den Kopf an ihrer Brust –

Am nächsten Morgen erwartet der Sekretär das Mädchen, das ins Geschäft geht.

Von seinem Fenster aus sieht der Dichter die beiden. Er runzelt unwillig die Stirn. Aus der freudigen Art, wie das Mädchen den Sekretär begrüßt und mit ihm plaudert, glaubt er zu entnehmen, daß dieses verdorbene Geschöpf den jungen Mann einfangen will.

Die beiden verabreden sich für den Abend.

Der Dichter wird in seinem Zimmer wieder von den Gestalten seiner Phantasie umdrängt, die immer schärfer Leben bekommen.

Durch seinen Kopf hindurch blendet eine Szene, wie der Stiefvater (Professorentyp) auf der Suche nach Lust bei Madame Melloni erscheint:

Sie führt ihm kupplerisch die Mannequins vor. Keine gefällt ihm.

Da führt ihm Madame Melloni das junge Mädchen zu. Von diesem ist der Stiefvater entzückt. Sie läßt die beiden mit kupplerischen Gebärden in ein Séparée eintreten. Hinter ihnen schließt sie die Tür.

Diese Imagination beherrscht den Dichter. Der Gedanke, daß der Stiefvater eines Tages in das Haus der Madame Melloni kommen und dort der Tochter seiner eigenen Frau aus ihrer zweiten Ehe begegnen könnte, ohne zu wissen, wer sie ist, erregt ihn so tief, daß er Hut und Mantel nimmt und fortgeht.

Er kommt zur Mutter, die sofort die Schande ihrer Tochter bestreitet, was der Dichter mit mitleidiger Ruhe entgegennimmt: Er glaubt es besser zu wissen. Er hat es ja selbst erlebt, wie die Tochter sich ihm angeboten hat. Er verabschiedet sich kurz.

Die Mutter ist betroffen und in neuen Zweifeln.

Da kommt der Sohn, der alles wieder mitangehört hat, verstört aus der Kammer. Er glaubt dem Dichter und stürzt aus dem Hause.

Zerquält bleibt die Mutter zurück, aufs neue von der Gedankenmacht des Dichters in ihren Gedanken beeinflußt, immer mehr von den Abschiedswor-

Documents

ten des Dichters beherrscht: „Wer weiß, vielleicht lebt Ihr erster Mann noch, ist gerade jetzt im Hause der Madame Melloni und wählt sich Ihre Tochter!"

Wie aufgescheucht hetzt sie davon – in das Haus der Madame Melloni.

Sie fragt zwei Mädchen nach ihrer Tochter, die, mit zweideutigen Gesichtern, auf eine der Türen deuten, die in die kleinen Salons führen.

Die Mutter will dort eindringen.

Die Mädchen versuchen, sie zurückzuhalten.

Madame Melloni erscheint.

Es folgt eine erregte Szene zwischen den beiden Frauen.

Da Madame Melloni energisch den Eintritt in das Zimmer verwehrt, dringt die Mutter schließlich gewaltsam ein.

Sie sieht in diesem Zimmer einen Mann mit dem Rücken zu ihr stehen, den sie in der Erregung tatsächlich für ihren ersten Mann hält.

Er streichelt gerade das Haar ihrer Tochter.

Sie stürzt zur Gruppe hin,

packt mit einem Aufschrei den Mann an, der sich erstaunt umwendet: es ist der Dichter selbst.

Madame Melloni, die der Mutter gefolgt ist, entschuldigt sich tausendmal bei dem Dichter über die Störung.

Angewidert von dem Gehabe der Kupplerin verabschiedet er sich brüsk.

Madame Melloni, die sich um ein Geschäft gebracht glaubt, ist wütend und wirft Mutter und Tochter hinaus.

Ihrer Existenz beraubt, der Not des täglichen Lebens ausgesetzt, verlassen die beiden Frauen das Haus der Madame Melloni.

Die Tochter beschwört die Mutter, nie mehr mit dem Dichter zusammenzutreffen, da er sie in ein Lügengewebe verstrickt und unglücklich gemacht hat.

* * *

Der Sekretär und das Mädchen treffen sich zur verabredeten Stunde.

Alle Sorgen und Bedrücktheit fallen von der Traurigen sofort ab, als sie in das bunte Getriebe des Vergnügungsparkes kommen und sich der heiteren, ungebundenen Lust des Gebotenen hingeben.

Der junge Mann ist vollends entzückt von der dankbar genossenen Freude, die ihm aus dem Mädchen entgegenstrahlt. Beide sind verliebt ineinander.

So sieht sie der Dichter, der selbst vor den andrängenden Gestalten und Gedanken Ablenkung im Lärm der Menge sucht.

156

Bestürzt über diese unerwartete Begegnung zieht er sich zurück, versucht zu Hause zu arbeiten.

Schärfer konturiert, größer als früher, um eine starke Nuance heller beleuchtet, tauchen die Gestalten immer wieder vor ihm auf.

Aber er kann nichts niederschreiben. Die Blätter vor ihm bleiben leer.

Der heimkommende Sekretär trifft ihn in abgespannter, unduldsamer Stimmung, die auch sofort energisch zum Ausbruch kommt.

Der Dichter warnt ihn vor dem Mädchen, das eine Dirne sei, ihn ins Netz zu locken drohe. Er warnt ihn davor, sich ernstlich zu verlieben.

Der junge Mann ist tief erschüttert.

Er verehrt den Dichter, seine Weisheit und Menschenkenntnis. Er will dem Mädchen, mit dem er sich für den nächsten Tag wieder verabredet hat, einen Absagebrief schreiben.

Aber er bringt es doch nicht über das Herz.

Er vernichtet den Brief wieder. –

Am nächsten Tag wartet das Mädchen auf den Sekretär.

Er kommt, aber sie fühlt sofort, daß etwas zwischen ihnen ist, daß er nicht derselbe wie gestern ist.

Sie trennen sich bald.

Tief unglücklich kommt das Mädchen nach Hause,

wo der vierzehnjährige Bruder bei ihrem Erscheinen wort- und blicklos sofort in seiner Kammer verschwindet, sich verschließt.

* * *

Im Haus ist bittere Not.

Der Junge versucht auf knabenhafte Weise auf der Straße etwas zu verdienen. Er hat das Schwesterchen bei sich.

Er kommt vor das Haus des Dichters, trifft dort auf den Sekretär, den er bittet, ihn zum Dichter zu führen.

Das Kind bleibt spielend im Garten zurück.

Der Junge wartet im Zimmer des Sekretärs.

Die Schreibtischlade steht halb offen: obenauf liegt ein kleiner Browning.

Er nimmt ihn, von Neugierde gelockt. Da kommt der Sekretär, der ihn zum Dichter holen will. Dem Jungen bleibt keine Zeit, den Revolver in die Tischlade zurückzulegen. In der Hast, ihn zu verbergen, steckt er ihn in die Tasche.

Der Dichter spricht mit dem Jungen, der von tiefer, knabenhafter Melancholie erfüllt ist.

Documents

Es ist nichts Tröstliches, was der Dichter dem Knaben zu sagen hat. Er sieht zu klar, daß dieser Junge nicht Kraft genug hat, das Leben zu bewältigen. Diese Wahrheit bedrückt den Dichter, der gerne helfen möchte.

Während er überlegt, was er für ihn tun könnte, tritt er an das Fenster, das in den Garten geht.

Da sieht er unten das kleine Mädchen am Ententeich.

Es ist weit über den Rand gebeugt, um nach den Enten zu greifen, und in Gefahr, jeden Moment in das Wasser zu fallen.

Er erschrickt sehr, deutet hinaus, so daß der Junge aufspringt, die Situation sieht und davonstürzt.

Der Junge kommt zum Teich gelaufen, packt das Schwesterchen und führt es fort. Sein Wesen ist völlig verstört –

* * *

Die Not im Hause des Mädchens ist aufs höchste gestiegen. Hunger ist eingekehrt.

Der Junge beobachtet, wie die Schwester sich zurecht macht, um fortzugehen.

Angstvoll fragt er sie, wohin sie gehe.

Sie hat den schweren Entschluß gefaßt, Madame Melloni aufzusuchen, um sie zu versöhnen und wieder für sich und die Mutter Arbeit zu bekommen.

Der Junge will sie verzweifelt zurückhalten, gibt aber den Kampf bald auf. Er bleibt in völlig verwirrtem Zustand zurück –

Als das Mädchen sich dem Hause der Madame Melloni nähert, kommt der Sekretär die Straße herunter.

Beim Anblick des Geliebten ist das Mädchen einem Zusammenbruch nahe.

Der junge Mann ist erschüttert.

Er drängt zur Aussprache und erkennt, daß der Dichter durch die Imagination seiner Gedankenwelt das Mädchen zu Unrecht beschuldigt hat.

Um so elementarer bricht das Bekenntnis seiner Liebe durch.

Wie mit einem Schlag von grenzenlosem Leid erlöst und in alle Himmel des Glücks geschleudert, liegt das Mädchen in seinen Armen –

In höchster Seligkeit der eben eingestandenen Liebe kommen sie in das Haus der Mutter, die mit dem kleinen Mädchen fortgegangen ist.

Während die Liebenden warten,

hockt der Knabe mit fiebrigen Augen in seiner Kammer, den Blick auf die Tür der Stube geheftet.

158

Leise öffnet er die Tür,

sieht die beiden in weltvergessener Umarmung –

Er taumelt in die Kammer zurück. Seine erhitzte Phantasie versteht die Situation so, wie sie sich ihm auf Grund alles Vorangegangenen darstellen muß: die Schwester hat jetzt ihre Schande ins Haus getragen –

Die Mutter kommt mit dem Kind heim.

Überglücklich erklären ihr beide ihre Liebe.

Der Sekretär hält um die Hand des Mädchens an, da –

erschießt sich der Junge in der Kammer.

Entsetzt, aufgewühlt stürzt der Sekretär zum Dichter,

der wieder mit den Gestalten seiner Dichtkunst lebt.

Der Sekretär schleudert ihm die Nachricht von der Katastrophe anklagend ins Gesicht:

Er, der Dichter, ist in Wahrheit an dem furchtbaren Unglück schuld!

Er, der Dichter, hat die Schicksale von ruhig lebenden Menschen durch die Vermischung seiner Phantasie mit der Wirklichkeit beeinflußt!

Er hat Böses gestiftet, er hat auch das höchste Glück des jungen Mannes zertrümmert, denn:

die Tragik dieser Stunde trennt ihn für immer von dem Mädchen! Stets würde der tote Knabe zwischen ihnen stehen!

Mit einem Fluch verläßt er den Dichter,

der in schwerster, tragischer Gemütsverfassung allein bleibt –

Wieder dringen die Gestalten verlangend, größer und schärfer sichtbar, auf ihn ein.

Sie wachsen im Format über den Dichter hinaus,

werden riesengroße, konturierte Schattenkörper,

erfüllen gigantisch den Raum,

grinsen höhnisch ihn an,

wohin er blickt,

während seine Gestalt immer kleiner und kleiner und schemenhafter wird.

Wie um sich vor den sechs Personen zu schützen, die von ihm alle Kraft und alles Leben nehmen und selbst dadurch immer lebendiger werden,

verdeckt er, von ihnen gewaltig umdrängt, die Augen.

Und nun rafft er sich auf.

Wie in einem Paroxysmus der Abwehr reißt er die Tür auf und jagt die Gestalten hinaus,

wirft hinter ihnen aufatmend die Tür zu!

In völliger Erschöpfung geht er aus diesem Kampf hervor und bricht im Lehnstuhl vor dem Schreibtisch zusammen –

Draußen vor der Villa des Dichters umschreiten die Gestalten in überrealem Format das Haus,

bis sie durch das feste Mauerwerk hindurch ins Innere wieder eindringen.

Der Dichter sitzt noch im Lehnstuhl, über den leeren Papierblock gebeugt, die Feder in der Hand, in sich in tiefster Konzentration versunken: das ist aus der Haltung des Körpers deutlich fühlbar.

Durch das Mauerwerk kommen die sechs Gestalten überlebensgroß und klar herein.

Gebieterisch nehmen sie hinter ihm Aufstellung.

Die Haltung des Dichters bleibt unverändert.

Aber seine Hand schreibt jetzt auf das vor ihm liegende Blatt groß und deutlich die Worte: SECHS PERSONEN SUCHEN EINEN AUTOR. Die Hand unterstreicht diese Worte.

Dann schreibt der Dichter weiter darunter: EIN THEATERSTÜCK VON LUIGI PIRANDELLO.

Das handschriftliche Titelblatt blendet in ein Theaterplakat von „Sechs Personen suchen einen Autor" über.

Es klebt an einer Anschlagsäule an der Ecke einer belebten Straße.

Neben der Anschlagsäule steht das junge Mädchen, dirnenhaft auffallend gekleidet.

Ein abenteuerlustiger Elegant bemerkt das Mädchen und fixiert es.

Das Mädchen lächelt ihn an und winkt leicht mit dem Kopf.

Der Sekretär, der gerade vorbeikommt, erkennt das junge Mädchen, das ihn aber nicht sieht,

da er sich hinter der Säule verbirgt.

Er beobachtet, wie der Elegant dem Wink folgt, die lockend Abgehende erreicht, sie anspricht und mit ihr zusammen weiterschlendert.

Tieferschüttert sieht er ihr nach.

Als er sich abwendet, fällt sein Blick auf das Theaterplakat.

Er senkt den Kopf wie in trauriger Beschämung –

In der Wohnstube der Mutter öffnet das kleine Mädchen ein großes Paket und packt aus einem Karton einen Teddybären.

Jubelnd läuft das Kind zur Mutter,

zeigt strahlend das schöne Spielzeug, das die Schwester geschickt hat.

Die Mutter verbirgt das Gesicht vor Qual und Schande.

Das Bild blendet über in die Bühne, in deren Kulisse der Dichter steht –

Auf der Bühne probt die Schauspielerin, die im Theaterstück die Mutter spielt, mit einem kleinen Mädchen, das ihr eben strahlend eine große Puppe zeigt, die ihm seine Schwester geschickt hat.

Die Mutter will dem Kind die Puppe wegnehmen.

Das Kind strampelt und wehrt sich.

Da läßt ihm die Mutter die Puppe, schluchzt auf und ruft: „Diese Schande! Diese Schande!"

Und verbirgt ihr Gesicht in den Händen.

Im vordersten Parkett sitzt der Regisseur an seinem Pult, ruft etwas zur Bühne hinauf.

Die Probe wird unterbrochen.

Der Dichter kommt aus der Kulisse auf die Bühne und streichelt das Kind, während er mit der Schauspielerin spricht und ihr seine Spielintentionen mitteilt. –

Vor dem Hause der Madame Melloni fährt ein elegantes Auto vor.

Ein älterer Herr steigt mit dem jungen Mädchen aus.

Sie gehen ins Hause.

Madame Melloni empfängt sie in ihrer kupplerischen Art und geleitet sie in eines jener kleinen Kabinette, die dem Amüsement ihrer Kundschaft dienen.

Eine kleine Tafel ist für zwei Personen gedeckt.

Eine Platte mit Vorgerichten steht auf dem Tisch. Sekt ist bereits kalt gestellt.

Das Mädchen befiehlt Madame Melloni, ihr die neuesten Hüte zu zeigen, sie gehe heute abend mit dem Herrn in die Pirandellopremiere.

Die Kupplerin schießt diensteifrig davon.

Der Herr schenkt Sekt ein, die beiden beginnen zu essen, trinken sich zu.

Das Bild blendet über in die Bühne.

Auf der Bühne soupiert die Schauspielerin, die das junge Mädchen darstellt, mit ihrem Stiefvater im Séparée der Madame Pace, das ähnlich dem Kabinett der Melloni ist.

Der Mann trägt die Maske, wie sie der Dichter als Typ des ersten Mannes der Mutter in seiner Phantasie gesehen hat (Professorentyp).

Beide trinken einander zu.

Der Dichter steht im Smoking in der Kulisse, sieht gespannt dem Spiel auf der Bühne zu.

In der Parkettloge sitzt das junge Mädchen mit dem Herrn, mit dem wir sie bei der Melloni eben vorher gesehen haben.

Sie hat ein großes Abendkleid an und sieht in sichtlicher Erregung und Spannung auf die Bühne, wo ihr eigenes Schicksal gespielt wird.

Jetzt setzt sich das Mädchen im Stück in dirnenhaft frechem Liebesspiel auf die Knie des Herrn.

Da wird die Tür aufgerissen,

die Mutter dringt gewaltsam ein,

vergebens von der ihr wütend folgenden Kupplerin zurückgehalten.

Das Mädchen springt vom Schoß des Herrn herunter –

die Mutter erkennt ihren ersten Mann, schreit mit einem fast wahnsinnigen Gesichtsausdruck weh auf!

Auch der Mann ist tief bestürzt und seine erste Frau erkennend aufgesprungen.

Sie ruft ihm anklagend zu: „Es ist meine Tochter, die du deiner Lust gekauft hast!" –

Sie reißt das Mädchen von dem Mann zurück,

der sie entgeistert anstarrt.

Die Frau bricht ohnmächtig in den Armen der Tochter zusammen.

Der Vorhang fällt.

In der Loge sieht das völlig aufgewühlte Mädchen wie betäubt von dem Erlebnis dieses Stückes auf seinen Begleiter, der zu applaudieren beginnt.

Das Mädchen starrt ihn plötzlich wie eine Erscheinung mit wachsendem Entsetzen an:

denn sein Gesicht verwandelt sich in die Physiognomie des ersten Mannes der Mutter, wie er in Wirklichkeit ausgesehen hat:

es ist der Mann mit der Beethoven-Maske!

Das Mädchen fährt mit einem jähen Aufschrei vom Stuhl hoch.

Der Mann, wieder mit seinem eigenen Gesicht, dem eines vornehmen älteren Herrn, sieht erschrocken auf.

Das in der Nähe sitzende Publikum im Parkett sieht betroffen zur Loge hin, während es weiter applaudiert.

Der Herr zieht das Mädchen, das in einen Schreikrampf verfällt, gewaltsam aus der Loge –

Unten vor dem Vorhang erscheint der Dichter und verneigt sich ernst und ruhig vor dem stürmisch applaudierenden Publikum.

Ende

The *Scenario*

for a silent film based on *Six Characters*

LUIGI PIRANDELLO & ADOLF LANTZ
Translated by Nina daVinci Nichols

This translation compares the original German Film-Novelle with two Italian translations, one by Antonio Illiano and Giovanni Bussino (1982) and the other by Roberto Tessari (1984); it incorporates research discussed in part 1 of this book. Passages in brackets represent variant readings prefaced with an "I" to indicate an Italian manuscript or a "G" to indicate the German one. Paragraphing varies slightly from the German original in order to convey implicit instructions for camera shots and scene breaks incorporated into the language of the text. Numbering of paragraphs (or "takes") corresponds to references in chapter 4 (Film-Novelle).

1. The Author, Luigi Pirandello, is seated at a desk in his study. He hands a sheaf of correspondence and other papers to his young Secretary; then he shakes hands with the young man briefly but politely. The Secretary bows respectfully and exits.

2. The Author goes to the window and looks out on a serene vista. Twilight falls on mansions encircling this elegant quarter of the city. He returns to the room and begins to pace its length, lost in deep thought. Then he sits down at his desk.

3. The room fills with a mist from which vague figures emerge slowly, indistinctly, their shapes shifting and illusory. They assail the Author like figures in a nightmare, or like incubi weighing him down with some unnameable sorrow. Then their forms begin to glow in the darkening room. The Author bends forward, leaning against his desk, besieged by these unruly ghosts.

4. Now darkness falls and a street lamp is lit outside in front of the house. A

ray of light from the lamp suddenly penetrates the study where the misty phantoms flutter around the Author. Then light chases the cloudy forms into the corners of the room where they vanish.

5. The Author straightens up as if liberated from a nightmare. He lights the desk lamp. His face reflects a profound exhaustion. He rises, looks out the window, then leaves the room.

6. The Author dresses in a hat and coat and prepares to leave the house. He passes through the entrance door and is unlocking the front gate when the same fantastic cloud of phantoms pours out of the house and disperses, as if dissipated by the wind.

7. The Author approaches a deserted alley barely lit by a smoky street lamp. Behind him the cloudy phantoms dissolve mid air. As he reaches the street lamp, a young woman appears, moving rapidly and staying close to the walls of buildings. She is dressed in black [I = mourning][1] and casts a shy glance in his direction as she passes him. That glance crossing his own makes him particularly attentive. Had he caught something indecorous in the glance of so young a woman, something suggestive?

8. Farther along the alley, at the entrance to a squalid old house, a sad [G = care-worn] woman, dressed in mourning, waits in the night. She is the young woman's Mother. The Author sees the Daughter run toward her Mother and throw herself at her Mother's breast. They embrace closely, then both disappear into the squalid doorway.

9. The Author is highly disturbed by what he has seen. He pauses a moment beneath the outer doorway, lifting his head to look at the windows of the decrepit house. Light from one of the windows filters through the shutters. The Author tries to peer between the slats into the interior.

10. He sees a wretched little room scarcely large enough for a bed and an old straw chair. The room is illuminated suddenly by a ray of light coming through a barely open door to the next room. A pale adolescent Boy, seated in an armchair, appears in this beam of light: it is the young woman's brother. Then, as if he has just heard someone enter the next room, the Boy jumps up, disturbed, and calls, "Mama"![2]

11. In the nearby room, the Mother frees herself from her Daughter's arms. This room, too, reflects poverty: there is a sewing machine, various types of piece goods in work, some lengths of fabric, and two beds. In one bed a pretty, blonde, five-year-old Girl lies sleeping; she is the Daughter's little sister. The Mother goes to the doorway between the two small rooms and says to the Boy, now sitting on a bed, "Be quiet. Go to sleep." She shuts the door.

12. Unable then to see into the darkened room, the Author goes off slowly, sunk in thoughts.

13. In the room, the Daughter digs into a purse for banknotes and tosses them [I = empties the contents of her purse] onto the table for her Mother. She watches sadly as her Mother places the money in a cupboard.

14. The Author continues his walk across the deserted alley, turning into a tree-lined boulevard lit by the moon and lined with electric lamps. While continuing on beneath the trees, the Author retains the image of that alley, as if its lurid walls and squalor were following him. He again sees the smoky lamplight, the Daughter in black slipping along the walls, and her sidelong glance; farther on he also sees the Mother in mourning in front of the doorway, the Daughter throwing herself in her Mother's arms, and their intimacy as they disappear into the vestibule. These visions follow him, taking on substance [G = then gradually receding and dissolving].

15. As the Author arrives at his own mansion, he sees his shadow lengthening before him on the sidewalk. He watches as it rises and becomes [G = merges with] himself. He turns back to see if the shadow is indeed his own. And again, as he unlocks the garden gate, there appears at his back a cloudy apparition of the young woman who clung to the walls of the deserted alley in the smoky light of the street lamp.

16. The apparition vanishes and the Author, turning around again, sees that his shadow has reformed ahead of him. He enters the garden. Two gigantic pine trees flank the entranceway like sentinels. In the sky above the treetops, the crescent moon hangs from a star [G = as if suspended in a sling].

17. As the Author climbs the outer stairwell, the light of the street lamp falls on the landing with the bewildering effect of a strange, gray-violet phantasmagoria. On the landing [G = above the threshold] a haze of subtle, indistinct phantoms once again forms around the Author and steals into the house with him. Before he lights a lamp in the vestibule, they begin to glow in the dark. Once the lamplight flares up, the phantoms flutter ahead of him like misty vapor and drift across the hall into the open doorway of his study. The lamp on his desk casts an increasingly sharp light and the mist flutters across the room. The Author sighs deeply and brings his hand to his forehead, covering his eyes.

18. Then, lifting his hand from his eyes, he turns and fixes a keen, penetrating gaze on a corner of the room where a blurred, evanescent image of the young woman he met earlier in the deserted alley quickly appears and disap-

pears. Her head is encircled by a kind of halo, the nimbus of poetry. She appears to him now as if a creature of his art [G = an already formed aesthetic creation], a being whom he would be compelled to bring to life. But for the moment he sees her animated only in the act of throwing her arms around her Mother, also transfigured, although her figure is not yet well defined [I = as yet in an uncertain manner].

19. The Author shudders as if to free himself from those figures of his imagination. Entering into the sphere of light cast by the lamp, he reaches for a cigarette. Then he sits. Before him on the desk lie white sheets of paper. His hand toys with his pen.

20. In the room, the Daughter stands at the bed where her little sister sleeps. The Girl awakens and smiles at her elder sister who is dressing; then the Girl kneels on her bed and holds out her arms to her elder sister. The Daughter takes the Girl in her arms. Meanwhile, the Mother is arranging a box holding a dress that she has just finished sewing.

21. A beautiful clear day. An automobile stops at the gate of the Author's .mansion. A chauffeur opens the car door and an elegant woman steps out of the car. The chauffeur rings the doorbell, and a porter comes to the gate. He replies to a question put by the chauffeur: "Madame Melloni lives across the way," indicating another mansion displaying a sign saying House of Melloni, Dresses and Coats, First Floor. The woman thanks him and asks another question to which the porter responds: "This is Mr. Pirandello's residence." The lady marvels, exclaiming, "Oh, the writer? Will he give me his auto-graph?" searching in her handbag for a notebook. But the porter puts her off. "Madame will know the best way to obtain the autograph."

22. The lady nods her head in assent, signals to her chauffeur to wait for her, and goes to the house indicated by the porter. She climbs to the first floor and pushes open a glass door with the inscription, House of Melloni.

23. Inside is a luxurious fashion house with several rooms. Two elegant salons are separated by an archway hung with draperies on either side. There is a large carpeted platform. Young mannequins come and go, engaged in modeling for the women seated in the salons. One after another, the manne-quins mount and descend the steps of a platform, crossing the salon with their light, stylish walk. Among them is the very young woman dressed in black whom the Author had seen first in the streets and then with her Mother in their poor lodgings. She is standing on the platform at the moment when the lady from the limousine enters the salon and seats herself among the women around whom the models are parading.

24. At the same moment, Madame Melloni appears, a characteristic type of the demimonde [G = shady character; I = *equivoco*]: shrewish, sly, stout, half-Spanish and half-Italian, chattering and gesturing. She posts herself behind the chair of the lady from the limousine, leaning on the armchair's shoulders and extolling the elegance of the Paris model that the Daughter is showing.

25. And because the Daughter fails to present the most advantageous features of a scarf draped across her bosom, Madame Melloni rebukes her sharply and shows the elegant woman how it should be worn more modishly. The Daughter, unnerved by the reproof, turns [G = continues her parading] and exits.

26. The lady rises and chats with the proprietess. She very much would like to have the autograph of the Author who lives across the street. Madame Melloni, zealous, the woman who can do anything, says quickly, "I'll get it for you; leave everything to me." Telling the lady to wait for her, she dons a large, showy hat, takes the lady's small notebook for the autograph, and goes out. Despite her stoutness, she descends the stairs rapidly.

27. The Author works at his desk. The butler enters to announce a visitor. The Author reads the calling card with amazement and indicates that the woman is to be shown in. Madame Melloni enters ceremoniously with well-simulated embarrassment. She explains her request and hands the Author the notebook. He smiles as he signs his name on a page. She thanks him and prepares to leave when her handbag slips from her hand and photographs of charming young women spill out.

28. Pretending dismay, she bends and collects the photos. Then while rising, she smiles ambiguously. She plays with the photos, fanning them out for the Author's view with the clever wink of an expert manager and procuress. He smilingly studies the photos on display. Suddenly, he is attracted by one of the photos. It is a picture of the young woman met in the deserted alley. He takes it. Yes, it is she, without a doubt.

29. Madame Melloni assumes an air of nonchalance. She senses the possibility of some business [an opportunity for pandering]. "She is a mannequin in my fashion house." To which the Author replies, "I'd like to speak to this girl." A smile filled with hidden understanding is her reply: "I will send her to you immediately."

30. The mannequins' dressing room. The Daughter is in underclothing. Madame Melloni enters, full of hypocritical amiability. She caresses the Daughter's cheek. "A gentlemen 'of a certain age' would like to speak with

you," indicating the house opposite. The Daughter refuses. Melloni's expression hardens. Turning abruptly to a closet, she pulls out a box containing a dress made by the young woman's Mother. She turns back toward the Daughter and says, "I have no further need for your Mother's work. Nor will I pay her for making this dress" [G = another cent for this dress]. And she exits.

31. Saddened, the Daughter continues to dress slowly. Madame Melloni returns and asks heatedly, "Well, will you go or not?" The Daughter nods, apparently acquiescent. Satisfied then, Madame Melloni takes the dress and returns it to the cupboard.

32. The Author's Secretary, carrying the mail, approaches the Author who is seated at his desk. Disturbed in his work, the Author looks at him severely. When he sees the impression his reproof makes on the Secretary, standing there respectfully, devotedly, as if intimidated by the Author's authority, the Author smiles, takes the mail politely and begins to examine it.

33. In the vestibule of Madame Melloni's house, the Daughter, strikingly dressed in that equivocal black, adjusts her hat before a mirror. The mirror clouds over as if some diabolical breath had just blown on the glass. Above this image, the blurred one of an old satyr appears and immediately begins to grin repulsively and obscenely. The Daughter bows her head and covers her forehead with her hand.

34. The Author's house. The Secretary receives the Daughter in the vestibule and escorts her to the study. The Author invites the Daughter to sit on a large leather sofa in front of the table. The Daughter at first is embarrassed. "Are you a dressmaker?" the Author asks. She shakes her head and says, "No, I am a mannequin. But my Mother works for Madame Melloni as a dressmaker."

35. After struggling with her conscience, the Daughter arrives at a resolution. As if following an order, she seats herself seductively on the arm of the couch occupied by the Author, a gesture underscoring her next words with a practical illustration, "We depend entirely upon Madame Melloni."

36. She tries to embrace the Author, but her style shows how completely inept she is in the arts of the courtesan. The Author eludes her attempt to embrace him, rises, and says, "I did not invite you here for that reason." The Daughter's face registers an expression of incredulity and amazement; she replies, "I was sent precisely for this." She turns away to hide a deeply disheartened expression on her features.

37. Moved by the young woman's entire situation, the Author dismisses

her, watching her thoughtfully until she nears the door. Then he rushes to detain her at the threshold, and gazing deeply into her eyes he says, "I could love you like my own creation." The Young Woman fails to understand him and freeing herself slips out hurriedly.

38. The Author remains lost in thought for a moment in the place [at the threshold] where she left him. He reflects intensely. Then he returns slowly to his armchair and sits. The armchair's high back hides him from the spectator's view. Smoke from his cigarette rises, mixing with the mist that once again fills the room. A provocative phantom of the Daughter appears, her outline growing increasingly clear as she approaches the Author's couch and offers herself to him.

39. It is evening. The Author's Secretary appears before the house in the alley where the Daughter lives. He is carrying flowers. He checks the number of the house and then enters.

40. Inside, the Mother and Daughter sit talking [G = and sewing] intently. The Little Girl plays at their feet. The Secretary enters. The Daughter casts a quick, confused glance at the flowers. She waits expectantly and excitedly, but the Secretary turns to the Mother, introduces himself to her, and offers her the flowers saying, "Mr. Pirandello begs you to call on him." He indicates that she is expected and offers to escort her. The Mother demurs nervously. Indicating that she is not dressed for a visit, she goes into the bedroom [I = next room].

41. The Secretary and the Daughter remain alone with the Little Girl. They look at each other awkwardly and then busy themselves playing with the child. It is obvious from the first that they are strongly attracted to one another. The Little Girl reaches for the flowers, playfully pulls one from the bouquet, and lays it in the Daughter's lap. She attempts to replace the flower, but the Secretary asks her to keep it. The Daughter looks at him with profound recognition [G = gratitude]. The two begin chatting animatedly.

42. Escorted by the Secretary, the Mother arrives at the Author's mansion. He invites her to tell him her life story. Recognizing that his interest demonstrates some regard for her daughter, the Mother asks for nothing more than a chance to unburden her heart. "I come from an honorable but poor family. I was married to a rich but eccentric man who lived a strange life amid his books."

43. Close-up of the Mother's head telling the story. Superimposed is an image of the first husband as she remembers him. He is an extremely intellectual type, distinguished and refined, with a tormented expression on his face,

rather like a beethovanesque mask. Seated among his books, he is absorbed in contemplation of a child's skull.

44. Close-up of the Author's head as he listens attentively to the Mother's story. Partial dissolve of the Author's head, which remains perceptible amid the surrounding mist of his phantoms. Superimposed (in montage) is an image of the Mother's first husband as the Author imagines the man according to the story he is hearing: a professorial type without particular distinction, unlike the [I = reality of the] man with the beethovanesque mask that was revealed in the Mother's story. The grinning skull that the professorial man contemplates is that of an adult.

45. The Mother continues with her story. Her lips articulate, "We had a Son . . ." and the image of her beethovanesque husband immediately appears seated at his desk. A child of about three runs to him, disturbing him in his work. Little hands reach for the skull.

46. The scene shifts back to the listening Author's face. Superimposed and obscuring it is a domestic scene evoked by the caption "we had a Son. . . ." The professorial man is seated with the Son on his knees; he twirls the skull between his hands as if it were a globe, running his fingers over the surface planes and hollows, its ridges and curves. In this microcosm he, like a visionary, discovers the face of the world.

47. The Mother's head reappears as she goes on with her story. Superimposed [fading into] the frame is a scene from the actual past: The beethovanesque Father and the Son play ball using the child's skull. The Mother enters; horrified at their game, she snatches the "toy" from her Son. He cries and the Father protests violently [G = indignantly]. Not understanding, the Mother rebukes him. The Father's exasperation grows into fury.

48. Amid this scene, the Father's Secretary comes in with a batch of papers and manuscripts. Dismayed by the scene but respectful and not daring to enter, he remains at the door and casts a pitying glance at the Mother. The sobbing child runs to him. Even the Mother seeks protection at the Secretary's side. The Father turns away furiously and then seats himself again at his desk. The Mother tries gently to take the child from the Secretary. Both bend over the crying boy, trying to comfort him.

49. The Father rises and goes to the group. He scrutinizes the Mother and Secretary with a subtle and penetrating gaze, then smiles mockingly as if to say, I understand you two very well. He brings their heads together as if trying to imagine the couple they would make and takes a cynical pleasure in

their embarrassment. Then he pushes them toward the door, keeping the child near him.

50. Disturbed by the memory, the Mother goes on weakly with her story. "He wanted me to marry the Secretary. He sent my Son to a foster home in the country to keep him away from me." The Author asks, "What became of them?" The Mother replies, "I never learned anything more of them. I don't even know if they are still alive."

51. The Author appears to be entirely caught up in the artistic destinies that the story's figures awaken in his fancy.

52. The Mother concludes her tale: "My second husband died six months ago. Now I live in poverty with the three children from that (second) marriage."

53. A picture of the living room of her poor house appears superimposed above her head in the same frame. She is working at her sewing machine. The Daughter is dressed, ready to leave for work. Under her arm she carries a box (containing a dress) for Madame Melloni. The Daughter embraces her little sister tenderly before leaving. The Young Boy of fourteen is immersed in a book, his tousled head resting in his palms.

54. The Mother and the Author appear in the same frame. She has finished her story. The Author, still under the story's influence, remains thoughtful. Suddenly, he raises his head and asks, "Do you know the kind of work your Daughter does for Madame Melloni?"

55. On seeing the expression on the Author's face as he looks at her, the Mother begins to suspect the kind of services that Madame Melloni exacts from her Daughter. The fearful revelation then strikes her with the overwhelming rapidity and brutality of a thunderbolt; [I = her pulse weakens] she nearly faints; her eyes grow wild.

56. The Author is ever more deeply immersed in the fate of these imaginary characters. "What if your first husband were still alive? And if one day finding himself at Madame Melloni's he meets his stepdaughter without the least suspicion of who she is?"

57. An image of the first husband, the professorial type, now fades in above the Author's head. The husband is seated on a couch much like the one the Author sat on earlier during the Daughter's visit. The Daughter perches seductively on the arm of the couch and begins to caress the first husband with the typical wiles learned by courtesans. And the Stepfather begins to enjoy the pleasures he has bought at Melloni's establishment.

58. The Mother, desperate, hides her face in her hands [I = pushes her hands through her hair], possessed by the thoughts the Author has planted in her mind. The images the Author begins to see taking possession of her superimpose themselves over the Mother's head. But with this difference: now it is the man with the beethovanesque mask who sits on the couch.

59. Utterly overwhelmed, the Mother flees from the house.

60. Moved by a sense of tragedy, the Author watches her leave. The room fills once again with a mist in which a phantom dance of six characters appears: the Daughter, the Mother, the Young Boy of fourteen, the Little Girl, the professorial Father of the Author's imagination, and Madame Melloni. The specters grow to huge, supernatural size. Then during their dance around the Author they diminish in size, bathed in an unreal light, and they group themselves on the Author's hand, which has grown to gigantic proportions. The Author's hand rises, holding the specters, and slowly his hand returns to normal size. Finally, he rests his hand on his brow, letting the six characters enter his forehead.

61. Now the Author's entire head appears, his hand at first hiding his forehead, then slowly coming away from it; then his entire figure appears, leaning against the desk still holding his hand in front of his forehead.

62. The Secretary enters. Recalled to reality, the Author says, "I would like you to take care of the young woman and her family. I am very interested in those people." The Secretary nods his head silently.

63. The Mother is returning to her house. Gripped by anxiety and despair, she rushes through the streets near her house. She thinks she recognizes her Daughter in a streetwalker accosting a man. She pursues the couple through crooked alleys until at last she can prove, to her great relief, that she had been mistaken. Yet, that man in the shadows whom she sees from the back, isn't he her first husband? And the slim elegant youth who meets a man in front of that building, might he not be the son of her first marriage, whom she has not seen since he was a child? Once again she must admit that her senses have deceived her and that the Author's ideas, influencing her own, have launched her on the tracks of phantoms who disturb and terrify her soul.

64. She arrives home. She finds the Daughter sleeping peacefully beside her little sister. In the next room, the Boy of fourteen is still awake. Exhausted and tormented, the Mother sinks onto the couch near the sewing machine.

65. An abrupt movement by the Little Girl arouses the Mother from her torpor and, as if suddenly struck by the conviction that this pure child ought

not rest near an elder sister who lives in sin, she snatches up the sleeping Girl, wraps her in a blanket, and sits with her at some distance from the Daughter.

66. The Daughter rouses herself, but still half-asleep, watches her Mother's movements. Then fully awake, she sits up and with eyes wide with fear, asks her Mother what this means. The Mother turns away to hide her tears at having to explain.

67. In the next room, the Boy stands behind his door listening, his eyes feverish. Meanwhile, the Daughter stands in a dressing gown before the Mother, who hurls accusations at her.

68. A disconcerting doubt takes possession of the listening Boy. His expression conveys pain; he obviously believes the Mother's overheard accusations.

69. The Daughter is desperate. She protests to her Mother and swears by the Holy Virgin that she is mistaken, that someone has slandered her, that she never had succumbed to the infamous proposals of Madame Melloni [to the temptations at Madame Melloni's establishment].[3]

70. These oaths begin to convince the Mother of her Daughter's innocence. The Daughter returns her little sister to bed. Now reconciled with her Mother, she hides her head in her Mother's shoulder. She has been forgiven.

71. The next morning, the Secretary waits on the street for the Daughter until she appears on her way to work. The Author at his window sees the two young people below and frowns. Watching the cheerfulness with which the Daughter greets the Secretary and chats with him, the Author easily could believe that this fallen creature is trying to ensnare the young man. The young people make an appointment for the evening.

72. The Author in his room is again assailed by the figures of his fantasy who are acquiring an ever more intense life and ever more discernible outline.

73. Superimposed over the Author's head, a scene appears in which the Stepfather (the professorial type) in search of adventure [I = inspired by lust] arrives at Madame Melloni's.[4] She, highly expert in these affairs, orders her models to file past him. None please him. Then she brings the Daughter to him. The Stepfather is charmed by her. Madame Melloni, with the flourish of a go-between, conducts them to a private room and closes the door on them.

74. These imaginary visions completely possess the Author. The idea that one day the Stepfather might meet his stepdaughter at Madame Melloni's, unaware of her true identity, so obsesses the Author that he puts on his hat and coat and goes out.

75. He arrives at the Mother's house. At his first words, she vehemently and

indignantly denies his imputation of her Daughter's shame. Although compassionate and humane, the Author is convinced he knows better from his own direct experience of the Young Woman who offered herself to him. He bids the Mother a brusque good-bye.

76. The Mother is assailed by fresh doubts. The Boy, who has heard everything, comes out of the nearby room. He believes everything the Author has said and dashes out of the house.

77. The tormented Mother remains alone. She cannot free herself from the Author's persuasive influence, which has supplanted her own thoughts. She especially is afflicted by his last words before leaving her: "Who knows if your first husband, very much alive, might not find himself at this moment at Madame Melloni's establishment, choosing your Daughter?"

78. Driven by these tormenting thoughts, the Mother rushes to Madame Melloni's. She asks two models where she may find her Daughter; and they, demonstrating with smiles of complicity that they know her well, indicate one of the doors to the private rooms. The Mother means to force her way in, but the models try to restrain her. Attracted by the noise, Madame Melloni enters and there is a violent scene between the two women.[5]

79. Madame Melloni fiercely and energetically tries to prevent the Mother from opening the door to the private room, but the Mother succeeds in exercising all her strength.

80. In the room she sees a man with his back to her and in her agitation she fully believes him to be her first husband. He is stroking the Daughter's hair. The Mother falls upon the couple, crying out wildly as she seizes the man, who turns in amazement. It is the Author himself.

81. Madame Melloni, who has followed the Mother into the room, apologizes profusely to the Author. Revolted by her pandering, he leaves abruptly.[6] Furious at having lost a potentially profitable client, Madame Melloni violently throws out Mother and Daughter.

82. Deprived of their livelihood, threatened with bitter poverty, the two women leave Madame Melloni's place. The Daughter begs her Mother never again to see the Author, who is the direct cause of their misfortune. He has enmeshed them in a web of lies.

83. The Secretary and the Daughter meet at an appointed hour. All the worries and anxieties of the unhappy Daughter leave her as they enter an amusement park and give themselves up to the gaiety and pleasure of the games. The Secretary is exhilarated by the joy radiating from the Daughter and delighted by the openness of her smiles. They are in love.

84. The Author, in search of relief from his obsession with his specters, also had come to the amusement park to distract himself amid the noisy crowd. He sees the young lovers and, disturbed by that unexpected sight, immediately returns home to try to work.

85. Larger than before, more precisely delineated and illuminated by an ever clearer and more realistic light, the phantom forms once again surge around him. He is incapable of writing a single word. The sheets of paper on his desk remain pure white.

86. When the Secretary returns, he finds the Author moody, depressed, gripped by an irritability quick to show itself. He warns the Secretary: that young woman is nothing but a streetwalker who is trying to trap him in her web. He should guard against falling in love with her or taking her seriously.

87. The Secretary is deeply disturbed. He respects the Author, honors his wisdom, and admires his profound insights into human nature. He will write to the Daughter to free himself from the appointment they made for tomorrow. He writes the letter but is unable to send it and destroys the offensive pages [G = ugly copy].

88. The next day, the Daughter waits for the Secretary. He arrives at the appointed time, but the Daughter immediately senses that something has come between them; he has changed. They part quickly. Deeply unhappy, the Daughter returns home. On her entrance, her brother, without a word or a glance in her direction, closes himself in his little room.

89. Misery reigns in the poor household. The Boy goes out into the streets to do whatever he can to earn some money. He takes the Little Girl with him. He reaches the Author's house where he meets the Secretary and asks to be taken to the Author. The Little Girl stays in the garden to play.

90. The Boy waits in the Secretary's room. A drawer of his desk is partly open. A revolver lies on top of a small package. Won over by curiosity, he takes the revolver. At that moment, the Secretary returns to find him and introduce him to the Author. The Boy has no time to return the revolver to the drawer. In a hurry to hide it, he slips it into his pocket.

91. The Author talks to the tormented adolescent. His words are not comforting. In fact, the Author sees only too clearly from the Boy's anxiety that he lacks the fortitude to confront life. Oppressed by this truth, the Author would like to help him. While he tries to think of how to do so, he approaches the window overlooking the garden. He sees the Little Girl standing at the edge of the duck pond. The Little Girl stretching out her arm to catch a duck leans out

175

over the edge of the pool in imminent danger of falling in the water. Alarmed, the Author points out the window until the Boy jumps to his feet, sees at a glance what is happening, and rushes out. He runs to the pond, snatches up his little sister and takes her away. He is extremely disturbed; his soul is in turmoil.

92. The Daughter's family is now in acute need and near starvation. The Boy watches the Daughter preparing to go out. Worried, he asks where she is going. The Daughter has reached a difficult decision: she will return to Madame Melloni to try to effect a reconciliation and obtain work once again for herself and her Mother. Desperately, the Boy tries to restrain her but then gives up the struggle. He remains in an extremely disturbed state.

93. The Daughter approaches Madame Melloni's house and meets the Secretary coming from the opposite direction. At the sight of her beloved, the Daughter nearly faints. He would like an explanation from her since he feels that the Author, having given substance to his imaginary phantoms, has wrongly accused her. He speaks to her so simply and so truthfully that the Daughter recognizes the authenticity of his love. [G = A confession of love bursts from him impetuously. Transported from the depths of infinite sorrow to the highest heaven of joy, the Daughter nestles in his arms.]

94. Freed from a nightmare and transported by joy, the Daughter throws herself in the Secretary's arms. Joined in happiness after the declaration, they return to the Mother's house; but she has just gone out with the Little Girl. While the couple wait for her, the Young Boy crouches on a sofa in his room, his feverish eyes fixed on the door. He opens it without a sound, surprising the two who are lost in a passionate embrace. Overwrought, the Boy retreats to his room. His active imagination leads him to interpret the situation in the light of earlier events; he concludes that his elder sister has brought her dishonor into their very home.

95. The Mother returns with the Little Girl. The radiant lovers tell her about their happiness. The Secretary is asking for the Daughter's hand in marriage when a gunshot rings out from the next room where the Boy has shot and killed himself.

96. Mad with terror, the Secretary rushes back to the Author, who is living with the creatures of his imagination. The Secretary confronts him with news of the tragedy, accusing him. He, the Author, is truly responsible for this horrible misfortune. He is the one who, mixing fantasy with reality, has influenced the destiny of these simple, ordinary people. He is the one who has

provoked an evil which has destroyed his Secretary's greatest happiness, since the tragedy of this hour has separated him from the Daughter forever. The dead Boy will always be between them. He leaves the Author with a curse.

97. The Author remains alone [I = with a heavy heart] in a dark mood and profoundly disturbed. Insistently, larger and clearer, the phantoms form around him. They grow until they tower above the Author, becoming gigantic and filling the room with their enormous shadows; they mock him at every turn while his own person shrinks, assuming a spectral unreality.

98. To flee the six characters who sap his strength and indeed become ever stronger at his expense and beleaguer him from every quarter, the Author rises abruptly [G = covers his eyes]. Reacting in defense, he opens the door violently and chases out the spirits; then he slams the door behind them drawing a deep breath of relief. Utterly exhausted by the encounter, he throws himself onto the sofa in front of his desk.

99. Outside the villa one sees the gigantic ghosts marching around the Author's house, besieging it with growing aggressiveness until at last they penetrate the walls and gain entrance.

100. Inside, the Author is seated in the armchair as at first, bent over a blank pad of white paper, pen in hand, and deeply immersed in thought. He concentrates his faculties to their full extent. The tension of his body reveals the intense workings of his spirit. The six specters, larger than life and wholly distinct, at this moment emerge from the walls into the study. Imperiously, powerfully, they line up at the Author's back. The Author remains in the same tense posture, but his hand now writes firmly in large letters the following words on the page before him: SIX CHARACTERS IN SEARCH OF AN AUTHOR. His hand underlines these letters and adds: A THEATRICAL WORK BY LUIGI PIRANDELLO.

101. The title page fades into a playbill saying, "*Six Characters in Search of an Author.*" It is attached to a pillar at the corner of a busy street. Standing near the pillar is the Daughter, dressed eccentrically [G = like a prostitute].

102. An elegant man in search of adventure notices and stares at her. The Daughter smiles at him, inviting him with a slight movement of her head.

103. Passing nearby, the Secretary recognizes the Daughter. She does not see him since he is hidden behind the pillar. The Secretary observes as the elegant man responds to the Daughter's signal, catches up to her, exchanges a few words with her, then walks along beside her.

104. Profoundly disturbed, the Secretary follows them with his eyes. As he

turns around, the playbill comes to his attention. He lowers his head with an expression of sadness and shame.

105. In the Mother's living room, the Little Girl opens a large package and pulls out a teddy bear. Exclaiming with delight, she runs to her Mother to show her the lovely toy that her sister has sent. The Mother, filled with grief and shame, hides her face in her hands.

106. At this moment, the scene fades into a scene of a stage. *The Author stands in the wings. An actress, playing the Mother's role, is rehearsing with a Little Girl who, radiant with joy, is showing her a huge doll that her sister has sent her. The Mother tries to take it away. The Little Girl stamps her feet, fighting back. At this, the Mother lets her keep the doll, sobbing out between tears, "Oh, the shame, the shame of it." And she hides her face in her hands.*

107. From a small table positioned in the first row of seats, the Director shouts something to the actors on-stage. The rehearsal then is interrupted. The Author comes from the wings, caresses the child on-stage, and that done, speaks to the actress playing the Mother, telling her something about how the scene should be interpreted.

108. A limousine pulls up in front of Madame Melloni's establishment. An elderly gentleman, accompanied by a young woman [the Daughter], steps from the car and enters the house. Madame Melloni receives them with her usual ceremoniousness and leads them to a small private room set aside for the diversions of her special clients.

109. A light meal [G = a platter of hors d'oeuvres] is laid out on a small table set for two. Champagne is cooling in an ice bucket. The Young Woman orders Madame Melloni to show her new collection [G = of hats]: she needs something to wear that evening to the opening of a new work by Pirandello. Solicitously, the procuress rushes off to comply. [G = Madame Melloni showers them with small attentions.] The gentleman pours the champagne; the two toast each other and begin to eat.

110. Fade into the scene developing on-stage. *The "Daughter" is having dinner with her "Stepfather" in a private room at the house of one Madame Pace, similar to the private room at Madame Melloni's. [G = The man wears a mask resembling] The lineaments of the man's face correspond to those of the professorial type in the Author's fantasy of the Mother's first husband. The "Stepfather" and "Daughter" exchange toasts. The Author, wearing a dinner jacket, stands in the wings, intently watching the scene on-stage.*

111. In an orchestra box, the Daughter sits with the elderly gentleman just

seen at Madame Melloni's. She wears a splendid evening gown. With tense concentration she watches the scene on-stage which represents her own life.

112. On-stage: the "Daughter," acting like a bold courtesan, perches on the man's knees. At that moment, the door crashes open and the "Mother" bursts into the room, followed by the procuress [Melloni] trying in vain to restrain the "Mother." The "Daughter" jumps off the man's lap. The "Mother" recognizes her first husband; an expression of sheer madness crosses her face as she shrieks in pain. At the same moment, the man jumps to his feet in amazement as he recognizes his wife.

113. She screams her accusation: "This is my Daughter whom you have bought to satisfy your bestial lust." She pulls her dumbfounded "Daughter" away from her "Husband," then utterly overcome, she drops into her daughter's arms in a faint.

114. The curtain falls.

115. In her box in the audience, the Daughter is stupefied by what she has seen on-stage and watched dully as her escort begins to applaud. Suddenly, her eyes fill with horror and she stares at her escort as if seeing a ghost. His face has metamorphosed into that of the Mother's first husband, the man with the beethovenesque mask. The Daughter leaps from her seat with a shrill cry.

116. The man, again appearing as the elderly aristocrat, looks at her in alarm.

117. People nearby, surprised by the outburst, turn toward the box as they continue to applaud, assuming the disturbance is part of the performance.

118. The gentleman leads the Daughter out of the box while she is screaming, contorted with hysteria.

119. The Author appears in front of the curtain and takes a calm, dignified bow while the audience applauds wildly.

The End

NOTES

1. The sense of the passage is that black may be a sign either of mourning or of a demimondaine. In both Italian manuscripts, the pejorative *equivoco* (of uncertain character) may refer to the costume or the person.

2. Manuscripts do not always indicate whether dialogue is to be rendered by captions.

3. In the Italian 1982 manuscript, responsibility for her temptation falls on the girl rather than the procuress.

4. The Italian *aventura* is close to chance or happenstance; therefore, the passage refers to someone ready for whatever comes along, rather than someone driven by lust. The 1982 Italian text often chooses an emotional term, where the later one substitutes a neutral description.

The *Treatment*

for *Six Characters*

LUIGI PIRANDELLO
& SAUL C. COLIN

Located in the Reinhardt archives, Theatersammlung der Österreichischen National-bibliothek in Vienna. Written in 1935 in English with the collaboration of Saul Colin, Pirandello's English-language secretary, and brought to New York by Piran-dello for Max Reinhardt. First published by A. Illiano and G. Bussino, "Pirandello: Progetti filmici sui Sei personaggi," Forum Italicum 16 (1982): 119–46.

A famous author, sitting at his desk. In the study there are six high-backed Gothic chairs. It is already night; the author's secretary [in the adjoining room] looks at the clock, noticing with anxiety the passage of time. He has been invited to a dinner with the author. Finally, the author, followed by a cloud of smoke, enters [this room], and hands a manu-script to the secretary, who reminds him of their dinner engagement. They hastily leave the house.

Two o'clock in the morning. The author and the secretary are leaving the home of their host.

The secretary is about to call a taxi, but the author expresses a desire to walk, and bids good night to the secretary, who lives nearby. The author looks at his watch, notices the lateness of the hour, and decides to take a short-cut.

He chooses a little street which is dimly lit by a lamp-post, and notices a young girl, dressed in black, standing under the lamp-post. She looks at him invitingly, but the author proceeds on his way. He passes a shabby house, in front of which an elderly, dolorous woman in mourning clothes is apparently waiting. The author conceals himself behind a tree and sees the girl rush to the woman, evidently her mother, and throw her arms about her. They both enter the house. The author moves close to the house so that he can peek through the windows. He observes a poorly furnished room, a bed and a chair. The room is lit by a light from the other room, the door between the rooms being open. In a chair in the first room, there is a pale adolescent, the brother of the young girl, who jumps up when he hears the door opened, and says, "Mother." The mother leaves the girl, goes to the boy, gently tells him to go to bed, and shuts the door, leaving the room in darkness. The other room, which is very small, contains only two beds and a sewing machine. A little blond girl, about five years old, evidently another daughter, is asleep in one of the beds. The girl empties her purse on the table; the mother takes the money and places it in a drawer as the girl watches her in despair.

The author leaves the narrow street, and continues his way on a boulevard leading to his villa. He is pursued by visions of the scene he has just witnessed, and in the middle of the wide boulevard, he sees, superimposed, the narrow street with the lamp-post, the girl, the mother, and the house. This image is repeated with his every step.

The author arrives in front of his villa. He sees his own long shadow on the pavement. His shadow is now thrown on the house, and momentarily takes the form of the girl. Image of the entrance to his villa and the garden with a large fountain. The author enters the garden.

The next morning, at 11 o'clock. The same image of the villa and the garden in full light.

An elegant automobile stops in front of the villa. A chauffeur opens the door of the automobile; a very distinguished woman steps out and rings the bell of the house. The butler opens the door, and the woman inquires about Madame Melloni. The butler points out a sign on the opposite side of the street, reading, "Madame Melloni, Robes et Manteaux." The lady sees on the door a little plaque with the name of the author. She asks him if this is the celebrated author, and whether she can have an autograph. The butler, refusing a tip, tells her that she will have to use her own initiative in getting the autograph. She nods with dignity and, asking her chauffeur to wait for her, crosses the street.

A fashionable dressmaker's apartment, several rooms, and an enormous sitting room where the lady is introduced. Several ladies are seated in this sitting room. Beautiful mannequins are going in and out. Several of them are parading on a little dais. One of the mannequins is the girl whom the author saw the night before under the lamp-post. Madame Melloni enters to greet the

lady. She is a plump matron, half Italian, half Spanish, loquacious and ges-
ticulating. She sits beside the lady and loudly reprimands the girl for not
modelling with enough chic. The girl is hurt; she makes another turn and
leaves the room. The lady tells Madame Melloni of her experience at the
author's house, and tells her that she must have an autograph. Madame
Melloni, an adventurous woman, puts on a large, colorful hat, and goes to the
author's house.

The author is sitting at his desk. He is greatly astonished when the secretary gives him Madame Melloni's card. He receives her very courteously and
writes his autograph in the booklet which she offers. Madame Melloni, thank-
ful, is about to leave, but drops her purse on purpose. Numerous photographs
of beautiful girls are strewn on the floor. She pretends to be very shocked,
hurriedly picks them up and contrives to display them in a fanlike arrangement. The author, looking at the pictures, recognizes one of them as the girl he
saw the night before. He picks it out, and Madame Melloni explains that she is
one of her mannequins. The author asks if he can see her. Madame Melloni
senses business, and promises to send her at once.

She returns to her apartment, and gives the lady the booklet with the
author's autograph.

She then speaks to the girl with exceedingly sweet and hypocritical polite-
ness.

In her office, she explains to the girl that an elderly man across the street
wants to see her immediately. The young girl, a beginner in the house, refuses
to go. Madame Melloni, after much argument, discharges her and tells her
that the last dress made by her mother is not going to be accepted. Faced with
this threat, the girl decides to go see the author.

The author's desk. The secretary enters with a stack of mail. The author not
wishing to be disturbed, makes an impatient gesture, but when he notices the
expression of hurt [on the secretary's face], he decides to sign the papers.

The author's house. The secretary and the girl are apparently attracted to
each other upon meeting. He shows her into the author's study.

The author offers her a big chair, and the secretary leaves the room. The
author asks her if she is a couturière. She explains that she is a mannequin,
but that her mother sews for Madame Melloni. Suddenly, the girl forces
herself to get up and sit down on the arm of the author's chair, saying that her
family depends on Madame Melloni. Her actions are very awkward. He asks
her whether she was sent for this express purpose, and the girl says that that

was Madame Melloni's intention. The author is shocked and disgusted, and asks her to leave the house.

He watches her leave, and his look seems to follow her through the walls.

He resumes his seat, and only the back of the chair is now visible.

Suddenly, a form resembling the girl's appears in one of the Gothic chairs; the form is similar, but the bearing is entirely different.

The author turns in his seat in an attempt to avoid the vision, but no matter which way he looks, the image is before him, and he also visualizes a new image of the girl's mother, her brother, her little sister and a more eccentric Madame Melloni.

A few days later, the secretary goes to the mother's home with a bunch of flowers in his hand. Before entering, he carefully checks the number of the house.

The mother and the girl are busy sewing. The little sister is playing. The girl is startled by the appearance of the secretary, and looks hopefully at the flowers, but the secretary offers them to the mother and tells her that the author wishes to speak to her immediately, if possible. The mother is greatly perturbed, and leaves the room to change her dress. The little sister, playing with the flowers, offers one to the girl, but she does not feel free to accept it. She takes the flower only when the secretary nods to indicate that it is all right for her to take it, and she is grateful.

The mother and the secretary arrive at the author's home. The mother sits in one of the Gothic chairs in the author's study. The author tries to find out about her past. She tells him that she was married to a very wealthy, but eccentric and intellectual man about twenty-five years ago. They had a son. (During the time she is relating her story, the image of her first husband, as she knew him, appears in one of the Gothic chairs, and, behind the chair, that of the husband, as the author imagines him.) One day the mother returned to her home and found the young son in the father's study, playing with a human skull. She was horrified, and tried to take the son away. An argument ensued between the husband and the mother. The husband's secretary interfered sympathetically. The intervention of the secretary led the father to believe that the mother was in love with the secretary. He decided that they had to marry, and arranged for both of them to leave for another city. The mother never saw her first husband and their son again. She had three children by her second husband. They always led a very modest existence, and, a few months ago, she became a widow. Their only source of income is

Madame Melloni. Suddenly, the author asks her if she knows what kind of woman Madame Melloni is. The mother, realizing what he means, is greatly upset. The author suggests the possibility of her first husband who might be alive, visiting the house of Madame Melloni, and meeting the girl without knowing who she is. Terrified, the mother runs out.

The author remains alone. The Gothic chairs are occupied by the same characters, but as the author begins to conceive them.

The secretary knocks on the door, enters the room, and the author tells him to take care of that family. He says that he is very interested in all those poor creatures.

The mother, going home. It is already night. She seems to see her daughter in every girl she passes on the street. In a couple passing by, she seems to see her first husband walking with her daughter.

She arrives home exhausted, and sees the girl asleep in bed with the little sister. The young boy is reading in the next room. She is struck with the thought that the little sister, who is so innocent, is lying near the girl, who is no longer pure. The mother lifts the little sister out of bed to put her in the next bed, and while doing so awakens the girl, who looks about to see what is happening. She understands, and exclaims, "Mother, mother it isn't true!" The young boy listens, horrified and suffering intensely. Finally, the mother becomes convinced of her daughter's innocence, and they all go to sleep.

The next morning. The secretary is waiting for the girl in front of Madame Melloni's house.

The author watches the scene from his window.

The secretary speaks with the girl. They both seem embarrassed. They make an appointment for that evening.

The author, disturbed by the thought of the girl remaining in Madame Melloni's house for another day, decides to see the mother again. He goes to the mother's home.

The mother is very rude to him, and tells him that she does not understand why he tries to put false ideas in her head, and that she is convinced of her daughter's innocence. The author insists that there is the possibility of a visit from her first husband to Madame Melloni's house, and tells her that the girl came to his very own study with less than honorable intentions, but, of course, at the insistence of Madame Melloni.

The young boy hears the conversation, and runs out of the house. The author says that something has to be done, and leaves the mother to her anxiety.

The same day. The author goes to Madame Melloni's house.

Meanwhile, the mother, tormented, runs to Madame Melloni's house, enters the apartment breathlessly, and, from behind a sofa, sees her daughter sitting with a man whom she imagines to be her first husband. She runs toward the sofa, and recognizes the author. Madame Melloni enters hurriedly and apologizes to the author, who is very much disgusted by the intervention of the Madame.

He leaves the house.

Madame Melloni, furious, discharges the girl, exclaiming that never had such an incident occurred in her house.

The daughter and mother go home, and the daughter begs the mother not to see the author again, as he is the cause of all their trouble.

That same evening, the secretary meets the girl, and they go to an amusement park where they are seen by the author, who goes there to find some relaxation and to forget his obsession with the characters. He sees in the girl's eyes that she has forgotten the miserable incidents of the day.

Early the next morning, the secretary finds the author at his desk with a blank sheet of paper before him. The author, who fears the consequences of a continued friendship between the secretary and the girl, tries to convince the secretary that the girl is not good for him. Besides, he fears the consequences of a tragedy which he foresees [occurring both] among the real characters and [among] the characters he is conceiving. The author decides to have nothing more to do with them.

The next morning, the secretary meets the girl. He had been unable to complete a letter which he had started to write to her, but the girl feels that something has changed in him.

She returns to her home, terribly unhappy.

The young boy goes out to try to earn some money by selling newspapers or something else. He has taken his little sister with him.

Near the author's house, on the street, they meet the secretary.

Suddenly, the boy gets the idea to see the author.

The little sister remains in the garden, playing near the fountain.

The boy waits in the secretary's room.

He sees an open drawer containing a revolver and papers. It is the first time he has held a revolver, so he goes near the window to examine it closely. The secretary is about to enter; the boy does not have time to return the revolver to the drawer, and puts it in his pocket.

He is shown into the author's study. The author, in spite of his former decision, talks with the boy and tries to calm his tormented young soul, but he finds that the boy does not have the necessary force of character to face life.

Looking out of the window, he sees the little girl leaning over the pond around the fountain, and playing with the little ducks. It occurs to him that a slight loss of balance could cause the little girl to drown.

The boy comes to the window, sees the precarious position of his sister, becomes frightened, runs out and takes her home.

Misery at [their] home is increasing every day. The girl decides to return to Madame Melloni, the only way she can see out of their misery. The young boy, sensing this, tries to restrain her, but she leaves.

The mother is in the park with the little girl.

The boy is alone in his room.

The girl meets the secretary on the street. She sees him with mixed joy and sadness, and he is greatly distressed to see her looking so unhappy. They walk through the park. They discover in each other their real sentiments. The secretary tries to explain how the author feels about them: that the author's intentions are not bad, but that he is carried away by the force of his imagination. The girl, profoundly happy, goes home with the secretary to tell her mother of her love for him, but the mother is out with the little girl.

The boy, feverish, thinks that the girl has brought her shame to their own home.

The mother comes in and listens to the girl's explanation.

Suddenly, they hear a shot. The boy has killed himself in the next room.

Horrified, the secretary runs to the author's house.

The author is in his study. He is tormented by the magnified image of his characters in their Gothic chairs, who sometimes take on such immense proportions that they seem to occupy the entire room, and sometimes to encircle the whole house.

The secretary runs in and relates everything that occurred, and blames the author for all that has happened.

After the secretary leaves, the author remains in his chair, limp and livid. Suddenly, he writes down, on a blank sheet of paper, "Six Characters in Search of an Author."

Some time later, the same title is seen on an advertising poster on a wall.

The girl, elegantly dressed, reads the poster. An elderly man, well-dressed, passes by. The girl looks significantly at him, and he stops to speak with her.

The secretary, behind a tree, watches the scene with horror.

The girl and the man leave arm in arm.

The mother's room. Everything is neat and clean. A delivery boy comes in with a package. It is a large teddy bear for the little girl from her sister.

* * *

The theatre where the play is being rehearsed.

The author is watching the rehearsal.

The actress playing the part of the mother is on the stage with [the little actress playing the part of] the little daughter who, exultant with joy, shows her a beautiful doll received from her sister. The actress [playing the part of the mother] seizes the doll and throws it across the stage, crying "Shame!" At the end of the rehearsal, the author gives some instructions to the cast and caresses the head of the little girl.

The next day, the cast has to rehearse the scene of the young boy's suicide.

The mother comes to the theatre to apply for a position as usherette. She has a letter of introduction from one of her daughter's friends. She has to wait for the manager who is busy. But, she does not know whose play is in rehearsal. She is sitting in a box in the empty theatre. At the climax of the scene (the actress playing the mother, the little actress playing the little girl, and the actor playing the secretary – all on the stage), the mother runs hysterically in front of the stage and tries to stop the rehearsal. At the sight of the mother's despair, everyone is breathless. And, when the mother discovers the author, she runs towards him, screaming, "Do you want to kill my little girl, too?" The author is profoundly touched.

The author's study. He is at his desk, a broken man. Suddenly, he sees in the high-backed Gothic chair the image of a dead little girl, and he decides to stop the play.

The manager of the theatre cannot understand the author's decision. He explains to the author that he is haunted by six characters resembling the author's characters, and that he is sure he cannot escape them.

The next day, the manager, confronted with possible money losses if the show should close, and harassed by the six characters, is taken ill, and the author decides to continue with the rehearsals himself.

A few days before the opening.

The mother's first husband, discovered by the secretary, and informed by him of the whole situation, comes to see the author. This is material proof that the author has foreseen the events. He wants to help the mother. He suggests that he (the first husband) take the little girl and look after her.

A pathetic scene [ensues] between the mother and her first husband. Finally, she agrees to put her daughter in a very exclusive girls' school.

The next day, the little girl is found drowned by accident in the pond.

The mother's despair is profound. She is probably going to live with her first husband and their twenty-five year old son, whom she hasn't seen since her second marriage.

The front of Madame Melloni's house.

The girl steps out of a limousine with an elderly man. Madame Melloni receives them with much curtseying. The girl wishes to choose a gown for the opening of the play that night. After choosing a gown, she and the man are having champagne in an adjoining room.

The theatre is crowded. The author cannot escape his characters, and the poor mother's family cannot escape its fate.

The author, backstage, is nervous.

We see the actress playing the part of the girl, seated on a sofa with a man who is [the actor portraying] the mother's first husband. She does not know who he is. She has the manner of the perfect courtesan. Suddenly, the door is opened, and the actress playing the part of the mother rushes in, followed by the actress playing the part of Madame Melloni. It is a very pathetic scene when (on the stage) the mother recognizes her first husband, and the man recognizes his former wife.

A box in the theatre.

The girl, elegantly dressed, is in the box with the elderly man.

When the curtain drops on the preceding scene, the girl begins to realize that the man in the box with her may be her mother's first husband. She screams and suffers a nervous collapse.

[The people in] the audience, some of whom are looking toward the box, applaud the play enthusiastically, thinking that this is a part of the plot.

The man in the box carries the girl outside.

Just then, the author appears on the stage, bowing to the audience, and watching the man carry the girl out.

Letter

Max Reinhardt & Joseph von Sternberg
to Saul C. Colin

This letter was written 11 February 1940 (translated in chapter 6). The original is located in the Reinhardt archive, Theatersammlung der Österreichischen National-bibliothek in Vienna; copied to the Reinhardt archive at SUNY Binghamton; first published in Max Reinhardt in Amerika, *edited by Edda Fuhrich-Leisler and Gisela Prossnitz (Salzburg and Vienna: Otto Muller, 1976), 241–44.*

den 25. November 1940.

Dr. Saul Colin,
30 Rockefeller Plaza,
New York City, N.Y.

Mein lieber Doktor Colin:

Ich habe Ihren Brief v.15. November und den ihm beigefuegten Kontrekt er-halten. Es hat beklagenswert lange gedauert. Die ersten Anfragen in dieser Angelegenheit wurden Ende August an Sie gerichtet. Ihre prinzipielle Zusage ist vom 3.Oktober datiert. Jetzt sind wir bereits Ende November. Trotzdem waere es heute noch Zeit, unseren Plan auszufuehren und sofort mit der Arbeit zu beginnen, wenn wir, wie ich *hoffte*, wirklich einen Kontrakt in Haenden haetten. Es ist aber nur ein "tentative contract", den Sie einsenden, und Sie erwaehnen in Ihrem Begleitbrief, dass Sie die Signatur der Erben Pirandellos einzuholen haben. Es erscheint mir klar, dass in diesem Umstande die eigentliche Ursache der unerfreulichen und leider bedenklichen Verzoe-gerung liegt. Es ist jedoch ebenso klar, dass wir vor dem endgueltigen und rechtsgueltigen Abschluss des Vertrages weder mit der kuenstlerischen Arbeit

191

noch mit den komplizierten technischen, organisatorischen und finanziellen Vorbereitungen beginnen koennen. Ich fuege hier eine Feststellung ein, in der Joseph von Sternberg selbst woertlich seinen Standpunkt formuliert und ich werde infolgedessen dieses Schreiben auch von ihm unterzeichnen lassen, damit wenigstens Sie Ihrerseits einer vollkommen geklaerten Situation gegenueberstehen.

"Nach Erwerb der Rechte zur Verfilmung des Stoffes "6 Personen suchen einen Autor" wird sofort fuer eine Gesellschaftsgruendung zur filmischen Horstellung gesetzlich eingereicht. Zur selben Zeit werden die praktischen Vorbereitungen zur Verfilmung getroffen. Die Hegie, Photographie und gesellschaftliche Leitung wird von Professor Reinhardt und Joseph von Sternberg ohne sofortiges Entgeld zur Verfuegung gestellt. Auch die Schauspieler werden auf der Basis von Beteiligung oder Minimumgagen von dem Reinhardtschen Ensemble beigestellt. Die Rechte zur Verfilmung, die uebrigens ein Jahr nach Herstellung des Experimentes wieder von Dr. Colin anderweitig verkauft werden koennen, werden mit 10% der gesamten Einnahmen unserer Gesellschaft, die mit dem Erwerb dieses Werkes gegruendet werden soll, entgeltet. Die Summe, die durch die 10%iger Beteiligung erreicht wird, ist in dem Verhaeltnis zu den anderen Beteiligungen eine ziemlich grosse. Nach Verfilmung, und nicht vorher, ist es gedacht, die fertige Arbeit durch ueblische Verleihgesellschaften vertreiben zu lassen. Die Verleihgesellschaft muss dann die Kosten der Kopien und Reklame uebernehmen, welche Kosten gewoehnlich eine Hoehe von $ 100.000.00 (hunderttausend Dollar) betragen. Jede Einnahme unserer Gruppe wird nach Zurueckzahlung der kleinen Barvorschuesse dazu verwendet, um gleichzeitig jeden Beteiligten zufrieden zu stellen, sodass die Filmrechte zur selben Zeit wie jede andere Beteiligung zur Auszahlung gebracht werden. Die bevorzugte Rueckzahlung der kleinen Barvorschuesse ist notwendig, da man sonst das Geld mit 50%iger Beteiligung aufnahmen muesste – , es aber geplant ist, das Geld zu keinerlei Profitwichtigkeit werden zu lassen, eine Tatsache, die im Interesse aller Beteiligten ist. Wir verpflichten uns, innerhalb von 6 Monaten (sechs Monaten) nach Erwerb der Rechte in Produktion zu gehen."

Diese Stipulationen entsprechen, wie Sie wissen, unserem bisherigen Briefwechsel, sie sind fair, sachlich begruendet, und zweiffellos im Interesse aller Beteiligten, also auch im Interesse der Erben Pirandellos. Sie haben sich inzwischen ueberzeugt, dass kein anderes Angebot vorliegt und dass keine der Filmfabriken gerade dieses Experiment wagen wird, wagen will und wagen kann. Abgesehen von der allgemeinen Depression und Unsicherheit, von der beaengstigenden Zusammenschrumpfung des Absatzgebietes sind es die enormen Overheads und die zeitgemaesse Vorsicht des Kapitals, die kuenstlerische Experimente heute noch mehr als vorher ausschalten. Der Vertrag sichert Ihnen ueberdies das Recht, eine eventuell bessere Zeit zu nuetzen und ein etwaiges Angebot der grossen Studios anzunehmen, wozu unser Experiment nur den Weg ebenen kann. Ich persoenlich glaube mit Sternberg, dass Experimente, die sich wie das unsere auf gerechter Gewinnbeteiligung aller Mitwirkenden aufbauen, die [nächste] Zukunft gehoert. Sie sind im Akkord mit dem unaufhaltsam fortschreitenden sozialen Umbau der Weltwirtschaft und sie werden reinere Werte beguenstigen, als sie aus den Kanaelen fliessen koennen, die zwischen Wallstreet und Hollywood liegen.

Nur Eines will ich gleich vorausschicken: wenn das Einverstaendnis der Erben *nicht*, wie Sie ankuendigen, in allerkuerzester Zeit (durch Kabel) erzielt werden kann, halte ich die Angelegenheit fuer negativ entschieden. Sie wissen, wie sehr im Theaterleben der Augenblick regiert. Und der Film ist ja nur ein allerdings maechtiger Ast am uralten Stamm. Was heute noch erwuenscht und moeglich ist, kann morgen durch einen politischen, wirtschaftlichen, kulturellen Windstoss fuer immer verweht sein, sogar in den Absichten des Kuenstlers, der doch ein besonders empfindliches Instrument seiner Zeit ist. Unsere Tage beschenken uns so ueberreichlich mit Umwaelzungen, die das Antlitz der Erde veraendern, dass ich nicht mehr darueber zu sagen brauche.

Der Zufall einer gelungenen Studentenauffuehrung hat einen der hervorragendsten Kuenstler des Screens (es gibt nur wenige) zu dem Plan angeregt. Sternberg ist ein Maler in der engsten und weitesten Bedeutung des Wortes und er ist im Medium des Films geboren. Er ist ueberzeugt, und mit ihm ich, dass die Leinwand eine augenfaelligere Scheidung zwischen wirklicher und erdichteter Welt ermoeglicht, und dass die Nahaufnahme die seelischen und geistigen Vorgaenge dominieren laesst, waehrend sie die oft ablenkende Umwelt nach Wunsch einfach ausschaltet. Damit koennen dem Werk neue und entscheidende Werte gewonnen werden.

Dass ich als eingeborener Theatermann die Buehnenatmosphaere des Steuckes und die Schauspieler dirigieren kann, hat sich in zahllosen Auffuehrungen bewiesen. Wir haben ferner eine Cast der besten jungen Kraefte des amerikanischen Theaters, die alle aus meiner Schule stammen, die ihre Studien bereits absolviert haben und reife Schauspieler sind. Mehrere sind durch

Vertraege mit den hiesigen Studios gebunden. Auch deshalb ist das Zeitelement ein ausschlaggebendes Problem.

Kurz: alle Bedingungen versprechen ein Gelingen das Experimentes und ich st[e]lle sie nicht noch einmal zusammen, um Sie zu ueberzeugen, woran ich nicht im geringsten zweifle –, sondern nur, um Ihnen das Material fuer Ihre Mitteilungen an die Erben des Dichters zu geben, was Ihnen vielleicht erwuenscht sein mag. Die begeisterte Hingabe aller Mitwirkenden, die gewoehnlich schwer waechst in den Hoefen dieser sonnigen Fabrikstadt, und das leicht zu ermessende Faktum, was der Ausgang des Experimentes fuer Sternberg und mich bedeutet, bieten eine gewichtigere Garantie als sie irgendein Producer in diesem Fall leisten kann, auch wenn ihm noch so viele Nullen anhaengen.

Zum Schluss noch ein Wort ueber das Treatment. Die Skizze, die Sie mit Pirandello entworfen haben, ist dichterisch wertvoll und artistisch ungemein interessant. Sie fuehrt aber noch tiefer und einseitiger in den komplizierten Schaffensprozess des Autors und entfernt das Werk noch weiter von der allgemeine verstaendlichen Wirklichkeit. Wir sollten in keinem Fall das Theatermilieu verlassen, dessen romantische und komische Wirkungen zuverlaessig erprobt sind. Wir muessen mit dem breiten Publikum rechnen und duerfen dem Experiment nicht auch noch die vorhandenen Stuetzen nehmen, die das Stueck bisher ueberall getragen haben.

Die einzelne wesentliche Aenderung (jede Kunstform bedingt gewisse adaequate Umformungen), die ich fuer wuenschenswert halte, ist die Ausschaltung des dreifachen Incests. Er ist ohnehin nur in der Andeutung vorhanden, aber die verhaeltnismaessig Wenigan, die ihn verstehen, sind meistons chokiert und die vielen Anderen sind verwirrt. Beides ist ueberfluessig, abtraeglich und leicht zu vermeiden. Es bleibt immer noch genug Dunkles, Gewagtes, Abgruendiges, das nicht zu entbehren ist und das die Kompensation der Komik erfordert.

Sternberg ist, wie ich bereits betont habe, ueberhaupt prinzipiell gegen jede einschneidende Aenderung, was aus der Opposition gegen die landlaeufigan Rezepte leicht verstaendlich ist. Ich bin weniger paepstlich, weil ich als Theatremann weiss dass die Bearbeitung von Stuecken zu allen Zeiten ein legitimer Bestandteil des lebendigen Theaters war und ist und dass wir diesen fortlaufenden Erneuerungen die staerksten Werte zu danken haben. Doch in diesen hiesigen Sudelkuechen ist Sternbergs Prinzip ein Gluecksfall ohne Analogie und von verheissungsvoller Vorbedeutung.

Letter from Max Reinhardt and Joseph von Sternberg

Darf ich erwerten, dass Sie die Ausfuehrlichkeit dieses Schreibens mit der Freundlichkeit erwidern, sofort zu antworten und uns nicht laenger auf Entscheidung warten zu lassen, die wir schon allzulange erhoffen und die so Wesentliches fuer uns alle entscheidet.

Mit herzlichen Gruessen

Joseph von Sternberg / Max Reinhardt.

Will Talkies Abolish the Theater?

("Se il film parlante abolirà il teatro?")

LUIGI PIRANDELLO
Translated by Nina daVinci Nichols

Corriere della Sera, 16 June 1929, and the Anglo American Newspaper Service of London and New York. Reprinted in Saggi, poesie, scritti varii, *edited by Manlio Lo Vecchio Musti (Milan: Mondadori, 1973); and* Pirandello e il cinema *by Francesco Callari.*

Anyone who has heard me talk about my travels knows how much I admire America and how well I like Americans. What interests me above all else about America is the creation there of new forms of life. Pressured by natural and social needs, life there succeeds in seeking and finding new forms. To see them being born gives the spirit an incomparable delight.

In Europe, the dead go on shaping life, crushing it with a weight of history, tradition, and custom. The stability of old forms obstructs, hinders, or arrests all vital motion. In America, to the contrary, life belongs to the living. Still, whereas life means constant motion, it must compose itself in forms. Because the two conditions are opposed, life is neither perpetual motion nor eternal consistency. Just consider: if life were in perpetual flux it would lack all consistency, while if it remained eternally consistent, it would be motionless.

Whereas life in Europe suffers from the excessive stability of its old forms, perhaps life in America suffers from an excessive mobility that prevents enduring forms. As a result, in response to an American gentleman who boasted to me, "We have no past, we thrust ourselves completely into the future!" I was able to say, "One sees, dear sir, that you rush to make yourselves a past." While forms remain alive and full of their own vitality, they represent a triumph of the spirit. To destroy them in their living state for the sole pleasure of replacing them is a crime equivalent to subjugating the soul. Certain original, almost natural forms expressing the spirit cannot be supplanted precisely because they express the nature of life itself. It is impossible, therefore, for such forms to age, and they cannot be replaced without threat to a natural expression of life. One such form is the theater.

My friend Evreinov, author of a play that was highly praised by Americans, says in one of his books that ultimately the whole world is theater. Not only do all human beings act out roles, whether assumed or assigned to them, but all animals act out roles too, as do plants, and in short, as does all of nature.

Perhaps this goes a little too far. Nonetheless, it is completely and utterly undeniable that theater, quite apart from its traditional literary form, is a natural expression of life. Yet in today's climate of universal infatuation with talkies, I have heard the heretical idea that talkies will abolish theater; that in two or three years time theater will cease to exist; that all theaters and music halls will be closed down because dramas and musicals will become either talking or musical films. Something similar was said by an American with that cheerful arrogance which comes naturally to them – even when Americans seem heretical, one listens sympathetically to what they say because their huge pride is genuine. It has the grace of an elephant whose little eyes laugh while its trunk swings around playfully; but beware it doesn't hit you! When the same heresy is repeated by a European, as I have heard it repeated, an enormous pride having lost its genuine grace becomes merely stupid and clumsy. Diabolically keen little eyes no longer laugh; you stand before eyes veiled with weariness. They are not shining with pride; they have dilated with fear. And that powerful and menacing joke of a trunk shrinks to the ridiculous size of a donkey's tail twitching to chase away flies or other nuisances and bothers.

Because they truly are worried and extremely frightened by this devilish talking machine, tycoons of the European film industry are like old fish who have agitated their fins and their tails too long in stagnant, marshy waters. They let themselves be caught by a fishhook and remain open-mouthed as if they are defenseless.

Meanwhile, both classical theater and the music hall can rest easy in the certainty that they will not be abolished for one simple reason. Theater is not trying to become cinema; cinema is trying to become theater. The greatest success to which film can aspire, one moving it even farther along the road toward theater, will be to become theater's photographic and mechanical copy, and a bad one at that. Like all copies, it must arouse a desire for the original.

Cinema's fundamental mistake from the beginning was to set off on the wrong and inappropriate road of literature, whether fiction or drama. Once on that road, cinema inevitably found itself in a double bind, that is,

1. in the impossibility of replacing words;

2. in the impossibility of doing without words.

And found itself with twin defects:

1. an intrinsic inability to find its own expression free of words, whether articulated or implied;

2. and a defect *as* literature which, reduced to a solely visual dimension, must inevitably diminish in spiritual values. These depend for their fullest expression on literature's own complex and proper medium of language.

Now, supplying cinema with mechanical words does not remedy the fundamental error; instead of curing, it aggravates the illness by pushing cinema even closer toward literature. Cinema is the silent expression of images and a language of appearances. By imposing words mechanically in an effort to become an exact, photographic copy of theater, film begins its own irreparable destruction. The copy necessarily will be bad since it has lost theater's illusion of reality, and for the following reasons:

1. because in theater a voice is produced by a live actor speaking, whereas on film it is produced only by photographic images of an actor.

2. because film images cannot speak; if they do, one only realizes that the tonalities and shadings of a live voice are irrecoverable. A speaking image disturbs us as something unnatural, and results in our denunciation of the mechanism;

3. because images are seen to move about in places that the film represents: a house, a motorboat, a forest, a mountain, a street, naturally always outside the film's projection room. The voice, nevertheless, sounds inside the room, as a result creating an unpleasant or unreal effect on anyone trying to remedy or lessen the evil by isolating the talking images, one at a time, and placing them on a primary level of perception. As one fine result, the effect of the picture is lost. The succession of talking images on the screen tires the eyes and detracts from the power of a dialogic scene. Ultimately, there also is a penalty to be

paid for the fact that on a primary level of perception, those huge images of lips are moving in a void; a voice is issuing not from a mouth but grotesquely from a machine. The voice is mechanical: a machine-made and inhuman voice, a slovenly mumbling of ventriloquism accompanied by the intolerable buzzing and hissing of gramophones. Even when technical progress succeeds in eliminating that hissing and achieves a perfect reproduction of the human voice, the chief trouble will in no way be remedied, obviously, since images remain images and cannot speak.

Achieving perfection on this road cannot lead cinema to abolish the theater, although it might abolish itself. The theater will retain its original vitality and, as with every living thing, might alter with time. A copy may come along, stereotypical, fundamentally illogical and unnatural to the very degree it seeks to challenge and replace theater's originality.

The same ridiculous misadventure is befalling cinema that befell the vain peacock in one of Aesop's most famous fables. While being flattered ironically by the diabolical fox for his magnificent tail and the majesty of his regal carriage, the peacock opened his mouth to make his voice audible and made everyone laugh.

So long as it remained a silent expression of images understandable to all, with a few brief captions easily translatable into all languages, then cinema with its huge international dissemination and its popularity with a vast general public offered a substantial threat to theater, recently a very serious threat. Certain directoral abuses tried to make theater primarily a visual spectacle, definitely tried to make it imitate cinematic techniques and processes. Several directors already have tested ways of darkening a stage gradually and letting another scene, accompanied by music, emerge from the blackout. Some directors have chosen a new repertory of lighter, less substantial plays that lend themselves easily to special stage effects, sudden changes of scene, and to devices especially created for a visual impact. These were signs of how greatly theater feared the popularity of cinema. The great danger to theater, however, lay precisely in such attempts to resemble cinema. And now, in reverse, cinema is trying to become theater. So theater has nothing more to fear. If I see nothing in cinema except an ugly reproduction of theater, and if I must listen to photographic images of actors speaking incongruously through the mechanically transmitted voice of a machine, then I prefer to go to the theater where at least there are real actors speaking with natural voices. A talking film that aspires to replace theater completely can only make me regret the absence of live actors before me playing tragedy or comedy, and regret their substitution by mechanical, photographic copies.

Far from harming theater, sound film will help theater because using language will, inexorably, erode cinema's internationalism. All people have eyes to see, but each people has its own language. Every film, therefore, will need to be distributed in differing editions from country to country, though all will not have markets able to bear the cost of a special edition. Moreover, even if translations of one edition could be based on plot summaries, all versions could not use the original dialogue since actors hardly can speak in all languages. So film will lose its international market. Nor can talking films use silent film directors; the new ones will be stage directors. So too, if characters from now on need to talk, actors with certain exceptions will not be silent film stars who lack the faculty – much less the art of recitation, or the ability to recite – that is, a voice. They will need to be stage actors. This same point applies to film subjects. Who will be able to create characters that talk? Certainly not writers of silent film subjects, but playwrights. So much then for the idea that talkies will abolish theater! In all ways, talkies will mean the triumph of theater.

Meanwhile, a grave misfortune has befallen cinema. The public after many years grew accustomed to the silent screen. Now that film has spoken however badly and grotesquely – intolerably enough, it would speak – anyone who returns to a silent film experiences a certain disillusionment, a disappointment, a dissatisfaction that earlier went unnoticed. Silence has been broken. It can never be restored. Cinema will need to be given a voice at any cost.

Cinema, however, persists blindly and in vain to flounder in the initial error of searching for its voice in literature. In order that characters born of a poet's fancy might speak, literature gave birth to theater. But film does not need to call upon theater. I have shown, and I think unquestionably, that cinema will never "arrive" by setting out on a literary road, if indeed it does not succeed in annihilating itself. Cinema must liberate itself from literature in order to find its own form of expression and accomplish its own true revolution. It should leave narrative to romance and leave drama to the theater. Literature is not film's proper element. Its proper element is music. It must free itself from literature and immerse itself completely in music, but not in the musical accompaniment of song. Song is words: and words, even when sung, cannot be images; if images cannot speak they certainly cannot sing. Film should leave melodrama to the opera and jazz to the music hall. I am referring to a music that speaks to all without words, music that both is and expresses itself through sound; cinematography can become a visible language.

Thus, pure music is pure vision: two paramount aesthetic senses of sight and hearing united in one sole pleasure. The eyes see, the ears hear, and the heart senses all the beauty and variety of feeling expressed by the sounds and represented in the images that such feelings arouse. They stir the subconscious with its inconceivable pictures, sometimes as terrible as those in nightmares, or as mysterious and changeable as those in dreams; images can come in vertiginous succession, or softly and restfully in time to the music.

The name for this true revolution is Cinemelography – a visible language of all kinds of music, from popular, to a genuine expression of sentiment by Bach, or Scarlatti, or Beethoven, or Chopin. What a wealth of images can be awakened by musical folklore, from a Spanish Habanera to the Russian Volga Boat Song, or the Pastoral Symphony, the Eroica, a Chopin Nocturne, or one of the brilliant waltzes. If until now literature has been a turbulent ocean on which cinema has navigated badly, tomorrow conquering the two pillars of Hercules – narration and drama – cinema will cross the ocean of music freely and, with sails unfurled, will at last be able to find itself and bring to shore prodigious miracles.

Si Gira! and Film Theory

LEO CHARNEY

Pirandello wrote *Si gira!* in the midst of the worldwide changes known loosely as "modernity." Beginning with the Industrial Revolution and gathering steam throughout the late nineteenth century, the attributes that characterized the nineteenth century rapidly gave way to technology, mass culture, and urban life.[1] Film resulted almost inevitably from these changes, as it made an art out of technology, above all mechanical reproduction, and oriented itself toward both city culture and mass experience.[2] Film, in this sense, became the emblem of modernity.

The experience of modernity was reflected in the work of numerous writers of the period, from the Italian Futurists to the Berlin critics of the twenties known as the "Frankfurt School." While Pirandello is not known primarily as a film critic, *Si gira!* expressed many themes ten or twenty years earlier than other thinkers on film and modernity in the twenties and thirties such as Russia's Dziga Vertov, Berlin's Siegfried Kracauer, and Pirandello's friend Walter Benjamin, whose well-known essay "Das Kunstwerk im Zeitalter seiner technischen Reproduzierbarkeit" acknowledged *Si gira!* in extravagantly complimentary terms.

Specifically, the novel emphasizes the following aspects of cinema: the clash of illusion and reality; the place of film in the urban mass culture of modernity; and above all the relation between art and mechanical reproduction, the subject matter Pirandello reflects in the camera operator's fear that he has been "reduced to this office of being the servant of a machine" (29).

In *Si gira!*'s first pages, Pirandello sketches the "clamorous and dizzy machinery" (5) of urban life that struck so many writers in this period. This focus marks the first resemblance between Pirandello's concerns and those of the Frankfurt School. In the voice of Serafino, Pirandello describes "the mechanical framework of the life which keeps us clamorously and dizzily occupied and gives us no rest. Today, such-and-such; this and that to be done hurrying to one place, watch in hand, so as to be in time at another" (4). "With each crossing of the street," wrote sociologist Georg Simmel in his 1903 study "The Metropolis and Mental Life," the city dweller is accosted by "the rapid crowding of changing images, the sharp discontinuity in the grasp of a single glance, and the unexpectedness of onrushing impressions."[3] Simmel's description of the city street could double as a description of cinema.

Yet Pirandello goes beyond the description of modernity to suggest, like Siegfried Kracauer in Berlin in the twenties, that urban culture is headed toward its own destruction. "I ask myself," Serafino Gubbio says, "whether really all this clamorous and dizzy machinery of life . . . has not reduced the human race to such a condition of insanity that presently we must break out in fury and overthrow and destroy everything" (5).

He echoes Kracauer's gloomy view of the city as apocalypse. "In the streets of Berlin one is not seldom struck by the momentary insight that one day all this will suddenly burst apart. The entertainment to which the general public throngs," he continues, "ought to produce the same effect."[4] Pirandello also saw the sort of change that Benjamin analyzed twenty years later.[5] For Benjamin, film brought the technologized age of mechanical reproduction to its apotheosis: not just mechanical reproduction *of* art but mechanical reproduction *as* art. Benjamin stressed that film, like photography, had changed the whole category of art, which, he wrote, "has left the realm of the 'beautiful semblance,' which, so far, had been taken to be the only sphere where art could thrive" (230). The work of art in the age of mechanical reproduction, Benjamin responds to his own title, can never be the same as the traditional work of art. Mechanical reproduction has transformed the nature, experience, and reception of art. Modernity has thrown the old categories out the window; it has altered the experiences of work, daily life, and aesthetic gratification, and it's too late to turn back.

This emphasis on the machine as emblem of modern society dominated the theory and practice of the Italian Futurists, who flourished from about 1909 to about 1915, precisely the years that encompassed Pirandello's writing of *Si gira!* The Futurists, like their counterparts in Germany and Russia, stressed the changes wrought by modernity: "Everything moves, everything runs, everything turns rapidly," wrote Umberto Boccioni in terms almost identical to Pirandello's.[6] The Futurists stressed speed, energy, noise, aggression – whatever values arose from the new culture of the machine. Filippo Marinetti's original 1909 manifesto for futurism exalted "the beauty of speed . . . the nocturnal, vibrating incandescence of arsenals and shipyards, ablaze with violent electric moons, the voracious stations devouring their smoking serpents."[7] The modern was defined as the technological. Social change necessitated artistic change: "Art, denying its past," wrote Boccioni, "must correspond to the intellectual needs of our time." This concept led to the valorization of film, a leap best expressed in the manifesto "Futurist Cinema": "Painting + sculpture + plastic dynamism + words in freedom + composed noises + architecture + synthetic theater = Futurist film."[8]

These Futurist manifestoes, like Pirandello's own sense of film's possibilities, emerged against the background of the successful yet traditional Italian film industry. In sharp opposition to the industry's commercial product, Pirandello senses film's potential, yet, like Kracauer in Berlin, he finds himself surrounded by films that seem retrograde, conservative, and pandering. In one concise sentence in *Si gira!* he expresses the plaintive query of many European intellectuals in this period: "If it is mechanical, how can it be life, how can it be art?" (88). In the same section of the novel, Serafino stands in the photographic department where "the work of machines is mysteriously completed" (84). "We are," the camera operator relates, "as it were in a womb, in which is developing and taking shape a monstrous mechanical birth" (85).

A sense of the worker's depersonalization by mechanical work haunts all the writers of this period, who identify it as the most pernicious by-product of modernity. "The individual," wrote Simmel as early as 1903, "has become a mere cog in an enormous organization of things and powers which tear from his hands all progress, spirituality, and value in order to transform them from their subjective form into the form of a purely objective life" (422). The worker loses his "subjective" individuality in favor of the impersonal, repeatable "objectivity" of the machine, the assembly line, and mechanical reproduction.

This sense that workers were deprived of meaningful, personal contact with natural materials filled the writings of such writers of the period as Theodor Adorno, Max Horkheimer, and Martin Heidegger, as well as, of course, Marx and Engels in the nineteenth century. Workers, wrote Kracauer, perform work "which fills their day fully without making it fulfilling."[9] They, therefore, seek an outlet in such emblematic urban entertainments as cinema.

Yet Pirandello's emphasis on the camera operator also reflects the historical importance of the cameraman. In the development of early American cinema, the "cameraman system of production," as Janet Staiger calls it, dominated the first ten years of film production.[10] Many early films were made in a relatively informal manner, in which a crew would simply go out and film something. In this context, the cameraman assumed particular control and authority. The cameraman, writes Staiger, "would select the subject matter and stage it as necessary . . . , photograph the scene, develop and edit it." This system placed the many functions of film production, which would later diversify into different tasks and guilds, under the control of the single cameraman. The cameraman of this period became the closest that analogue film has ever provided to the traditionally conceived "artist" who retains single-handed control over all aspects of the artwork's production, a notion that later "auteur theory" strove to ascribe to the directors of mid-century Hollywood cinema.

This centrality of the cameraman emerges above all in the films and writings of Soviet filmmaker Dziga Vertov, who unlike Pirandello unequivocally reveled in the cameraman's ability to master and reorder the phenomenal world. For Vertov, the possibility of losing himself in the work of the camera freed him from the limits imposed on the human body by human time and space. Where Pirandello mourns the impersonality of the camera operator's work, Vertov finds it one of modernity's great leaps forward. He coins the term "Kino-eye" to denote the union of machine and operator that Pirandello also observes. "I am kino-eye," wrote Vertov. "I am a mechanical eye. I, a machine, show you the world as only I can see it."[11] For Vertov, this conflation of camera and cameraman was unequivocally positive: "Now and forever," he continued, "I free myself from human immobility, I am in constant motion, I draw near, then away from objects . . . I put together any given points in the universe, no matter where I've recorded them. My path leads to the creation of a fresh perception of the world" (17–18).

Further, the films referred to in *Si gira!* resemble those early films, which Pirandello would likely have seen, that Tom Gunning has called the "cinema of attractions."[12] Before the development of full-length narrative cinema, when films were shown as brief "attractions" for a nickel in urban nickelodeon parlors, they often confined themselves to simple, nonnarrative images designed to shock, thrill, or incite curiosity – for instance, the late-1890s Lumière short of a train arriving at a station; or a 1903 Edison short in which an elephant is electrocuted, falls over, and dies, "neither further explained, nor dramatised" (AA 37); or "magnified images of cheese mites, spiders and water fleas" that inspired protests from reformers repulsed by "slimy and unbeautiful abominations" (AA 39).

These "attractions," like Pirandello's paradoxically real fiction of the hunter and the tiger, displayed "real" events that nevertheless fulfilled the distracting functions of fictional entertainment. The irony that suffuses Pirandello's dramatic treatments of illusion and reality is here transposed to his conception of cinema. Film, Serafino Gubbio's fulminations make clear, is *both* illusion and reality. Real people do real things, yet they do so under the guise of, and inside the technology of, illusion. In a sense, this notion anticipates Christian Metz's later supposition that film seems real because the movement of the people in it is actually real; the cinema, for Metz, may involve many illusions, but "the real presence of motion" gives it an irrevocable link to the real behavior of real people, memorialized by the camera.[13]

Yet Pirandello's grasp of this paradox actually surpasses Metz's, for perhaps only Pirandello, in his fascination by life's necessary intertwining of reality and illusion, could so fully appreciate this dilemma. Throughout *Si gira!* he respects film's radical possibilities while remaining wary of its strange underside. In this way he provides for film historians the perspective of a skeptical yet trenchant intelligence trying to come to grips in film's earliest years with the changes in both art and society that surround him. This position, through Pirandello's distinctive imagination and preoccupations, does not simply connect Pirandello to the contexts of his time but marks his singular contribution to them.

Notes

1. This passage eliminates two redundant pronouns but otherwise is the same as C. K. Moncrieff's translation of *Si gira!* Specific citations in this chapter refer to C. K. Moncrieff's edition.

2. *Si gira!* was begun in 1903 under the working title, *Filauri* (perhaps a reference to Filauro, a village in Sicily); it was retitled *La tigre* in 1913, then published serially in 1913 as *Si gira!* in *Nuova antologia.* The title was changed again to *Quaderni di Serafino Gubbio Operatore (The Notebooks of Serafino Gubbio, Cameraman)* in 1916. The novel was republished in 1925 at the height of Pirandello's fame, with the original title.

The novel may have been revised several times, but especially between 1913, when Pirandello first proposed its serial publication to the monthly literary magazine *La Lettura,* and 1914 when they rejected it again because of its "philosophical monologues narrated in the first person," its lengthy "exposition," and "lack of action" (Callari, 20).

The publication history alone shows that Pirandello knew the medium as an insider and had begun to think deeply about its cultural implications far earlier than film theoreticians have suspected. Here and throughout the book, however, Francesco Callari's information on early relations with film remains authoritative since he alone had access to unpublished records held by Pirandello's estate.

3. The *Treatment* is discussed in chapter 6 and reprinted in part 2.

Pirandello's debut on film, in fact, occurred earlier under circumstances that remain mysterious. In 1978, a short film of Pirandello was discovered among others made by the painter Nino Bertoletti for the company Pathé-Baby "and forgotten." No one knows whether it was shown, and if so, to whom, but since it remained among the painter's possessions (and in a condition of extreme deterioration), it probably had only private screenings (Callari, 12).

4. Literally, "the opposite." Since Pirandello was reading German philosophy at the university in Bonn, the perception may derive from Nietzsche's proposition in *Wille zur Macht (The Will to Power)* that what we call truth is nothing but illusion and reality in an eternal dynamic: "eternal contradiction is the father of all things." Pirandello breaks down the distinction between illusion and reality and dramatizes the dynamic itself in his plays and fiction. See daVinci Nichols, "Pirandello and the Poetics of Desire."

The extent to which his thinking is a result of his studies in German classical philosophy is outlined by Benjamin Bennet in *Modern Drama & German Classi-*

cism. But Pirandello's insight into the aesthetic implications of an eternal tension between opposites is a cornerstone of his essay *L'umorismo* (*On Humor*, 1908) discussed in the preface to this book and referred to throughout.

5. His close friend Arnaldo Frateili's claim that Pirandello was entirely antipathetic to the medium unfortunately has been repeated in numerous references as the whole truth. Pirandello's son, Stefano Landi, supposedly said that his father's motive for writing film was essentially but obviously not entirely economic since they collaborated on many film projects. Also see Stefano Crespi, "L'esperienza cinematografica," *Pirandello, vita e pensiero* 50 (1967): 847–53.

6. This view of Pirandello is shared by Rossano Vittori, in *Il trattamento cinematografico*, 19.

7. Quoted by M. P. Helder, "Luigi Pirandello over perspectieven der Filmkunst" ("Perspective on Film"), 340.

8. English speakers, unaware that consciousness in Italian also means conscience, tend to minimize the convergence of moral, cultural, and psychological meanings that the word "conscience" held for Pirandello.

9. Whereas other critics have treated (or not treated) Pirandello's complex thought as "metaphysical" or "philosophic," Anthony Caputi's book naturalizes Pirandello in the course of appreciating his insistence on experience as the basis for his art.

10. Apochrypha has it that the only time Joyce returned to Ireland after his grand exile was in 1914 to negotiate the opening of a cinema in Dublin; he hoped box office receipts would keep him solvent without subsidies from his brother Stanislaus. That part of the story is plausible.

11. See Mario Verdone on Futurists and film in Works Cited. Some indication of Pirandello's minimal support for Futurist experiments can be gleaned from the fact that his company, Teatro d'Arte, produced only one of F. T. Marinetti's works, *Il Vulcano*, three times: 31 March 1926 (Rome); 13 April 1926 (Milan); 21 June 1926 (Turin). He also may have produced *Pantomime* once. Returning the gesture, Pirandello's play *La salamandra* (The salamander) was staged instead by the Futurist Pantomime Theater, directed by Enrico Prampolini, music by Massimo Bontempelli, 1928. See Tinterri, *Capocomico*, 190.

12. To cite an example, Marinetti appeared along with other Futurist artists in the film *Vita Futurista* (1915), by Emilio Settimelli. And Pirandello very notably mocks himself and refers to his own works (e.g., in *Six Characters*), well before he thought of a role for himself in the film scenarios.

13. That is, "Serafino" puns on "seraph" or "angel," while "Gubbio" is the kind of name given a clown or *pagliaccio*.

14. The conclusion can be drawn directly from the film manuscripts and from *Si gira!* already in work while Pirandello was writing *L'umorismo*.

15. See Kenneth M. Hodess' analysis ("In Search of the Divided Self," 133) of the plays in the light of Freudian speculations later formalized by Ernst Kris.

16. Anne Paolucci provides an eloquent summary in *Pirandello's Theater*, 12.

17. Pirandello's *Six Characters* may have influenced Ingmar Bergman's film *Fangelse* (1948), turning on a story within a story. A professor proposes a film to a filmmaker; their encounter is related by the film's director to a journalist. The latter recounts the story of a prostitute, her fiancé, and his sister. The director observes the three and tells the professor that the film cannot be made. For the connection between Pirandello's play and Bergman's film, see Taylor, *Cinema Eye, Cinema Ear*, 144. Cited in Nulf, "Luigi Pirandello and the Cinema," 24–25. In fact, Bergman was one of many filmmakers who negotiated unsuccessfully with Pirandello's estate for film rights to the play.

18. Pirandello's primary enterprise remained the creation of the self, and so of the artist, and ultimately then, the consequence of the artist's self creation for his art. Decades of criticism about his insistence on depicting art-in-the-making (see Balakian, "*Six Characters* and Surrealism") might be carried to this next step in order to see the significance of his introspections in the works rather than in the man.

19. This title of one of his late novels, *Uno, nessuno, e centomila* (1926) seems to pun on Nietzsche's subtitle of *Thus Spake Zarathustra: A Book for All and No One*.

20. Gaspare Giudice, *Pirandello: A Biography*. Subsequent references to Giudice are to this work unless otherwise noted.

21. "We are as it were in the womb, in which is developing and taking shape a monstrous mechanical birth. And how many hands are at work there in the dark! There is a whole army of men and women employed here: operators, technicians, watchmen, men employed on the dynamos and on the other machinery, drying, soaking, winding, colouring, perforating the films and joining up the pieces" (*Shoot!* 85).

22. Callari (*Pirandello e il cinema*, 90) tells the same story, naming *I promessi sposi* as the novel to be adapted. Distinctions between Pirandello's proposals and those made by others remain unclear for this early period.

23. "La filosofia del cinematografo" appeared in *La Stampa*, 18 May 1907. Papini's insightful understanding of film as a news medium, comparable to our television, and as the perfect medium for recording the spectacle of "life as lived," makes the article a valuable documentation of the period. It is entirely possible that Pirandello read the essay and adopted its refutation of the camera for some of Gubbio's dissertations.

24. Between 1910 and 1911, for instance, there appeared *Cine-Foto, Cinema, Film e Lux, La Proiezione, La Face*, and *La Vita Cinematografica*.

25. The men mentioned often in these pages formed a loose community of

"originals" in filmmaking who maintained a professional and personal association to Pirandello. Martoglio was poet, playwright, filmmaker, and manager of a Sicilian dialect theater that performed several of Pirandello's short plays. As later discussion shows, he belonged to the inner circle of theater people Pirandello trusted when his own fortunes took him away from Italy.

For the relations between Martoglio and Pirandello, as well as Martoglio's role in film, see Sarah Zappulla Muscara, "Pirandello, Martoglio, Bracco ed il cinema muto," 293–310; and Sarah Zappulla, *Pirandello e Martoglio*.

26. It is said that Griffith owned a pirate print of *Cabiria*, which he scrutinized before filming *Intolerance*. True or not, Pastrone's film had enormous influence in its day (Leprohan, *The Italian Cinema*, 31 ff.).

27. Not to deny that many authors contracted for screenplays or allowed films to be made from their works; among them were Giovanni Verga, Guido Gozzano, Lucio d'Ambra, Luciano Zùccoli, Marco Praga, and Gabriel D'Annunzio.

28. Leprohan (*The Italian Cinema*, 40) claims that Martoglio's cutting to juxtapose scenes of high life and low life strongly influenced the Russians.

29. The industry was centered in Turin from 1904 to 1914, but by 1910 it had already begun to shift to Rome.

30. Callari (*Pirandello e il cinema*, 156) questions the authenticity of the existing script, chiefly since its melodramatic subject and "unliterary form" do not correspond to an earlier fiction. The twin heroes, older and younger, "dead" and alive, can be seen as thematically close to doubling in several later stories, plays, and films.

31. See Balakian, "*Six Characters* and Surrealism," 185–92, for a discussion of Pirandello's insistence on presenting art in the making.

32. In this connection, especially, Walter Benjamin's admiration for *Si gira!* is apparent in his essay, years later, looking at film and modernism, "Das Kunstwerk im Zeitalter seiner technischen Reproduzierbarkeit."

33. On this theme and still relevant, Federico Sciacca, *L'estetismo, Kierkegaard, e Pirandello*, 31.

34. This essentially is another form of the novel's *umorismo*, balancing statement with extreme, deadpan irony so as to imply the opposite; but the theory itself is parodied on many levels from structural to metaphoric, from novel versus film to the very Cavalena marriage of opposites.

35. Pirandello repeats the doubled older and younger male in more plots than are feasible to list, many of them discussed in subsequent pages. Note that, atypically, *both* doubles are "philosophers."

36. The subject was thoroughly researched for Reinhardt's theater long ago by J. L. Styan, *Max Reinhardt*. "Reinhardt's *grosse shauspielhaus* was the size of a circus," 9.

37. Douglas Cole spotted this and other parallels between *Si gira!* and Michelangelo Antonioni's film in "Antonioni and Pirandello and *Blow-Up*," 25–27.

38. The theme of reciprocal recognition between self and other, crucial to the formation of personality, is also central to Pirandello's earlier novel, *Il fu Mattia Pascal* (*The Late Mattia Pascal*) (1904). Pirandello studied psychology quite thoroughly at the University in Bonn, in particular the theories of Alfred Binet, and he continued to investigate the subject throughout his life. He seems to have absorbed Freud osmotically, but still more remarkably, he sometimes appears to have anticipated Lacan on the psychological construction of the self *by* the other, a quite different project leading to my view of *Si gira!* as a novel poised on the brink of postmodernism.

39. See Olga Ragusa, *Luigi Pirandello*, for an assessment of the essay's centrality to his work, as well as the introduction to Pirandello's *L'umorismo*.

40. This and all subsequent references are to the text of the 1925 edition of *Six Characters*, recently reissued by Eric Bentley in *Pirandello's Major Plays*.

41. Donati Corrado expresses a similar idea in his *La solitudine allo specchio*, 24.

VARIATIONS ON A THEME

1. Several critics quote the line, each attributing it to a different source; Giudice says it occurs in a letter to Pirandello's daughter Lietta.

2. Helen Auger, "Pirandello's New Play for Duse."

3. No one quotation from the *Secret Notebook* suffices here; Giudice notes several applicable quotations in his article, "Ambiguity in Six Characters"; da-Vinci Nichols quotes others in "Pirandello and the Poetics of Desire." See Corrado Alvaro, "Tacciuno Segreto di Luigi Pirandello."

4. For Lacan on the construction of the self by another's desire, see *Ecrits*, especially 3, 50, 135.

5. About Pirandello's finances, a perpetual worry after 1903: his father lost an investment of 400,59 lire in a sulphur mine that flooded. The sum included 70,000 lire of Antonietta's, her dowry. After Antonietta's father's death in 1909, her condition worsened (Giudice, 64, 85).

6. Going beyond the monographs *Arte & Scienza* as well as *L'umorismo*, Ragusa in *Luigi Pirandello* discusses Pirandello's attraction to occultism, hermeticism, and other parapsychological phenomena, again like Strindberg's.

7. In "In Search of the Divided Self: A Psychoanalytic Inquiry into the Drama of Pirandello" Kenneth M. Hodess says the plays were "ahead of their time in reflecting a modern psychoanalytic awareness of the dynamics of interpersonal relationship," and he explores this in Laingian, as well as Janusian, terms.

Considering the earlier psychoanalytical study by Charles Kligerman, entitled "A Psychoanalytic Study of Pirandello's 'Six Characters in Search of an Author,'"

Hodess's more important contribution may be his suggestion that "many aspects of [Pirandello's] personality and life history closely parallel the schizoid personality structures and personal relationships that he portrays in his drama," "In Search of a Divided Self," 136. This observation provides a point of departure for analyzing the filmscripts in later chapters.

8. Auger, "Pirandello's New Play for Duse."

9. About his autonomous characters, he also enjoyed teasing interviewers. "You remember that woman [Ersilia] in *Naked*. . . . Remember how that play ends? That's her fault, not mine. I wanted to finish the play in my own way. It seemed my right as a self-respecting dramatist. But, no, she wouldn't have it. For days and nights we wrestled and fought over the denouement, and in the end she won. There's the play, just as she wanted it" (Auger, "Pirandello's New Play for Duse").

10. Barry Jacobs analyzes this in his "Psychic Murder and Characterization in *The Father*," drawing on Strindberg's essay, "Psychic Murder (Apropos Rosmersohlm)." Translated by Walter Johnson, *Tulane Drama Review* 13, no.2: 113–18. The essay may have been translated into German by 1914 when Pirandello immersed himself in parapsychological study.

11. "Il lume dell'altra casa" was bought by Paramount in 1930, and included in an anthology of films by Luigi Filippo D'Amico called *Il mondo di Pirandello* in 1967 (Callari, *Pirandello e il cinema*, 92).

12. E. Gordon Craig was not alone in claiming that Musco was the greatest actor in the world; Ragusa said the same thing in *Sicilian Comedies*, 8. Angelo Musco's forte was Sicilian dialect theater, which provided Pirandello occasion for his meeting.

13. "Lettere," in *Omaggio a Pirandello: Almanacco letterario Bompiani*, edited by Leonardo Sciascia (Milan: Mondadori, 1987), 17.

14. On the subject of Hollywood ideology, see Mario Verdone on developing theories of modernism and cinematography, and Jennifer Stone, "Cineastes' Texts."

15. *La rosa* starred Bruno Barilli, Olympia Barroero, and Lamberto Picasso, who worked later on several Pirandello projects and starred in Pirandello's company's production of *Six Characters*.

16. Interview with Helen Auger, 4 March 1923. Many of his short stories moved either into drama or film, or both. See, for instance, Signora Frola and Ponza as figures in fiction, then in *Cosí è (se vi pare)*, then as ghosts in the *Prologue*, discussed in chapter 3.

17. *Il berretto a sonagli* was sufficiently "daring" for Rome in 1916, as Pirandello tells his son Stefano, to have made its success something of a surprise (Bassnett-McGuire, *File on Pirandello*, 18). It was not, after all, French farce but Sicilian paradox. Musco played Professor Toti to great acclaim and with the full range of ironic self-effacement that Pirandello apparently had in mind.

18. Psychoanalytical reading of the theme emphasizes escape from a tyrannical father through an impossible fantasy of rebirth as one's own father. But this is the situation of the writer, whose act of writing, therefore, may be exorcising a feared and hated father. Chapter 3 reviews the theme again.

Rittenberg and Shaw's "On Fantasies of Self-Creation" has been useful.

19. Pirandello knew L'Herbier's work directly and wrote to Eric Allatini about it first with some misgiving. By the time he shot *Feu Mathias Pascal* he already had made two shorts and seven full-length feature films of which *El dorado* (1921) and *L'Inhumaine* (1924–25) are considered the most important (Stone, "Cineastes' Texts," 47 and 51).

20. Quoted in Italian by Tullio Kezich in "Mattia Pascal: uno, due e tre," in *Omaggio a Pirandello*, 77–84. The further reference is to Sciascia's, *Pirandello dall'A alla Z*.

21. The experiment is a famous demonstration of what can be achieved through the order, sequence, and duration of each frame; Vsevolod D. Pudovkin recorded it in *Film Techniques and Film Acting*, 290.

22. Evelyn Gerstein, "Four Films of New Types," 296–297.

23. The critics Compassi and Sabel, preferring the later *Il fu Mattia Pascal* film, object to comic touches on the grounds that they destroy continuity and coherence. Their criticism of Chenal's *L'homme de nulle part* is compared in chapter 5.

24. Fragments of the unfinished novel dated to 1910 appear in Bompiani, *Omaggio a Pirandello*, 20–22.

25. Pirandello talked to a journalist in 1934 about a play he was writing for Duse called "The Mother," saying it more closely approached pure art than anything he had written. Nothing says he had in mind his experience with the ghost mother, but immediately thereafter he comments on *La vita che ti diedi* (*The Life I Gave You*), about the very subject of reciprocal desire that he explored first in his "Colloqui coi personaggi" (Auger, "Pirandello's New Play for Duse").

26. See Giudice, "Ambiguity in *Six Characters*." The *Secret Notebook*, especially, describes the act of "recognizing" otherwise unformed images of passion or fantasy by clothing them in a familiar dress of circumstance.

27. Dario Niccodemi's company performed *Six Characters* at the Teatro Valle with Niccodemi as the Director, and Vera Vergani and Luigi Almirante in principal roles (Bassnett-McGuire, *File on Pirandello*, 39). Pirandello, fortunately, had been developing a self-saving aloofness to the reception of his plays, which were hardly popular. While *Liolà* (1916) and *Cosí è* (*Right You Are*, 1917) had been received politely, if rather quietly, *Il giuoco delle parti* (*The Rules of the Game*, 1918) had met with outright hostility from a confused audience, as well as from critics. Pirandello alternated between villifying them for their blindness and praising them for their acumen.

28. Jennifer Lorch, "The 1925 Text of 'Sei personaggi in cerca d'autore' and Pitoëff's Production of 1923," argues that Pirandello's 1925 revision was influenced by Pitoëff's production in 1923. Lorch compared photographs of Pitoëff's production with changed stage directions in the 1925 text.

The sequence of editions is as follows: 1921, 1923–24, 1925, 1931. The 1923 and 1924 revisions are editorial and hence virtually undistinguishable from the 1921 text. Lorch's analysis is confirmed by Alessandro Tinterri, the authoritative scholar on Pirandello as *capocomico*, in "Two Flights of Steps and a Stage Direction: Pirandello's Staging of 'Six Characters in Search of an Author' in 1925."

29. Quite separately, Pirandello added the famous postscript about acting and marionettes to his second edition of *Il fu Mattia Pascal*. There may be no connection, but the direction of his thinking seems to become more stage-oriented than when he first formulated the Bergsonian idea about marionettes in *L'umorismo*.

30. See Michael Rossner, "La fortuna di Pirandello in Germania e le messin-scene di Max Reinhardt," 42. The point about "influence" raises related and implicit problems about Reinhardt's texts and their translations. Rossner says the German translation which Reinhardt used fails to credit a translator but names Emma Hecht and Margit Veczi rather than Hans Feist, as tradition otherwise claims. The problems of Reinhardt's text are discussed in chapter 6.

31. These included Silvio D'Amico; the playwright Massimo Bontempelli; the actor Lamberto Picasso; the writer Orio Vergani; and Pirandello's son, Stefano Landi. The company's name was soon changed to Teatro d'Arte di Roma; and after March 1927, to Compagnia del Teatro Argentina.

Pirandello's wish to create a stable state theatre in Italy threads through many more comments, essays, and letters than is feasible to list. After twelve years of effort he still went on testing one plan after another, with and without Mussolini's help, with sporadic success. For instance, he tells a journalist in 1934 that he and Paolo Evani *"were about to"* model a company on that of the Belgian Marais Theater; it would perform plays by Italian authors and rotate between Rome, Milan, and Turin (fragments from the *New York Times* clipping file, late December 1934 and early January 1935, emphasis added).

32. That the poet knew words better than action, he admitted years later in an interview with M. P. Helder, "Luigi Pirandello," 340–42.

33. Pirandello especially admired Evreinov's *Theater in Life*, 1913. He refers to him with respect in a conversation with associates of Piscator in Berlin.

34. Pirandello wanted to retrieve serious theater from (1) the stultifying grip of commercial playhouses, dominated by *capocomici* (or impressarios) attracted to a star system and a profit motive, and (2) excesses of independent groups either too amateur or too radical to represent a true alternative. Futurist groups, for instance, "regarded the text as merely another element in the production along with scenery,

costumes, and lighting." They were ruled by a theatricalist director who used "the entire production as a springboard for his imaginative innovations" or for pro-Fascist propaganda (Sogliuzzo, *Luigi Pirandello, Director*, xxv).

35. Censorship rules against obscenity prevented his playing in any but private theaters or in the Italian language, so he wrote explanations to help his audiences.

36. In fact, the vocabulary, "life versus art," or "form versus flux," is not Pirandello's but Adriano Tilgher's in his criticism of the play. The formulation has become "fixed" by tradition.

37. Benito Ortolani, editor of the correspondence dating from Pirandello's meeting with Abba until his death, introduces each year of letters with an eloquent summary and commentary from which we borrow freely. The authors' immense debt to Professor Ortolani for permitting us to read his text in page proof cannot be overstated. Reference throughout is to pagination and dating in the Italian page proofs.

38. Amleto Palermi (11 July 1889 to 20 April 1941), another Sicilian in the circle of artists respected by Pirandello and Martoglio, was a journalist, man of the theater, and recognized filmmaker and director who had made thirty-seven films by the time he called on Adolf Lantz to handle the particulars of German cinematic vocabulary and to be a guide through the Berlin community. Lantz's function for the highly experienced Palmeri provides us with a sense of Lantz's strictly technical function for Pirandello later. He also was responsible for the film's strange German title, *Die Flucht in die Nacht* (Callari, 313).

39. Giulio Cesare Castello, in "Pirandello e il cinema," an undated clipping in the files of *Cinema*.

40. In 1926, the film was released in Austria under the title, *Die lebende Maske;* in France as *Le fou;* and distributed in English-speaking countries as *The Living Mask.* Thereafter, five different films were made (see the Chronology and Callari, *Pirandello e il cinéma*, 96).

PROLOGO

1. Dated 25 June 1941. The journal appeared five times per year but is no longer published. The article and document are the only evidence of the *Prologo*'s original publication.

2. The relevant section of the report by Senator Corrado Ricci reads:

Our schools, public festivals and cinemas require films of an essentially scientific, historical and patriotic nature; we must oblige the cinema-owners to include one or several of these films in their programmes, and attempt to correct public taste, which has been corrupted by films whose moral and aesthetic qualities have all too often left much to be desired. (Leprohan, 58)

3. The Berlin film company was Geschaftsstelle Verband Deutscher Film-autoren-Berlin (Callari, 36).

4. Random quotations of his support of Mussolini, so detrimental to his professional connections in America, need to be seen in the light of his basic alienation from all systems, institutions, and organizations. The letters to Marta Abba, for instance, reveal his wavering between admiration for and disgust with the regime, depending upon Il Duce's individual actions rather than his overall policy or platform. On his early fascism, see Giudice, 154 ff. On his test of fascism later according to Mussolini's handling of the arts, see Ortolani, *Lettere*, 7 ff.

5. While Pirandello was touring Europe, a theatrical syndicate grew strong enough to push out the eleven founders of the Teatro d'Arte, along with other groups, so that bookings on his return were made extremely difficult. Pirandello, therefore, set out again, touring South America, again returning to disaster at home in 1928. State control ended all syndicates but substituted a crippling monopoly and aggravated mismanagement up and down the organizational ladder (Ortolani, Introduction).

6. *Corriere della Sera*, Milan, 19 April 1928, quoted in Bassnett-McGuire, 63. The play, *La nuova colonia*, was based on the novel *Suo morito*. (Her husband) and in 1926 had been optioned for a film (see the Chronology).

7. "Luigi Pirandello and his great cinematographic innovation" (4 October 1928). The accuracy of this report, like its completeness and degree of editorial revision, are unverifiable.

8. The interview goes on as follows: "I have the utmost faith in Murnau. Only he is capable of understanding me. . . . Yes, the Germans." Il Maestro continued, following his train of thought:

> Reinhardt, and Piscator too. Piscator does marvelous things. But to me, he imitates the Russians and therefore overdoes it. Imagine, the Russians produced Goldoni's *La Locandiera* in a cubist style. These are crimes committed against the spirit of an artistic creation. In Germany, especially, I saw miracles. Stages which can be raised or lowered to any level, lights which bathe everything in a sort of unreal, fantasmagoric glow, originating from the most unexpected places – wonders, I tell you wonders. (*Il Popolo d'Italia*, 4 October 1928)

9. Both Olga Ragusa and Oscar Budël discussed this long ago. Recently, Caputi places the subject of parapsychology in the context of Pirandello's introspections rather than his separate interests (see Works Cited).

10. Reference is to passages in *L'umorismo* cited earlier, and to daVinci Nichols' article on the principle of forming and deforming, "Pirandello and the Poetics of Desire," 307–25.

11. Apparently, Pirandello's German was literary and conversational. He acquired his German for purposes of study in Bonn between 1889 and 1891; he also traded German lessons for Italian ones with a young Bonn native (Giudice, 36–44).

12. A specific awareness of audience, in fact, only begins to appear in film criticism during the 1930s and in Fascist use of film for propaganda.

13. Kracauer discusses the genre in a chapter, "The Prostitute and the Adolescent," providing summaries of enough models with which to compare both Pirandello's *Prologo* and his *Film-Novelle*.

14. Kracauer identifies the genre with an implicit narrative of emerging German history, analogous to one of male passivity and symbolic defeat; thus he sees the genre as a mass culture phenomenon. Eisner and others rather contend that Weimar cinema, while appealing to contemporary audiences, was essentially an avant garde product by and for filmmakers and scholars. But the debate may be irreconcilable since "structures of identification in the German cinema are so unstable that no spectator position – outside of the traditional categories of nation and class – can be deduced or analyzed with any degree of certainty" (Petro, 13–15).

15. The novel as history "deforms" itself in that novels by definition are invested in the historical and prosaic. Pirandello said the novel expressed everything he ever wanted to say, a wry comment on heroes or himself ending in silence. With this work, Pirandello answers the problem of high modernism, otherwise expressed by James Joyce, Robert Musil, and others. For a perceptive comment on Moscarda, see Cambon, "Pirandello as Novelist," 337–42.

FILM-NOVELLE

1. Pirandello is supporting his wife in a sanitarium; his children and their enterprises; Marta Abba; her attempts to found a permanent repertory theater; his secretary, agents, and collaborators; and himself in a style telling that his genius did not extend to managing money. Habit and pride led him to patronize fine hotels and restaurants in spite of what he saw as a constant threat of penury (Ortolani corroborates, 83).

2. Pirandello's correspondence to Abba from this year on to his death, along with Ortolani's invaluable summaries, shed new light on Pirandello's state of mind and his immersion in the film industry.

3. Pirandello was introduced to Joe May by Adolf Lantz and either proposes or adapts his story, "L'abito nuovo" (The new suit) (letter 19 June 1929). May, who was working for UFA, "liked the script a great deal," but when the time came for production, Jannings was in a sanitarium in Austria (Callari, *Pirandello e il cinema*, 225).

The following year Pirandello notes that Joe May hired Lantz so as to give him a few months work when he otherwise was dependent upon Pirandello. But then May himself "fell into disgrace with UFA" and went to look for work in America (letter 2 May 1930).

4. Alfred Hitchcock was under contract at British International Pictures from 1927 and made four silent films at their "British Hollywood," the studios at Elstree. Could he and Pirandello have met? There is no evidence either way.

5. One especially annoying negotiation, he says, illustrates the mentality of the German companies, as well as Pirandello's treatment as the representative of his country whom no one in Berlin wants to see or talk to. Terrafilm at first told Hans Feist (Pirandello's German translator working also in film) that they would accept *Six Characters* if Pittaluga would consider it as one of the six subjects they were contracted to work on. (Pittaluga, we recall, is the sole producer-distributor in Italy.) Pittaluga not only accepted the proposition, but answered that they were prepared to pay half the costs of filming. Meanwhile, Pirandello discovered that Pittaluga's fervent interest served his own political ends: cooperation would ingratiate the fascist regime and place the "blame" for the deal with ENTE-UFA, the supposedly semiprivate company actually financed on the sly by the state (Callari, *Pirandello e il cinema*, 62).

6. He describes his feelings on entering his lonely, silent apartment: "I heard the gentle ticking of your little alarm clock on my table; I closed my eyes and I recalled how the clock sat on your nightstand, when I used to wind it before saying good night and leaving your room; I began to cry, to cry as I had never done in my lifetime" (letter 24 March 1929).

7. In only two of his hundreds of letters to her does Pirandello end with something like resolution (Ortolani, 207). "You don't really want to understand the condition in which I remain; but if for you its been nothing, Marta, to separate from me, for me instead . . . Enough, Addio" (letter 29 April 1929).

8. By March 1930, severe depression causes Pirandello to give many signs of a death wish and veiled hints at suicide. He writes: "In my current state, only a word from you could revive me, but it doesn't come, it doesn't come. Instead only this atrocious evening comes, in which even the solitude in which I'd like to immerse myself is denied me. 'How are you, Maestro,' Lantz's wife mews in French, putting her head in from the hall. 'Well, Madame, Very well, thank you!' Die, I scream inside me" (letter 31 March 1930).

9. Interview, "The World Her Stage," *Colliers*, 13 November 1937.

10. Specific reference later on to the Italian film, apparently undistinguished, is *Il caso Heller*, directed by Alessandro Blasetti (letter 7 July 1933). Otherwise, records of her appearance in film conflict; she may have made no films.

11. Ortolani's summaries for each year of Pirandello and Marta's correspon-

dence provide a wealth of such advice from Pirandello to Marta. For instance, from the first Pirandello had urged Marta to learn French and English so as to expand her acting possibilities.

12. With her father's help and many of Pirandello's contacts, Marta formed her own production company, staging several of Pirandello's plays written for her, and touring Italy and the Continent. She and Pirandello however managed to meet periodically and never lost contact. His almost daily letters to her continue until his final illness.

13. The plays written for Marta develop women's characterizations more fully than do the earlier ones, including the theater plays. For example, *Come tu mi vuoi* (*As You Desire Me*) describes the heroine's books as a means of realizing her physical being rather than, as is more typical, her psychological stance alone and relative to others.

14. Richard Eichberg was the head of an independent subsidiary of British International Pictures, with whom Adolf Lantz made three films: among them (with co-writer Helen Gosewish) were *Song* (1928) and also *Grosstadtschmetterling* (Big city butterfly, 1929), both starring Anna May Wong. Pirandello may have written two or three scripts for Eichberg, one with Lantz and one without. See the Chronologies. Pirandello goes to London "with Eichberg to contract for two more films," unnamed (letter 1 April 1929). The film written with Lantz for Anna May Wong, *Vergine madre*, included a small part for Marta's sister, Cele Abba (letter 21 March 1929). Details about production and release are conflicting (letter 12 April 1929). Also see note 16.

15. Fragment of a newspaper article in English 2 January 1931, immediately before Pirandello leaves Berlin. Possibly from the *New York Times* or the *New York Post*, "Signor Pirandello Enjoys Life and Spaghetti."

16. Vittori (109) claims that Pirandello mentioned the film in "an article" but does not cite it. Also, there are contradictory notes about Pirandello's dealing with Richard Eichberg of British International Pictures. Pirandello says Eichberg decided to do another film with Anna May Wong using a subject prepared by him and Lantz (letter 5 May 1929). Then he hears from Lantz that "the Eichberg connection is completely broken" (letter 16 June 1929). Ortolani says, however, that only Lantz has been dealt out of the film. No records discuss the film's production.

17. "Yesterday I spent about three hours in the company of the famous Russian metteur en scene, Alexsander Tairov, who is like Germany's Max Reinhardt; he is enthusiastic about my theatre and now that censorship has been removed he plans to stage not only the new play *Questa sera si recita a soggetto* (*Tonight We Improvise*) but also *Six characters*, *Enrico IV* and *Così è*" (letter 26 May 1929). Ortolani (230) says this never happened, despite Tairov's interest and the director Anatoly Lunacharski's support.

18. Both Swallow (75) and Montague (13 and 72) record the conference but are emphasizing only Eisenstein. To summarize:

Eisenstein leaves Moscow for a premier in Berlin of his film *Staroie i novie* (Old and new), August 1929. He then proceeds to La Sarraz, belonging to Mme. della Mandroit who offered her villa for the International Film Conference of film-makers. Among the sponsors of the conference were Andre Gide, Stefan Zweig, and Pirandello. Participants included Walter Ruttmann from Berlin; the Italian futurist Enrico Popolini; Montgomery Evanson from the United States; Hiroshi Hijo from Japan; the surrealist Hans Richter; Jack Isaacs from London; probably Dziga Vertov, and others named directly in the discussion.

19. Street film was an absorbing subject to most of the innovative German filmmakers of the time, as comment on the *Prologo* and the *Film-Novelle* imply. Otherwise, Fritz Lang added himself to the list of movie makers wanting to film *Six Characters* (letter 17 May 1930).

20. Comments here draw on Eisenstein's theories discussed by Swallow, on Pirandello's theories referred to throughout this chapter especially, and on cinema history.

21. See Jana O'Keefe Bazzoni's article on the centrality of carnival to Pirandello's thinking, "The Carnival Motif in Pirandello's Drama."

22. Pirandello expressed particular delight in knowing that Chaplin agreed with him about sound (Callari, 109). *Modern Times* rejected sound in 1936. Chaplin wanted to make a film of *Uno, nessuno, e centomila* (One, No One, and a Hundred Thousand) during the 1950s, but his difficulties with the IRS intervened.

23. In one letter to Marta Abba, Pirandello reconstructs a wild and long-winded prediction by a passing acquaintance about the impact of sound: "In two or three years everything will be cinema. . . . Only photographed shows will go before the public. . . . Openings will take place there and then be passed along to the public. It seemed as though I was speaking to a madman . . . but I let him talk, declaring that for my part I've always believed in miracles and that therefore I was well disposed to believe in this" (Ortolani, 174).

24. Fragment of an undated clipping from the files of *Cinema*, 1930–39.

25. Eisenstein in *Film Form* (Cleveland: World Publishing Co, 1957), 189, quoted by Nulf, "Luigi Pirandello and the Cinema."

26. "I don't ever want to hear about Al Johnson [*sic*] again . . ." (letter 16 April 1929). *The Jazz Singer* (1927) directed by Alan Crosland and starring Al Jolson. The interview cited was with the London correspondent for *Corriere della Sera*, 19 April 1929.

The film used a vitaphone sound system with more or less synchronized score and songs, but this system rapidly gave way to a more sophisticated track system. Except for the German Tobis Klongfilm organization, Hollywood owned most of the patents for sound equipment, and "royalties paid them by other countries soon became crippling" (Robinson, 170).

27. At Paramount's Joinville Studios outside of Paris, films were being made in fourteen or fifteen languages. Other practices that were used to reach the widest audience included limiting sets to interiors or generalized places and choosing scripts with universal themes and situations (Robinson, 174ff.).

28. The essay began as the first of several articles promised to the Anglo-American Newspaper Service at "6,000 pounds each, one a month." (This probably was 6,000 lire.) It is published in *Corriere della sera*. The essay well demonstrates his genie of contradiction as well as his volatility at the time. See Document 6.

29. The ideas about film and melography are proposed in varying forms: in his essay "Se il film parlante abolirà il teatro?"; again in an interview in London with Anglo-American Newspaper Service, London–New York, June 1929; in a further interview with *La Nación*, Buenos Aires, 7 July 1929, where he discusses sound and drama; and finally in *La Stampa*, Torino, 9 December 1932.

Callari notes that a few contemporary makers of art films, like the early Walt Disney, appear, in retrospect, to have reinvented and applied Pirandello's ideas. He fails to place Pirandello in the French ideological debate about sound representation.

30. Vittori (25) cites Giudo Cesare Castello on Pirandello's filmography in "Filmografia ragionata di Luigi Pirandello," *Cinema*, no. 135, 10 June 1954. Both take exception to Callari's view that "mutual incomprehension" between the artist and film professionals was the only reason for Pirandello's disillusionment with film. Directors often distorted the subjects or screenplays he provided.

31. Heder in *Filmiga*, 1934. The interview was conducted in English when Pirandello was en route to Stockholm to receive the Nobel prize. The fact, if it is a fact, bears on his estimate of his poor English. He understands the words, he tells the interviewer, but that is not to understand the language.

32. Adolf Lantz (1882–1949) was basically a technician working with innovators like Joe May, Willy Zehn, Max Mack, and Alexander Korda for a series of companies including UFA, Decla-Bioskop, Pielfilmges, Oswaldfilm, Domofilm, Maximfilm, and Gloriafilmgesellschaft. His last film, *Sonnenstrahl* (Sunbeam), was shot in 1933 in Vienna shortly before he left Austria for London, where he died.

Lantz's son, Robert Lantz, the prominent New York producer and literary agent, remembering his father's association with Pirandello, agrees that Lantz's contribution remained technical. "Surely nobody dictated to Pirandello how to do it [the *Film-Novelle*] or anything else," Mr. Lantz quipped in an interview with the authors, 15 May 1990.

33. See Roberto Tessari's introduction in Vittori, *Il trattamento*. Tessari notes that most early assessments of the *Film-Novelle* were superficial, with the possible exception of a reading by Ferdinando Chiarelli in *Intercine 7* (1935), which detected a characteristically "Pirandellian theme of reality and illusion." Tessari worked from the French translation of the scenario by E. Goldey. Vittori verified this text against the original German in the British Museum in London, providing an Italian translation and a critical commentary. For further details, see headnotes to the documents in part 2.

34. Kenneth M. Hodess (1988) analyzed the play in the light of Ernst Kris's *Psychoanalytic Explorations in Art* (New York: International Universities Press, 1952). The scenario, however, advances Kris's theory still more remarkably. Kris

> builds the connection between art work and dream work by equating artistic ambiguity with an overdetermination of the primary process. Poetic metaphor, seen as an integration of different levels of experience, was equated to the metaphorical expression of dream imagery, where elements and objects in the dream are analogous to others in the individual's constellation of "real" experience. (Quoted by Hodess, 134)

35. The use of Strindberg's term here is to suggest that both Strindberg and Pirandello were dramatizing their own psychic processes and treating them as parapsychological phenomena. See Jacobs (1969).

36. "A torture chamber," a literal translation of *La stanza della tortura*, Macchia's study showing that Pirandello's theater is a series of torture chambers whether the scene is set in a garden, rehearsal hall, a bourgeois parlor, or a tomb (Macchia, 12).

37. *Die buchse der Pandora*, based on two Wedekind plays, *Erdgeist* (Earth spirit) and *Die buchse der Pandora* (Pandora's box), which Pirandello apparently studied. On Pabst, see Eisner (296); on Pirandello's reading, see *The Notebooks* (120).

38. Giudice says Pirandello's childhood traumas remain at the core of the man's thinking, but Klingerman's psychoanalytical reading of the theater plays, followed by that of Eric Bentley, and most recently that of Kenneth Hodess, draw specific analogies between Pirandello's suppressed sexuality and the sexuality underlying heated arguments in his novels and plays. Hodess (133–45) also points to the "development of psychological exploration as a major thematic element in twentieth century drama."

39. Talks with Otto Kahn of Paramount concerning *Six Characters*, the "talking machine" film, and cinemelography continued for months, always leaving Pirandello with the impression that Kahn's wishes and promises were crucial to decisions at ɪ ư.ːmount since he provided the money (letters 30 April 1929).

40. The film was first cut, then banned, by the Higher Film Censor Board (*Oberprufstelle*). See Bock (217n).

TREATMENTS FOR THE TALKIES

1. From "Se il film parlante abolirà il teatro?" See Document 6 for the complete essay.

2. This is Pirandello's first explicit mention of having given in to "talkies" (letter 27 May 1930).

3. Men behind the major studios and distributors in the post–World War I war period were for the most part immigrants who had once owned nickelodeons and who had "learned to fight for survival." Carl Laemmle (Universal), William Fox (Fox), Louis B. Mayer (MGM), the Warner Brothers, and Adolph Zukor (Robinson, 1973).

4. As one curious result, films began to take on a studio style that reflected the vision of its principal producers. To mention Thalberg, for instance, was tantamount to referring to the glamorous, opulent scope of MGM, backed by Chase National Bank (Robinson, 180).

5. Apparently, the czar Pittaluga asked Righelli to make the first sound film knowing that the director already had obtained Pirandello's story. Pittaluga wanted to capitalize on Pirandello's distinction without approaching him directly. Three other talkies produced immediately before *La canzone dell'amore* were deliberately 4withheld from release until after *La canzone* was released (Callari, 315).

The film was a welcome financial success in its French version, *La dernière berceuse,* as well as in its German, *Liebeslied* (Love song), both films released the following year.

6. No one has written about this recurrent romantic theme in Pirandello's work. Distinct to the retrospectives of modernist writers about themselves as children, the children in Pirandello remain castaways, or "mistaken identities," or changelings, or orphans, and in *Six Characters,* desperate victims of their parents' heedlessness.

7. In fact, the advent of sound resulted in Hollywood's complete ascendancy in the industry because it owned most of the patents for sound equipment. Except for the German merged organization Tobis Klongfilm, other companies paid crippling royalties. Tobis Klongfilm patents allowed them to make historic films including Fritz Lang's *M* (1931); Pabst's *Westfront 1918* and *Kameradshaft* (Comradship, 1930); Kurt Weill's *Dreigroschenoper* (1931); and von Sternberg's *Der blaue Engel* (*The Blue Angel,* 1930) (Robinson, 170–71).

8. Even with a capital of 200 million lire, financing the venture probably presented insuperable obstacles.

9. The adaptation by Dimitri Ostrov for the Shuberts ran for six months, opening on 28 January 1931 and closing on 30 May. The source of this and the following information is publicity materials from MGM's house publication called "Five Advance Features, Scene and Player Cuts." Howard Dietz was promotion manager.

10. A curious Italian article speculates on the friendship between Pirandello and von Stroheim that might have developed as a result of their shared "sensibilities," the latter not specified. The notion is strange since von Stroheim (1885–1957) came to Hollywood from Vienna in the early 1900s. He acted in *Birth of a Nation* and directed a trilogy on adultery between 1919 and 1921; he directed a second trilogy between 1923 and 1927. Critics agree that *Greed* (1924) was his masterpiece.

11. Apocrypha says the play was based on a contemporary actual case of a professor of Greek in Verona, reported missing on the Italian front. His wife spots a man named Canella – their name was Brunelli – and insists he is her husband; ultimately, she manages to convince him. The theme, however, resembles that of the Martin Guerre legend.

12. Stephen Rathbun, the *New York Times*, 3 June 1932. For Pirandello's comment that Garbo "herself has interpreted one of [my plays] very well," see the interview with Andre Rousseaux in "Candide" in the *Paris Topical Weekly*, reprinted in *The Living Age* (New York) 347 (February 1935): 512–14.

13. MGM House publication called "Five Advance Features, Scene and Player Cuts," by Howard Dietz, promotions manager.

14. In a letter to Marta Abba (15 May 1931), he says he's beginning to understand English "well." Three years later, speaking perfectly comprehensible English, he told one journalist in London (1934) that the language had defeated him. He understood the words, but grasping a language had little to do with mere words, he said (Helder, 341).

15. For several accounts of Pirandello's presence during filming, see *Omaggio a Pirandello* and Renato Tomasino's *Analisi, archeolgie e dispositive per un archivio di pratiche dell'immaginario* (Palermo, *Acquario*, 1989).

Callari says Pirandello was not on the set; Frateili in his recollections says Pirandello was. Only two trips to America are documented: one in 1923 with his theater company and the second in July 1935.

16. Producer Albert Servillo at the Brooklyn Sports Stadium, beginning 1 September 1935. Source: advertisement in MGM clipping file, undated, for *As You Desire Me*.

17. Based on letters dated 7 May 1931 and 24 May 1931. Whether the Shaw-Pitoëff debacle over staging *The Apple Cart* was the true reason, Shaw left Paris sooner than he expected because of his wife's illness. He hoped Pirandello would visit him in London.

18. The fact that the MGM representative had seen a version of the *Film-Novelle* in the French journal *Cinema* provides evidence of the document's dissemination after its publication. Otherwise, Pirandello's dickering over fees probably needs to be seen not only against his fantasies of sudden wealth but against his resentment

that Pittaluga, who made 7 million lire with *La canzone dell'amore*, never turned to Pirandello for other subjects (letter 14 March 1931). He instead went to "Petrolini, Blasetti, Rosso di San Secondo and others," each of whose films lost as much as the income from *La canzone*. Pirandello cites this in his letter as an example of the "mismanagement" that afflicted film and theater in Italy.

19. The translation, owned by the Pirandello estate and Robert Lantz (Adolf's son), was loaned to us for research purposes. We decided against including it in the manuscript section since its poor quality and anonymity add nothing to scholarly investigation. It rather prompted daVinci Nichols's decision to retranslate the original German.

20. The tone of this long letter is extremely excited and full of detail, unavailable elsewhere, revealing Pirandello as a maker of deals.

21. The deal with Cines involved four subjects, including *L'esclusa* (The outcast), one subject per year, finalized at 70,000 lire from Pirandello's asking price of 100,000 lire (letter 6 May 1932).

22. Pirandello said he would be on the set to forestall "the mess that Cines had made of *La canzone dell'amore*." This time he intended to insure the best possible representation of his name before the public. Pirandello reassures Marta that they will make a film elsewhere (letter 22 May 1931).

Marta finally did not make *Acciaio*. She may have been offered another role instead, while Ina Pola made *Acciaio*. Pirandello's interceding for Marta yielded an offer that she play Spera in an English film of *La nuova colonia* (*The New Colony*), while she was rehearsing the stage role, but she had no English (letter 18 March 1932). Pirandello urged her from the start of their association to study languages, and that spring his wish was that she would work with a companion-instructor in French and English (letter 26 March 1932). Her poor English almost cost her the stage role in *Tovarich*, as later comment shows. In any case, in this period plans were under way for a Marta Abba Company tour of Spain and South America.

23. According to one critic, *Acciaio* links Pirandello as scenarist to Cesare Zavattini and other neorealists; he adds, however, that Pirandello's reality filters through *his* experience of the world, not a common one (Mario Verdone, *Gli intellecttuali e il Cinema*, Roma: Edizioni dell'atteneo, 1952).

MOMA in New York included *Acciaio* and Chenal's *L'homme de nulle part* in a series of screenings of Italian films in 1978. Sponsors included the Istituto di Cultura; Cineteca Nazional; and Cineteca Italiana, Milano.

24. The French production included a publicity stunt similar to stunts for Pirandello's theater plays, *Ciascuno a suo modo* and *Questa sera si recita a soggetto*. Players "spill over into the theatre lobby, the orchestra, offstage, and even into the street in front of the theatre building itself" (Ragusa, *Sicilian Comedies*, 15). Performances of the play in America, typically antipathetic to satire and farce, apparently suffered from ponderous direction of the cuckold and adultery themes.

25. Katherine Roberts featured Marta Abba with her photo in *Colliers*, 13 November 1937, "The World Her Stage." The subhead reads: "An Italian actress, speaking English with a Russian accent and playing the part of a Grand Duchess in Paris – that was America's introduction to Miss Marta Abba in *Tovarich*. Miss Abba will at a moment's notice play anywhere in almost any tongue." The hyperbolic information, as opposed to the newspaper style, sounds like the public relations effort of Saul Colin, Pirandello's secretary at the time. See chapter 6.

26. Given Carl Laemmle's reputation for experimenting with early sound, and then for turning to the horror genre, his attraction to *Six Characters* seems inevitable, with benefit of hindsight, of course.

27. Marta's interview with Il Duce about theater a month earlier held out no such hope of his interest. Pirandello's letter comforting her says: "The man doesn't merit your pain. He's rude and gross human stuff, made to command with disdain the mediocre and vulgar people who are capable of anything and without scruples. He can't stand to have people of other quality around him; he especially accuses those with the courage to tell the truth about [his] surrounding himself with 'ugly characters' [a phrase Mussolini leveled at Pirandello]. A brutal man like Him is needed in times like these to maintain the myth that we've made of Italian leadership stretching back to the Romans. But don't expect what he cannot give, don't forget what and for whom are his sympathies, which his aspirations, even in terms of art, as he's already shown" (letter 14 February 1932).

28. Pirandello worked on *Trovarsi* and *Quando si è qualcuno* (*When One Is Somebody*). The fall also passed easily in Paris since Marta was nearby, playing in *Come tu mi vuoi*, and they could visit.

29. Pirandello describes Mussolini as ill, exhausted, his skin color yellow, grayheaded, and not only physically but spiritually depressed (letter 6 December 1932).

30. The premiere performance on 20 September 1933, at Teatro Odeon di Buenos Aires, in Spanish, translated by Homer Gugleilmini. The first Italian production followed at the Teatro del Casino Municipale, San Remo, 7 November 1933, with Marta Abba's company.

31. One conference was on Ariosto and Cervantes in Montevideo. In 1933 he attended the Congress of Writers in Bologna especially since Mussolini appeared after all to devote some attention to the state of the arts. He presided over the Volta Congress in 1934 and traveled extensively throughout Europe before and after receiving the Nobel prize.

32. Not being on the scene precluded his having the ear, for instance, of city theater cooperatives that had been forming against state control and might have offered him a fresh source of support well before he finally approached them.

33. UFA has Italian and German affiliates. When Bernsteil returns to Italy after a

trip abroad, he apparently hears rumors about German activity on the projected film (letter 23 September 1928).

34. For a sense of his idiosyncrasies during the last two years of his life, see Giudice (196ff).

35. This was the first production in a German version by Hans Redlich entitled *Die Legend von Vertauschten Sohn*, Landtheater, Braunschweig, 13 January 1934. Chancellor Hitler, present at one performance, seemed to be pleased. Therefore, the Italian literary and cultural world was stunned when it was announced in Berlin that the Minister of Culture, on the advice of critics and members of the public, had decided to ban the work because it was "subversive and contrary to the interests of the German people's state."

The first Italian production at the Teatro Reale dell'Opera, Rome, 24 March 1934, was reviewed in *Il Messagero*, Rome, 25 March. "The evening was not a pleasant one. The storm was already on its way at the end of the first act. . . . Pirandello followed the progress of the disastrous performance from a side box in the second row" (Bassnett-McGuire, 72–73).

36. *Kaos*, 1983–84, by Paolo and Vittorio Taviano, was produced by Giuliani G. De Negri for RAI-Radiotelevisione Italiana, RaiUno e Filmtre, Roma, based on six stories: *Il corvo di Mizzaro* (The crow of Mizzaro), 1919; "L'altro figlio" ("The Other Son"), 1905; "Male di luna" (Moonsickness), 1925 (originally "Quintadecima," 1919); "La giara" ("The Jar"), 1909; "Requiem aeternam dona eis, Domine!" (Give them eternal rest, Lord!), 1913; and "Colloqui coi personaggi" (Conversations with characters), 1915. See Chronology II.

37. The congress took place in October 1934, and it was sponsored by the Italian Academy. Pirandello produced and directed d'Annunzio's play, *Figlia di Iorio* (Iorio's daughter), for the occasion.

38. Callari (326) says the silent film should be attributed to Frateili, who adapted the script from Pirandello's original story for the play. The contract for the sound film was administered by persons referred to only as Mauri and Antamoro with a rider for a German language version entitled, *Der Mann, der nicht nein sagen kann* (The man who couldn't say no), made and released in 1937.

39. Released simultaneously in French (as *L'homme de nulle part*) and Italian; credited to Pierre Chenal, Christian Stengel, Armand Salacrou for Ala-Colosseum, Roma and Generale Production, Paris. The film was produced in the studios of Caesar, Rome. Dialogue by Roger Vitrac was edited and revised by Pirandello. Pierre Blanchar played Pascal's double roles, and Isa Miranda played Adriana, renamed Luisa. See two relevant pieces of criticism in *Cinema* (no byline) prima serie, no. 117, 10 May 1941; and Mario Pannunzio, "Chenal di fronte a Pirandello," prima serie, no. 10, 25 November 1936.

40. The 1964–65 "liberal treatment" (Callari, 417) was directed by Mario Monicello. Marcello Mastroianni, as a sixty-year-old Pascal, begged the issue of self-regeneration. In the 1980s Pascal "should have fled at least to South America or New Zealand" instead of Rome for the sake of credibility (Kezich, 77). Italian and French critics were negative at the Cannes Film Festival, 15 May 1985.

41. Quoted by Rousseaux (514). Pirandello's collection of stories, *Novelle per un anno*, actually contained fewer than 365 tales.

42. The play, with Marta Abba as the adulterous wife Signora Perella, adapts a plot motif that can be traced back through Middleton's *Chaste Maid of Cheapside*, through Machiavelli's *Mandragola*, to Roman comedy. Pirandello's beast element probably should be related to these earlier satires rather than to his own narrative source for the play, "Richiamo all'obbligo" ("A Call to Duty"), that is, to the marital obligation. Ragusa finds the play unpirandellian (*Sicilian Comedies*, 13).

THE *TREATMENT* FOR MAX REINHARDT

1. Eisner in *The Haunted Screen* claims that Weimar film aesthetic combining abstraction and stylization is neither modernist nor realist, but a synthesis of expressionism in the fine arts and the popular theater of Reinhardt. The argument is summarized in Petro, 28.

2. The premiere was in Berlin at the Lessing-Theater on 31 May 1930. Bassnett-McGuire bases her information about the riot that broke out on newspaper accounts. These, however, had been manipulated. Pirandello's letters from 1 to 7 June fill in the missing details; they also convey his shocked state of mind and his decision to leave the city.

3. According to his letters, Pirandello did not imagine that Feist's anger at being insufficiently rewarded for his work had taken such virulent form. He and Feist had squabbled on and off during the Berlin years, even though Feist may have been instrumental in Pirandello's decision to come to Berlin. But then, Feist brought Pirandello to court for breach of contract in a battle over his right to translate Pirandello's work and according to Ortolani remained a bitter enemy.

It is possible, too, that Feist was not serving as Pirandello's German translator during the years in question. Michael Rossner, in his study of Reinhardt's texts of Pirandello, introduces the names of Emma Hecht and Margit Veczi as translators.

4. The play *Phaea*, by Fritz von Unruh at the Deutsche Theatre, reviewed September 1930 in *Theatre Arts Monthly* 14(9): 730.

5. Pirandello's letter remarks on the director's ability, "with errors," to use Italian in his telegram, perhaps an assurance to Marta that Reinhardt would appreciate her Italian performances (letter 29 April 1934). After the performance he shared his opinion with her: "Good first Act, the other two forced and false." This seems to be his only recorded judgment of Reinhardt's productions, par-

ticularly important in the light of the liberties he took with Pirandello's text, which will be discussed below.

Abba, in any case, profited from the men's excellent relations by playing Portia that summer in Reinhardt's *Merchant of Venice* in Venice at the Campo San Trovaso theater.

6. Gottfried Reinhardt, *The Genius* (302), says his father closed deals with Warner (after *A Midsummer Night's Dream*) to direct *Hamlet, Twelfth Night,* and *King Lear,* deals that subsequently collapsed. According to an article in *Variety* on 4 May 1938, Warner bought out the contract for $300,000.

7. Of course, by the mid 1930s nearly 95 percent of U.S. film production was the output of five major organizations: MGM, Paramount, and Warner Brothers ranking highest, and these under the financial control of Morgan and Rockefeller networks, from the early 1930s until World War II (Randall, 179).

8. *New York Herald Tribune,* 15 December 1934. Pirandello alludes to *Six Characters.* The following month he tells the *New York World Telegram* reporter, 16 January 1935, that he received about twenty cable offers from Hollywood immediately after receiving the Nobel prize. He is eager to "revolutionize his films," the first being *Six Characters.* If present plans proceed he will appear in the picture, but it won't be necessary for him "to speak any English because the part is a silent one."

9. "Pirandello Backs War with Ethiopia," the *New York Times,* 21 July 1935 (with photo of Pirandello arriving on the Conte di Savoia). The interview was openly antagonistic to him as a supporter of Mussolini and perhaps of Nazism. Several remarks which sounded righteous and somewhat racist mention that Saul C. Colin served as Pirandello's representative and interpreter. It is therefore impossible to know precisely what Pirandello actually said.

The article pointed out that Colin had sailed from France on the Normandie two weeks earlier; the purport was that Mussolini did not want Pirandello to book on a foreign liner. Pirandello denied the charge of state pressure, offering to show his passport and declaring that he liked Italian ships better than French ones and would return on an Italian liner as well. The interview apparently had to be okayed by Romolo Angelone, the commercial attaché.

Privately, Pirandello confessed to feeling assaulted by the New York press concerning Italian action in Ethiopia but thought he defended himself well (letter 21 July 1935).

10. Pirandello's letters of the period still complain about Colin's impetuousness and insensitivity to the task of negotiating with important people. "Each time I reprimand him," Pirandello tells Marta in one letter, "he grows contrite, assures me of his good will, and binds me to him again" (letter 25 February 1933). Colin also seemed to miss no opportunity to have himself photographed with the rich and famous; there is one photo taken long afterward, for instance, with President

and Mrs. John F. Kennedy. The impulse to aggrandize himself is apparent in his trying to ingratiate himself with Albert Einstein, according to Eric Bentley's recollection, and in adopting the title of "Doctor."

11. On Pirandello's first trip in December 1923 for the New York run of *Six Characters*, his antidemocratic bias, along with his outspokenness about American attitudes toward consumerism and money, made him appear an eccentric, if not an elitist. He remained interested in, but essentially foreign to, American ways. See his three short stories on American subjects, mentioned in Giudice (134).

12. This is from a newspaper fragment, perhaps a wire service, dated 5 January 1929. Another, earlier fragment dated 17 November 1928, from the *Evening Post Foreign Service* (dateline, Berlin), includes an example of Pirandello's typical tact. After commenting that America was "the greatest country in the world for the masses, but not for the individual," he apologized for expressing "any opinion on such short acquaintance with a country. . . . It seems presumptuous, too cocksure for a foreigner to consider himself capable of understanding the psychology of a country."

13. Only the headline and subhead of the story remain. Fragment of a 1935 photo essay in the *New York Evening Post*, 24 July 1934.

14. The letter is signed by Umberto Mauri, "administrator," nowadays roughly equivalent to executive secretary. Pirandello had appointed Mauri as Paris representative the previous year (Callari, 52).

15. This information comes from reprints of clipping fragments. The critic Alberto Rossi wrote the first article cited, entitled "Pirandello e l'America," published 15 February 1936 in *Il Dramma*, Torino, vol. xii, no. 228, 32. The second article for *Il Tevere* was signed by "C.E." and titled only "Intervista a Pirandello" (Interview with Pirandello), Rome, 7–8 October 1936. Both are *partially* quoted in Italian in Callari, who excerpted only those sections of the interviews he found relevant. Callari also excerpts only the line quoted in this text from Colin's letter to Pirandello (51).

Vittori (32) insists that Pirandello, in the second interview for *Il Tevere*, is referring to the *Film-Novelle* and not the *Treatment*.

16. The comparison was originally undertaken by Michael Rossner, "La fortuna di Pirandello in Germania e le messinscene di Max Reinhardt," no. 40–53. Analysis here also incorporates observations based on an acting copy of the playscript for Reinhardt's Hollywood Studio productions.

17. The relevant reviews comparing Reinhardt's productions to Pirandello's (in 1925) are by Alfred Kerr in *Berliner Tageblatt*, 13 and 19 October, and General Anzeiger, 19 October; reprinted in D'Amico and Tinterri, *Pirandello capocomico*.

18. Of course, since Pirandello was addressing Marta and reassuring her that the actress playing the Stepdaughter could not compete with Marta's perfor-

mance, his hyperbole on that count may have spilled over onto his judgment of the play as a whole.

19. Colin's obituary in the *New York Times* of 23 April 1967 gives the years of his involvement with Pirandello as 1929 to 1935. Born in Bucharest, he held a Ph.D. from the University of Paris (1931), and after working for Pirandello became assistant general manager of RKO in Paris. From 1935 to 1945, he tried his hand as a producer on- and off-Broadway as president of Continental Productions. He was known as a lecturer on international theater, an adaptor of foreign literary works for the stage, a New York–based drama critic for periodicals in London and Paris, and finally as president of the Dramatic Workshop founded by Erwin Piscator and originally based at the New School in New York. Unlike Adolf Lantz, Colin essentially was a go-between and administrator rather than a filmmaker.

20. Here and below, letters from 1931 are extracted. Marta Abba must have warned Pirandello against overly trusting Colin, since he responds by reassuring her that Mr. Colin "writes as my secretary, and I pay him for this . . . all correspondence must come to me and be signed and regulated by me," and more in the same vein (letter 18 July 1931).

21. "I can't even have this blessed secretary take care of the nightmare of all these letters waiting on answers. Services, yes my good Lantz has done many a service for me; in some respects, it's good for me that he doesn't know a word of Italian or French because I am forced to speak in German and regain the use of this tongue that was really lost to me; but on the other hand, it is truly troublesome to have him as a secretary since he is unable to handle any correspondence outside of Germany" (letter 1 May 1930).

22. After extensive travel and negotiation in Rome, London, and New York that year, at Pirandello's expense, Colin finally managed to arrange the deal with an agent referred to as Miller. The play launched Marta in London and New York in October 1936.

23. Correspondence in 1935 and 1936 reads like a minor criminal register against Colin for everything from "indiscretion" with the press regarding an announced "deal" rather than an "option," to padding his expenses by $1,000, as much as Pirandello says he earned from Gilbert Miller's production of *Trovarsi*.

24. The article continues: "There was no doubt of Max Reinhardt's agreement. He'd like to do an intimate film, perhaps a Molnar play." Eileen Creelman, *New York Sun*, 22 January 1937, unpaginated fragment in clipping file.

25. The *Los Angeles Times*, 28 February 1939, gave a rave review to Reinhardt's Hollywood Actors Studio performance of *Six Characters*, especially singling out Robert Ryan as the Father, Walter Brook as the Director, Ruth Sandholm as the Mother, and Nanette Fabray as the Stepdaughter.

A playbill for performances on 9 and 11 January 1939 reads, "Max Reinhardt version adapted by Karla Martell." Whether this ambiguous wording means Martell translated into English remains moot. Similar wording is used on other of the company's playbills where translation seems clearly to be intended. It is highly likely, however, that this same version was used in 1940.

26. The 1934 text substantially copies the 1924 translation into German. The working script for the Hollywood Studio is in English, its interpolations and colloquial passages in quite rough English; no translator is credited. The script was authenticated by Reinhardt's wife, Helen Thimig, as belonging to the actor playing The Leading Man. It is held at the University of Kansas, Ada Clark Collection, Spencer Library.

27. Von Sternberg established his place in film history with his gangster film series in 1927–28, "Underworld," "The Dragnet," and "The Docks of New York." His costume and spectacle pictures also apparently rivaled anything Germany produced, beginning with Douglas Fairbanks's "The Mask of Zorro" (1921) and others including "The Shiek" (1921). For the information about Stefano Landi, see Callari, 350.

28. The German original is housed in the Theatersammlung der Österreichischen Nationalbibliothek in Vienna and is copied to the Reinhardt archive at SUNY, Binghamton. It was reprinted also in Fuhrich and Prossnitz, *Max Reinhardt in Amerika*, 241–44.

29. In an interview with the authors, Robert Lantz, son of Adolf Lantz, lay the failure to make a film at the door of censorship rules about incest: "after all, certain things you just couldn't do at the end of the silent era." To his mind, not even Ingmar Bergman is the right director; "the ideal director would have been [Federico] Fellini."

Robert Lantz was the young man of fourteen who went almost every night to the Klosterstrasse Theatre to see *Six Characters* and report on the crowds to Pirandello; noted with fond amusement in his letter of 4 May 1930.

APPENDIX

1. As general references on this period, see Stephen Kern, *The Culture of Time and Space, 1880–1918* (Cambridge: Harvard University Press, 1983); Miles Orvell, *The Real Thing: Imitation and Authenticity in American Culture, 1880–1940* (Chapel Hill: University of North Carolina Press, 1989); Wolfgang Schivelbusch, *The Railway Journey: Trains and Travel in the 19th Century*, trans. Anselm Hollo (Oxford: Basil Blackwell, 1980); and Cecelia Tichi, *Shifting Gears: Technology, Literature, Culture in Modernist America* (Chapel Hill: University of North Carolina Press, 1987).

2. There is a vast literature on early cinema. See *Early Cinema: Space–Frame–*

Narrative, ed. Thomas Elsaesser (London: British Film Institute, 1990). On film and modernity, see Eileen Bowser, *The Transformation of Cinema, 1907–1915* (New York: Scribner's, 1990); Miriam Hansen, *Babel and Babylon: Spectatorship in American Silent Film* (Cambridge: Harvard University Press, 1991); and Charles Musser, *The Emergence of Cinema: The American Screen to 1907* (New York: Scribner's, 1990).

3. Georg Simmel, "The Metropolis and Mental Life," *The Sociology of Georg Simmel*, ed. Kurt Wolff, trans. H. H. Gerth (New York: Free Press, 1950; orig. 1903), 410.

4. Siegfried Kracauer, "Cult of Distraction: On Berlin's Picture Palaces," trans. Thomas Y. Levin, *New German Critique* 40 (Winter 1987): 95; originally *Frankfurter Zeitung,* 4 March 1926.

5. Walter Benjamin, "The Work of Art in the Age of Mechanical Reproduction," *Illuminations*, ed. Hannah Arendt, trans. Harry Zohn (New York: Schocken, 1969; orig. 1936).

6. Cited in Norbert Lynton, "Futurism," *Concepts of Modern Art*, ed. Nikos Stangos (New York: Harper & Row, 1974), 99.

7. *Concepts of Modern Art*, 97–98.

8. Cited in *Futurist Manifestos*, ed. Umbro Apollonio (New York: Viking, 1973), 219.

9. "Cult of Distraction," 93.

10. See David Bordwell, Janet Staiger, and Kristin Thompson, *The Classical Hollywood Cinema: Film Style and Mode of Production to 1960* (New York: Columbia University Press, 1985), especially 116–17.

11. *Kino-Eye: The Writings of Dziga Vertov*, ed. Annette Michelson, trans. Kevin O'Brien (Berkeley: University of California Press, 1984), 17.

12. Tom Gunning, "The Cinema of Attraction: Early Film, Its Spectator and the Avant-Garde," *Wide Angle* 8(3 and 4) (1986): 63–70; and "An Aesthetic of Astonishment: Early Film and the (In)Credulous Spectator," *Art and Text* 34 (Spring 1989): 31–45.

13. Christian Metz, "On the Impression of Reality in the Cinema," *Film Language*, trans. Michael Taylor (New York: Oxford University Press, 1974).

Works Cited

Abba, Marta. Introduction to *The Mountain Giants and Other Plays by Luigi Piran-dello*. New York: Crown Publishers, 1958.

Albert, Alberto Cesare. *Il teatro nel fascismo: Pirandello e Bragaglia*. Rome: Bulzoni, 1974.

Alonge, Roberto. "Le messinscene dei Sei personaggi in cerca d'autore." In *Piran-dello tra realismo e mistificazione*. Napoli: Guida, 1972.

Alvaro, Corrado. "Commento al 'Taccuino Segreto di Luigi Pirandello.'" *Sipario* 7, no.80 (Dec. 1952): 19–20.

—— "Taccuino Segreto di Luigi Pirandello." *Almanacco letterario Bompiani, 1934* and *1938*. Milano: Mondadori, 1957–58.

Angelini, Franca. *Il teatro del Novecento da Pirandello a Fo*. Rome: Laterza, 1976.

Auger, Helen. "Pirandello's New Play for Duse." *New York Times Magazine*, 4 March 1923.

Balakian, Anna. "Pirandello's *Six Characters* and Surrealism." In *A Companion to Pirandello*, edited by John Louis DiGaetani. New York; Westport, Connecticut; London: Greenwood Press, 1991.

Bassnett-McGuire, Susan. *File on Pirandello*. London and New Hampshire: Meth-uen, 1989.

Bauer, Alfred. *Deutscher Spielfilm Almanach, 1929–50*. Munich: Filmladen Chris-toph Winterberg, 1976.

Benjamin, Walter. "The Works of Art in the Age of Mechanical Reproduction." In *Illuminations*, edited by Hannah Arendt and translated by Harry Zohn. New York: Schocken, 1969. ("Das Kunstwerk im Zeitalter seiner technischen Re-produzierbankeit")

Bentley, Eric. *The Pirandello Commentaries*. Evanston, Illinois: Northwestern Uni-versity Press, 1991.

——. *Pirandello's Major Plays*. Foreword by Albert Bermel. Evanston, Illinois: Northwestern University Press, 1991.

Berea, Giancarlo. "Pirandello e i surrealisti." *Cinema*, n.120, June 1941.

Bernadini, Aldo. *Cinema muto italiano*. Rome: Laterza, 1980.

Bishop, Thomas. *Pirandello and the French Theatre*. New York: New York University Press, 1960.

——. "Pirandello's Influence on French Drama." *Pirandello: A Collection of Critical Essays*, edited by Glauco Cambon, 34–46. Englewood Cliffs: Prentice-Hall, 1966.

Bock, Hans-Michael. "George Wilhelm Pabst: Documenting a Life and a Career."

Works Cited

In *The Films of G. W. Pabst,* edited by Eric Rentschler, 217–35. New Brunswick, New Jersey: Rutgers University Press, 1990.

Brunetta, Gian Piero. *Cinema italiano tra le due guerre: fascismo e politica cinematografica.* Milan: Mursia, 1975.

——. *Storia del cinema italiano, 1895–1945.* Milano: Mursia, 1987.

Büdel, Oscar. *Pirandello.* New York, 1965; London, 1966: Bowes & Bowes.

Callari, Francesco. *Pirandello e il cinema.* Venezia: Marsilio Editori, 1991.

Cambon, Glauco, "Pirandello as Novelist," 337–42. *A Companion to Pirandello Studies,* edited by John Louis DiGaetani. New York: Westport, Connecticut; London: Greenwood Press, 1991.

Cambon, Glauco, ed. *Pirandello: A Collection of Critical Essays.* Englewood Cliffs, New Jersey: Prentice-Hall, 1966.

Campassi, Osvaldo, and Virgilio Sabel. "Chenal, L'Herbier, e 'Il Fu Mattia Pascal.'" *Cinema* 117 (Rome), 10 May 1941.

Caputi, Anthony. *Pirandello and the Crisis of Modern Consciousness.* Urbana and Chicago: University of Illinois Press, 1988.

Castello, Giulio Cesare. "Pirandello i el cinema." *Cinema* (Italy), 1930–39, 178.

Cole, Douglas. "Antonioni and Pirandello and Blow-Up." *Literature Quarterly* 17, no.2 (1989): 25–27.

Cometa, Michele. *Il teatro di Pirandello in Germania.* Palermo: Edizione Novecento, 1986.

Corrado, Donati. *La solitudine allo specchio.* Roma: La Lucarini, 1980.

D'Amico, Sandro, ed. *Lettere ai Familiari di Luigi Pirandello.* In *Terzo Programma,* vol.3. Milan: Mandadori, 1961.

D'Amico, Alessandro, and Alessandro Tinterri. *Pirandello Capocomico.* Palermo: Sellerio, 1987.

daVinci Nichols, Nina. "Pirandello and the Poetics of Desire." In *On Character in Modern Drama,* edited by Nina daVinci Nichols (*Annals of Scholarship* 9, no.3 (1993): 307–25.

deCastris, A. L. "The Experimental Novelist." In *Pirandello: A Collection of Critical Essays,* edited by Glauco Cambon, 91–102. Englewood Cliffs, New Jersey: Prentice Hall, 1966.

Del Ministro, Maurizio. *Pirandello: scena, personaggio e film.* Rome: Bulzoni, 1980.

DiGaetani, John Louis, *A Companion to Pirandello Studies.* New York; Westport, Connecticut; London: Greenwood Press, 1991.

Eisner, Lotte H. *The Haunted Screen: Expressionism in the German Cinema and the Influence of Max Reinhardt.* Berkeley and Los Angeles: University of California Press, 1969.

Evreinov, N. N. *The Theatre in Life.* Translated by Alexander I. Nazaroff. Reprint of 1927 edition. New York: B. Blom, 1970.

Works Cited

Frateili, Arnaldo. "Pirandello Uno e Due." *Almanacco letterario Bompiani*. 1938. Milano: Mandadori, 1957–1958.

Fuhrich, Edda Leisler, and Gisela Prossnitz. *Max Reinhardt in Amerika*. Vienna: Amerika Hause, 1973.

——. *Reinhardt in Europa und Amerika*. Salzburg: Reischl-Druck, 1976.

Genovese, Nino, and Sebastiano Gesu. *La Musa inquietante di Pirandello: il cinema*. Palermo: Bonanno, 1990.

Gernstein, Evelyn. "Four Films of New Types." *Theatre Arts Monthly* 11 (April 1927): 296–97.

Gianola, Elio. *Pirandello e la follia*. Genoa: Il Melangolo, 1983.

Giudice, Gaspare. *Pirandello: A Biography*. Translated by Alastair Hamilton. London: Oxford University Press, 1975.

——. "Ambiguity in *Six Characters in Search of an Author*." Translated by Jana O'Keefe Bazzoni. *Theatre Three*, no.7 (fall 1989): 69–88.

Hodess, Kenneth M. "In Search of the Divided Self: A Psychoanalytic Inquiry into the Drama of Pirandello." In *Pirandello in America*, edited by Mario B. Mignone, Rome: Bulzoni, 1988, 133–45.

Illiano, A., and G. Bussino. "Progetti filmici sui sei personaggi." *Forum italicum* 16(1982): 1–2.

Jacobs, Barry. "Psychic Murder and Characterization in Strindberg's 'The Father.'" *Scandinavica* 8, no.1 (May 1969): 19–34. Journal published in Norwich, England.

Kezich, Tullio. "Mattia Pascal: uno, due e tre." *Omaggio a Pirandello*. Edited by Leonardo Sciascia, *Almanacco letterario Bompiani*. Milano: Mondadori, 1986, 77–84.

Kligerman, Charles. "A psychoanalaytic Study of Pirandello's 'Six Characters in Search of an Author.'" *Journal of the American Psychoanalytic Association* 10 (October 1962): 731–44.

Kracauer, Siegfried, *From Caligari to Hitler: A Psychological History of The German Film*. Princeton: Princeton University Press, 1947. Reprint Noonday Press, New York, 1959.

Lacan, Jacques. *Ecrits*. Translated by Alan Sheridan. New York: W. S. Norton, 1977.

Lambrecht, Gernard. *Deutsche Stummfilme, 1903–1931*. Berlin: Deutsche Kinemathek, 1967–69.

Laurella, Enza. *Pirandello e il cinema: atti del convegno internazionale*. Introduced by Stefano Milioto. Agrigento Center for National Studies, 1978.

Leff, Leonard J., and Jerold L. Simmons, *The Dame in the Kimono: Hollywood, Censorship, and the Production Code from the 1920s to the 1960s*. New York: Grove Weidenfeld, 1990.

Works Cited

Leprohan, Pierre. *The Italian Cinema.* New York: Praeger, 1972.

Lizzani, Carlo. *Il cinema italiano, 1895–1979.* Rome: Editore riuniti, 1979.

Lorch, Jennifer. "The 1925 Text of 'Sei personagi in cerca d'autore' and Pitoëff's production of 1923." In *Yearbook of the British Pirandello Society,* no.2, 1982, 32–47.

Macchia, Giovanni. *Pirandello, o la stanza della tortura.* Milano: Mondadori, 1981.

Marx, Samuel. *Mayer and Thalberg: The Make-Believe Saints.* New York: Random House, 1975.

Micheli, Sergio. "Itinerario cinematografico di un commediografo di successo." *Quaderni di cinema* 33 and 34 (May–August, 1987).

——. *Pirandello in cinema: da "Acciaio" a "Kaos."* Rome: Bulzoni, 1989.

Mignone, Mario B. *Pirandello in America.* Rome: Bulzoni, 1988.

Milioto, Stefano, ed. *Pirandello e il cinema.* Agrigento: Centro nazionale di studi pirandelliani, 1978.

Montague, Ivor. *With Eisenstein in Hollywood.* New York: International Publishers, 1967.

Murray, Bruce. *Film and the German Left in the Weimar Republic.* Austin, Texas: University of Texas Press, 1990.

Muscara, Sarah Zappulla. "Pirandello, Martoglio, Bracco ed il cinema muto." In *La Musa inquietante di Pirandello: il cinema.* Edited by Nino Genovese and Sebastiano Gesu. Palermo: Bonanno, 1990, 293–310.

Nietzsche, Friedrich. *The Birth of Tragedy.* Translated by William Kaufmann. New York: Modern Library, 1968.

Nulf, Frank Allen. "Luigi Pirandello and the Cinema." Unpublished dissertation. University of Georgia, Athens, GA, 1969.

O'Keefe Bazzoni, Jana. "The Carnival Motif in Pirandello's Drama." *Modern Drama* 30, no.3 (September 1987): 414–25.

Ortolani, Benito. *Le Lettere di Pirandello a Marta Abba.* 2 vols. in the series *I meridiani.* Milano: Mondadori, 1994; and *Pirandello's Love Letters to Marta Abba,* abridged. Princeton: Princeton University Press, 1994.

Paolucci, Anne. *The Recovery of the Modern Stage for Dramatic Art.* Carbondale and Edwardsville: Southern Illinois University Press, 1974.

Papini, Giovanni. "La filosofia del cinematografo." *La Stampa* (18 May 1907): 22–23. Journal published in Turin, Italy. Clippings file, New York Public Library at Lincoln Center.

Pennica, Gilda. *Pirandello e la Germania.* Palermo: Paslumbo, 1984.

Petro, Patrice. *Joyless Streets: Women and Melodramatic Representation in Weimar Germany.* Princeton, New Jersey: Princeton University Press, 1989.

Pirandello, Luigi. "Colloqui con la madre morta" and "Lettere." In *Omaggio a Pirandello,* edited by L. Sciascia, *Almanacco letterario Bompiani.* Milano: Mondadori, 1987.

——. *The Late Mattia Pascal.* Translation by William Weaver, 1904. New York: Doubleday, 1964.

——. *On Humor.* Translated by A. Illiano and D. P. Testa. Studies in Comparative Literature, no.58. Chapel Hill: University of North Carolina Press, 1974.

——. *Saggi, poesie e scritti varii.* Edited by Manlio Lo Vecchio Musti. Milan: Mondadori, 1973.

——. *Shoot!* Trans. C. K. Moncrieff. New York: Dutton, 1926, and Howard Fertig, 1975.

——. *Tutte le opere.* Edited by Francesco Flora. Milan: Mondadori, 1937.

Pirandello, Luigi, and Adolf Lantz. *Sechs Personen suchen einen Autor, Film-Novelle.* Berlin: Reimar Hobbing, 1930.

Proser, Matthew N. "The Hidden Image in Pirandello and Shakespeare." *A Companion to Pirandello Studies.* Edited by John Louis DiGaetani. New York: Greenwood Press, 1991.

Pudovkin, Vsevolod Illarionovic. *Film Techniques and Film Acting: The Cinema Writings of V. I. Pudovkin.* New York: Lear, 1949.

Ragusa, Olga. *Luigi Pirandello: An Approach to His Theatre.* Edinburgh: Edinburgh University Press, 1980.

——. *Sicilian Comedies: Two Plays by Luigi Pirandello.* New York: Performing Arts Journal Publications, 1983.

Randall, Richard S. *Censorship of the Movies.* Madison: University of Wisconsin Press, 1968.

Rauhut, Franz. "Il Motivo Psicologico in Pirandello." *Veltro* 12 (1968): 99–121.

Reinhardt, Gottfried. *The Genius.* New York: Alfred A. Knopf, 1979.

Rittenberg, Stephen, and L. Noah Shaw. "On Fantasies of Self-Creation." Paper read at the 783d meeting of the New York Psychoanalytic Society, New York, 8 May 1990.

Robinson, David. *The History of World Cinema.* New York: Stein and Day, 1973.

Romeo, Carlo. "Da specchio a occhio: Il cinema nella poetica pirandelliana." *Cristallo: Rassegna di Varia Umanita* 30, December 1988.

Rondolino, Gianni. *Torino come Hollywood.* Bologna: Cappelli, 1980.

Rossner, Michael. "La fortuna di Pirandello in Germania e le messinscene di Max Reinhardt." *Quaderni di Teatro* (Florence) 34 (November 1986): 40–53.

Savio, Francesco. *Cinecitta anni trenta.* Rome: Bulzoni, 1979.

Sciacca, Michele Federico. *L'estetismo, Kierkegaard, e Pirandello.* Milano: Marzorati, 1974.

Sciascia, Leonardo. *Pirandello e il Pirandellismo.* Palermo: Salerio, 1953.

——. ed. *Omaggio a Pirandello, Almanacco letterario Bompiani, 1938 and 1987.* Milano: Mondadori, 1987.

Sogliuzzo, A. Richard. *Luigi Pirandello, Director.* Metuchen, New Jersey; and London: Scarecrow Press, 1982.

Stone, Jennifer. "Cineastes' Texts." In *Yearbook of the British Pirandello Society*, no.3, 1983, 45–66.

——. "In Search of a Dead Author." In *Pirandello in America*, edited by Mario B. Mignone. New York: SUNY Stony Brook, 1986.

Strindberg, August. "Psychic Murder (Apropos *Rosmersohlm*)." Translated by Walter Johnson. *Tulane Drama Review* 13, no.2:113–18.

Styan, J. L. *Max Reinhardt*. New York: Cambridge University Press, 1982.

Swallow, Norman. *Eisenstein: A Documentary Portrait*. New York: Dutton, 1977.

Taylor, John Russell. *Cinema Eye, Cinema Ear*. New York: Hill and Wang, 1964.

Tessari, Roberto. "Sei persone in fuga da un autore." In *Il Trattamento cinematografico die* Sei Personaggi, *testo inedito di Luigi Pirandello*. Edited by Rossano Vittori. Firenze: Liberoscambia editrice, 1984.

Tinterri, Alessandro. "Two Flights of Steps and a Stage Direction: Pirandello's Staging of 'Six Characters in Search of an Author' in 1925." In *Yearbook of the British Pirandello Society*, no.3, 1983, 33–37.

——, ed. *Il teatro italiano dal naturalismo a Pirandello*. Bologna: Societa editrice il mulino, 1990.

Verdone, Mario. "Luigi e Stefano Pirandello soggettisti e sceneggiatori di cinema." *Teatro contemporaneo*, no.11–12, October–May 1986.

Vicentini, Claudio. *L'Estetica di Pirandello*. Milan: Mondadori, 1970.

Vittori, Rossano. *Il trattamento cinematografico dei* Sei Personaggi, *testo inedito di Luigi Pirandello*. Firenze: Liberoscambio editrice, 1984.

von Sternberg, Josef. *Fun in a Chinese Laundry*. London: Columbus Books, 1965.

Zappulla, Sarah. *Pirandello e Martoglio: carteggio inedito*. Milano: Pan Editrice, 1980.

INTERVIEWS IN NEWSPAPER AND MAGAZINE CLIPPINGS FILES

Auger, Helen. "Pirandello's New Play for Duse." *New York Times Magazine*, section 4, 4 March 1923.

Untitled clipping. *Il Tevere* (dateline Berlin). Rome, 7 October 1936.

Creelman, Eileen. "Max Reinhardt Reluctantly Turns His Eyes from External Road to Hollywood." *New York Sun*, 22 January 1937.

Gerstein, Evelyn. "Four Films of New Types." *Theatre Arts Monthly* 11 (April 1927): 296–97.

Helder, M. P. "Luigi Pirandello, over perspectieven der Filmkunst." *Filmiga*, December 1934, 340–42.

Kerr, Alfred. *Berliner Tageblatt*, 13 October 1925; *Deutsche Tageszeitung*, 13 October 1925; *General Anzlifer*, 19 October 1925.

La Guttuta, Joseph. "Pirandello Looks at Life." *Theatre Magazine*, March 1931, 28–29.

New York Times. Untitled fragments of two interviews with Pirandello. Clipping file, no byline, no specific dates. December 1934 and January 1935.

Works Cited

Roma, Enrico. "Pirandello e il Cinema." *Comoedia*, 15 July–15 August 1932.

Rossi, Alberto. "Pirandello and America," *People's Gazette*, 15 February 1936.

Rousseaux, Andre. "Conversation with Pirandello." *The Living Age* 347 (February 1935).

"An Interview with Luigi Pirandello on the Italian Film." *La Stampa*, 9 December 1932. Journal published in Turin, Italy.

MATERIALS IN SPECIAL COLLECTIONS

Cinecittà, Rome, for filmographies.

Museo dell attore, Genoa. Special collection for files on Pirandello as director, including his correspondence with theater colleagues.

Reinhardt's German script *Sechs Personen suchen einen Autor*, Reinhardt Archives, SUNY Binghamton, New York.

Scrapbooks; clippings files; *Cinema*, Italy, 1930–39, at the Theatre Collection, New York Public Library for the Performing Arts.

Script and director's material on *Six Characters* produced at Reinhardt's Hollywood Workshop: The Ada Clark Collection, Spenser Library, University of Kansas.

University of California Davis, Pirandello files of the estate executor, Toby Cole.

Index

Index

Index

247